D1544071

For Reference

Not to be taken from this room

A

DICTIONARY

OF

MUSLIM

NAMES

BY

SALAHUDDIN
AHMED

NEW YORK UNIVERSITY PRESS
Washington Square, New York

First published in the U.S.A. by
NEW YORK UNIVERSITY PRESS
Washington Square
New York, NY 10003
Printed in India

Library of Congress Cataloging-in-Publication Data
Ahmed, Salahuddin.
  The dictionary of Muslim names / Salahuddin Ahmed.
     p.   cm.
  ISBN 0-8147-0674-6 (cloth) . — ISBN 0-8147-0675-4 (pbk.)
  1. Names. Personal—Islamic.   1. Title.
CS2970.A34   1998
929.4 ' 4 ' 091767103—dc21

و لله الأسماء الحسنى فادعوه بها

"The most beautiful names belong to Allah. So call on him by them." (*surat al-A'raaf* 7:180).

و علم آدم الأسماء كلها

"And He (Allah) taught Adam all the names." (*surat al-Baqarah* 2:31)

CONTENTS

Introduction   *page* ix
Male Names   1
Female Names   233
Bibliography   347

بسم الله الرحمن الرحيم

In the name of Allah, Most Gracious, Most Merciful

INTRODUCTION

Due to the resurgence of Islam and the revitalisation of Muslim culture,[1] there is a growing interest in the study of Muslim names. Throughout the world Muslims share similar names, be they in the Middle East, the Indian subcontinent, South-East Asia or even new migrants in the West.

The predominant language in Muslim names is Arabic, followed by Persian (Farsi), the two major languages which transmitted Muslim culture in its early stages and later expansion to the various parts of the world. An important source of Muslim names consists of the ninety-nine attributes of Allah[2] mentioned in the Qur'an and the *hadith*.[3] According to Islamic belief, the relationship between man and his Creator is that of servant and master. A Muslim feels gratified and honoured to be named as a servant of one of the attributes of Allah, e. g. Abdur Rahman عبد الرحمن (*'abd al-Rahmaan*), Servant of the Most Gracious; or Abdur Rahim عبد الرحيم (*'abd al-Raheem*), Servant of the Most Merciful. The *hadith* states that the best names are derived from the roots, 'thanking Allah' and 'servant of Allah'.[4] A Muslim is pleased to

---

[1] See e.g. Habibi, Nader, 'Popularity of Islamic and Persian Names in Iran before and after the Islamic Revolution', *Int. J. Middle East Stud.*, XXIV, pp. 253-60 (1992).

[2] On the authority of Abu Huraira who said: "The Messenger of Allah said: 'Allah has ninety-nine names; whoever remembers them will enter paradise.'" (Bukhari: Adab no. 2736).

[3] Sayings and practices of Muhammad (s). The letter 's' in this context signifies 'May Allah bless him and give him peace'.

[4] See Abd-el-Jawad, Hassan, 'A Linguistic and Socio-cultural Study of Personal Names in Jordan', *Anthropological Linguistics*, XXVIII, p. 86 (1986).

Introduction

discover his/her name, or a derivative of it, mentioned in the Qur'an or *hadith*. The two well-known names of the Prophet (s) mentioned in the Qur'an, Muhammad and Ahmad, are a favourite choice for boys. However, it is accepted that part or parts of a Muslim name derive from the local language, culture or place of residence.

The purpose of this book is to give the meaning or bearing on Islamic heritage of the Arabic or Persian words which form parts of Muslim names. Muslims like their names to carry some significant meaning or heritage relating to Islam. By way of illustration, this book gives references to the names of Muslims who left their mark on history in different ages, in different fields, and in various parts of the world. Therefore it is not merely a compilation of Muslim names but a reference work pertaining to the broad field of Islam. To the general reader the names alone may not appear as significant as when they are identified as having been borne by an *Imam*, a *Khalifa* (Caliph), a *Sahaabi* (Companion of the Prophet (s)), a *Mujahid* (fighter for the cause of Islam), a *Sultan*, a saint, an author or a jurist who shaped the history of Islam.

It is important to note that the first thing that Allah taught Adam was names.[5] In the Qur'an, when the wife of 'Imraan gives birth to her daughter (who later became the mother of Prophet 'Isa), she says to Allah: "I have named her Maryam" مريم(إني سميتها (*surat Aal-'Imraan* 3:36). This *aayat* of the Qur'an reminds us that an important parental duty is the suitable naming of a new-born baby. In the well-known *hadith*, Muhammad (s) advised Muslims to be careful when

---

[5] "And He taught Adam all the names, then showed them to the angels, saying: Tell me the names of these if you are right. They said: 'Glory to You. We have no knowledge saving that which You have taught us. You, only You, are the Knower, the Wise.' He said: 'O Adam! Tell them their names.' When he had told them their names, He said: 'Did I not tell you that I know the secrets of heavens and earth? And I know that which you disclose and which you hide'." (*surat al-Baqarah* 2:31-33).

Introduction

selecting names for their children: "On the Day of Resurrection, you will be called by your names and the names of your fathers; so keep beautiful names."[6] A distinguishing feature of Muslim names in general is that they are inspired by the teachings of Islam in the Qur'an and *hadith*. "[N]ames [are] selected because they [are] religiously acceptable and [are] rejected because they [are] religiously unsound."[7] Ideally, part or parts of a Muslim name are in Arabic, are mentioned in the Qur'an or the *hadith* and reflect their Islamic heritage, thereby fulfilling the rightful aspiration of a true Muslim.

Unfortunately, a large number of Muslims bearing names which comprise Arabic or Persian words are unaware of the meaning, or the bearing on Islamic heritage, of their names, particularly if they are not familiar with Arabic or Persian. Muslims unfamiliar with these two languages need to realise that names comprising Arabic or Persian words without suitable meaning or bearing on Islamic heritage do not fulfil the aspirations of true Muslims. In the present age of individualism there is a tendency among some parents to select names consisting of uncommon Arabic or Persian words which are phonetically appealing but in truth devoid of any real meaning. As a consequence, some names are sheer inventions which cannot be traced in dictionaries and are grammatically incorrect. It is very important that parents and guardians should devote enough time in selecting suitable names for new-born boys and girls by consulting authentic books on names and re-checking them from standard Arabic-English and/or Persian-English dictionaries.

It should be noted that there are certain rules or patterns regarding the formation of Muslim names. Naturally, classical Arabic names were formed in accordance with the customs of Arabia whence Islam spread. Traditionally, Arabic names prevalent in Arabia conform to the following

---

[6] Bukhari: Adab no. 6178.

[7] See Sheniti, Mahmud, 'Treatment of Arabic names', *International Conference on Cataloguing Principles Report*, 1961, p. 268.

Introduction

parts or components:

(1) *Kunya* or nickname, e. g. *Abu* (father) or *Umm* (mother) of the first born son or daughter. Muhammad (s) was known as Abul Qasem, father of Qasem, the name of his son. But in the Indian subcontinent, this type of *kunya* is used informally only in family circles but is not a part of formal names. It is possible that a childless person may have a *kunya*. For example, the Prophet's (s) wife Ayesha, although childless, was known as Umm Abdullah (mother of Abdullah). Even a new-born baby can be given a *kunya* in the form of father or mother of so-and-so. Sometimes *kunya* is used in a figurative or metaphorical sense. In the non-Arab countries, one may find only a figurative *kunya*, e. g. Abul Fazl (*fadl*)[8], endowed with bounty.

(2) *Ism* or proper name, e. g. Muhammad.

(3) *Nasab* or lineage, son (*ibn, bin*) or daughter (*bint*) of so-and-so. Some people are known by their *nasab*, e. g. Ibn Rushd (1126-98), the great philosopher, known in Europe as Averroes; Ibn Batutah (1304-78), the famous traveller and explorer, known as the 'Arab Marco Polo'; Ibn Khaldun (1332-1406), the famous historian, known as 'father of historiography'. In the Indian subcontinent, *nasab* is not normally used. "[T]he traditional *nasab* is still retained in some Arab countries, especially in Tunisia and Morocco where the word *ibn* is now replaced by *ben*."[9] Sometimes, the father's name may form part of a name without using *ibn*, e.g. Jamal Abdun Naser, meaning 'Jamal, son of Abdun Naser'.

(4) *Nisba* or relationship to the place of birth, residence, descent or sometimes the name of the *madhhab* (school of jurisprudence) which one follows. "*Nisba*: an adjective ending in *i* and preceded by *al* indicating

---

[8] A renowned author in the Mughal court during the reign of emperor Akbar.

[9] See Sheniti, Mahmud, 'Treatment of Arabic names', *International Conference on Cataloguing Principles Report*, 1961, p. 273.

xii

Introduction

place of origin, descent, or membership of a tribe or sect, [e.g.] al-Hashimi."[10] Muhammad Ibn Ismail (810-70), the famous author of one of the *sahih hadith*, is known by his *nisba* al-Bukhari from his place of birth, Bukhara.

(5) *Laqab* or honorific title given to a person. Many of the Prophets were known by their *laqab*, e.g. Prophet Adam as Abul Bashar (father of mankind), Prophet Ibrahim as Khalil Allah (friend of Allah), Prophet Musa as Kalim Allah (one who conversed with Allah), Prophet Muhammad as Al-Amin (the trustworthy). Khalifa Abu Bakr was known as Al-Siddiq (the truthful), while Khalifa Umar was known as Al-Faaruq (one capable of distinguishing truth from falsehood).

One may notice that in the course of time, the pattern or style of Muslim names adapted itself to local traditions or cultures as Islam spread to new countries beyond Arabia. Thus the naming patterns in the Indian subcontinent, Indonesia, Malaysia, Turkey are quite different from the Arab countries. In some Muslim countries, e.g. Egypt, Iran and Turkey,[11] family names are well established, but in the Indian subcontinent a complete liberty in selecting names means that there is no necessary continuation of the surname from father to son. Also, there is little distinction between a surname and first name and they are freely interchanged. Regarding names which are prevalent in the subcontinent, one should note that as well as Arabic names, those in Persian (Farsi) also became popular during the long period of Muslim rule when it

---

[10] See Chaplin, A.H., 'Names of Persons', *National Usages for Entry in Catalogues*, p. 1. "[A]ny name can be made an attribute by adding the Arabic letter ya' in duplicate at its end...When used as a part of a person's name, the *nisba* usually refers to a tribe or sub-tribe, to a father or grandfather, to a country or town or village..." See Sheniti, Mahmud, 'Treatment of Arabic names', *International Conference on Cataloguing Principles Report*. 1961, p. 271.

[11] See Schimmel, Annemarie, 'Some Notes on Turkish family Names', *Islamic Names*, p. 80.

xiii

Introduction

became the state language. Commenting on the pattern of Turkish names, one scholar writes: "The Turks introduced the fashion of adding Arabic abstract nouns to the common names, which they were unable to pronounce without a vowel at the end of a word, so that these came back into Arabic use with an i or y as popular names, Lutfi...Sabry... Hamdy... Fathy...and so forth. These forms spread widely in the Ottoman Empire and became names on their own."[12]

In any culture, the naming of a person is susceptible to gender showing significant difference in the attitude of parents when naming a boy or a girl. In general, Muslim parents tend to give male children names of religious significance or those bearing qualities of manhood, courage and bravery, while female children are given names bearing on Islamic heritage or depicting feminine qualities, e.g. beauty, modesty, virtue.

The title A Dictionary of Muslim Names should not suggest that the names included are used only by Muslims. It is common knowledge that Arab names and culture are shared by Arab Christians as well, e.g. Karam (see reference in the text and note). Furthermore not all the names included in this book, bear strict religious significance in Islam. There are many which simply reflect qualities, e.g. bravery or virtue, that are 'universal' but at the same time associated with Muslim identity in harmony with other cultures. In a proper evaluation of Muslim names, one should keep in mind the fact that Islamic heritage and Muslim culture transcend both Arabic language and Arab culture.

It is well known that transliteration from one language to another is no easy task. In order to appreciate the different versions in English spelling of Arabic or Persian Muslim names, one should consult Islamic Names by Schimmel. The method and style adopted in setting out the

---

[12] See Paxton, Evelyn, 'Arabic Names', *Asian Affairs*, LIX, p. 199 (1972). "Some Turkish names, especially short ones ending with t, e.g. Hikmat, Ezzat, or i, e.g. Hilmi, Fahmi, were widely used a few decades ago and are still in use." See Sheniti, Mahmud, 'Treatment of Arabic names', *International Conference on Cataloguing Principles Report*, 1961, p. 273.

Introduction

names in this book are as follows:

(1) Names are divided into two sections, male and female. The few names which are common to boys and girls have been included in both sections. If a female name is simply the feminine form of a male name, the reader is referred to the latter entry which provides the full meaning and annotation.

(2) Names are arranged in English alphabetical order according to their most common spelling.

(3) The origins of each are indicated by 'A' for Arabic, 'P' for Persian and 'T' for Turkish.

(4) Spellings in the original language, i. e. Arabic, Persian or Turkish, are also given using the Arabic alphabet.

(5) The correct pronunciation of names is indicated through their formal transliteration.

(6) For the names in Arabic, the three root letters often are given so that a reader can consult a standard Arabic dictionary, where words are arranged under the root letters system. Moreover, by consulting the root letters a reader may find other names originating from the same roots, e.g. from *hamd* حمد: Ahmad, Hamid, Mahmud, Muhammad.

(7) The brief meaning of each name, its bearing on Islamic heritage and, where relevant, annotations are provided.

(8) If part of a name or its derivative is mentioned in the Qur'an, the relevant *aayat* (verse) in Arabic containing that word is quoted with English translation, citing the *sura* (chapter) and *aayat* numbers.

(9) Where appropriate, eminent persons of the same name are mentioned.

It should be noted that many names are not exclusively male or female. Ideas and notions concerning the gender of names vary and change from country to country and also from one generation to another. Furthermore it is always likely that names currently out of use may regain popularity in a later period, while new names may come into circulation. However, some names never grow old and remain

Introduction

favourites, e.g. Muhammad for a boy and Ayesha (the Prophet's wife) for a girl.

This work is the product of several years' research but does not claim to be exhaustive. If any significant errors or omissions are found, I shall be glad to be informed of them.

I am indebted to a large number of books, dictionaries, articles and international reports which are cited in the footnotes and bibliography. For the English translation of the verses from the Qur'an, I have received liberal help from the well-known English translations by Yusuf Ali and Marmaduke Pickthall. I wish to record my deep appreciation of the helpful comments that I received in preparing this book from a number of friends, especially Mahmoud Jaame', Ismat el-Ayoubi, Mamdouh Agawani and Samir Shousha. My special thanks are due to Raphael Cohen who revised the text and offered useful suggestions regarding its presentation and I acknowledge the spontaneous appreciation and kind support I received from the publishers of this book, particularly from Michael Dwyer. I express my deep sense of gratitude to Christopher Hurst for overall supervision of publication and particularly thorough revision of the Introduction of this book. I received considerable support and encouragement from my wife Nazli (Mahmudunnisa), daughter Rumana, sons Omar and Shahan and son-in-law Mizanur Rahman. This work is the product of the teachings and inspiration I received from my late parents Ziauddin Ahmed and Zaheda Khatun.

Faculty of Law   SALAHUDDIN AHMED
University of New South Wales
Sydney, Australia
July 1998/Rabi al-Awwal 1419 H

xvi

MALE NAMES

A

Aalam (A) عالم (*'aalam*) (علم): world; sing. of *'Aalameen* عالمين. الحمد لله رب العالمين "Praise be to Allah, Lord of the worlds." (*surat al-Faatihah* 1:1). See Dunya دنيا (f.). Comp. Alam علم, flag. See Aalam (f.).

Aalamgir (P) عالمگير: world conqueror. Title of Mughal emperor Awrangzeb (1658-1707).

Nur-e-Aalam (P) نور عالم: light of the world.

Nur-ul-Aalam (A) نور العالم: light of the world.

Aali (A) العالى (*al-'aalii*): high, tall, towering, lofty, exalted, high-ranking, sublime, superior, excellent. See Ali علي, high.

Aalim (A) عالم (*'aalim*) (علم): learned, scholar, expert. Al-Aalim العالم, the Knower: one of the names of Allah. ان الله عالم غيب السماوات والارض "Allah is the Knower of the Unseen of the heavens and the earth." (*surat Faatir* 35:38). See Aleem عليم, scholar.

Aamir (A) آمر: commander, ruler, leader, master, chief, superior. الآمرون بالمعروف والناهون عن المنكر "Those who enjoin the right and who forbid the wrong." (*surat al-Tawbah* 9:112). Comp. 'Aamir عامر, prosperous: Ameer أمير, prince.

1

Male Names

Aamir[1] (A) عامر (*'aamir*) (عمر): prosperous, full of life, large, substantial. 'Aamir ibn Sharaahil al-Sha'bii (d.103 AH): well-known *hadith* scholar.

Aaqil (A) عاقل (*'aaqil*) (عقل): wise, judicious, intelligent, prudent, sage. Comp. Aqeel عقيل.

Aarif (A) عارف (*'aarif*) (عرف): learned, expert, authority, saint, the highest position a mystic can attain. See Areef عريف, learned.

Aarifin (A) عارفين (*'aarifeen*): saints; pl. of Aarif عارف.

Shams-ul-Aarifin (A) شمس العارفين: sun of the saints.

Aasim (A). See Asim عاصم.

Aasir (A) آسر: captivating, fascinating. Comp. Asir أثير (*atheer*), honoured.

Aban (A) أبان (*abaan*): clear, distinct. Comp. Abyan أبين, clearer. Aban ibn Sa'id: a *sahaabi*.[2]

Abbaad (A). See Abbad.

Abbad (A) عباد (*'abbad*) (عبد): worshipper. Abbad ibn Khalid al-Ghifari: a *sahaabi*.

---

[1] "An inhabited place". See Colebrooke, T. E., 'On the Proper Names of the Mohammadans', *Journal of the Royal Asiatic Society of Great Britain and Ireland*, XIII, p. 242 (1881). Also see Abd-el-Jawad, Hassan, 'A Linguistic and Socio-cultural Study of Personal Names in Jordan', *Anthropological Linguistics*, XXVIII, p. 93 (1986).

[2] See Haykal, M. H., *The Life of Muhammad*, p. 350.

Male Names

Abbas (A) عباس (*'abbaas*): one who frowns a lot. *'Abasa* عبس, 'He Frowned': title of the 80th *sura* of the Qur'an. Al-Abbas: uncle of Muhammad (s), the forefather of the Abbasid dynasty which ruled the Muslim empire from 750-1258. Abu al-Abbas al-Saffah (750-54): founder of the Abbasid dynasty.[3] Shah Abbas I (1588-1629): King of Persia.[4]

Abbasi (A) عباسي (*'abbaasii*): an Abbasid. A *nisba* (relation)[5] through ancestry to the Abbasid dynasty. See Abbas عباس.

Abboud (A). See Abbud.

Abbud (A) عبّود: devoted worshipper of Allah.

Abd (A) عبد (*'abd*): servant (male). The word Abd is used with the attributes of Allah to form compound names, e.g. Abd Al-Aziz, servant of the All-mighty. Comp. Amat أمة, female servant.

Abdullah[6] (A) عبد الله (*'abd allah*): servant of Allah. Father of

---

[3] It is "the most celebrated and longest-lived Arab dynasty in Islam." See Hitti, Philip K., *History of the Arabs*, p. 288.

[4] "The Isfahan of Shah Abbas...was unmistakable evidence of the power, wealth, confidence and dynamism of Safavid Persia." See Fernandez-Armesto, Felipe, *Millennium*, p. 214. "[S]ome of the greatest achievements [of the reign of Shah Abbas I] are preserved in the unparalleled architectural beauties of Isfahan." See Bosworth, C. E., *The Islamic Dynasties*, p. 173.

[5] "Belonging unto the house of Abbas." See Steingass, F., *A Comprehensive Persian-English Dictionary*, p. 833.

[6] This name is a favourite throughout the Muslim world. The *Hadith* mentions that it was recommended by Muhammad (s) as very pleasing to Allah. See Muslim: Adab no. 2132.

3

Male Names

Muhammad (s); a son[7] of Muhammad (s). In the Qur'an, Prophet 'Isa called himself Abdullah. قال انی عبد الله, "He ['Isa] said: I am the servant of Allah." (*surat Maryam* 19:30).

Abdallah (A). See Abdullah.

Abdel (A). See Abd.

Abduh (A) عبده (*'abduh*): His [Allah's] servant. An epithet of Mūhammad (s). سبحان الذی اسری بعبده ليلا من المسجد الحرام الی المسجد الاقصا الذي باركنا حوله لنريه من آياتنا "Glorified be He Who took His servant for a journey by night from the Sacred Masjid to the Farthest Masjid whose precincts We blessed, in order that We might show him some of Our Signs." (*surat Bani Israa'il* 17:1). Shaykh Muhammad Abduh (1849-1905): Egyptian religious reformer, author of *al-Islam wa al-Nasraaniyyah*.[8]

Abdul (A). See Abd.

Abed (A). See Abid عابد.

Abedin (A). See Abidin عابدين.

Abid (A)[9] عابد (*'aabid*) (عبد): worshipper, adorer, devout. ولا انا

---

[7] See Lings, Martin, *Muhammad*, p. 19.

[8] He was "a liberal reformer...advocated the compatibility of Islam with science." See Fernandez-Armesto, Felipe, *Millennium*, p. 570.

[9] As Abid means worshipper, names such as Abid Ali are improper unless it is Abid al-Ali Worshipper of The All-High (an attribute of Allah). Similarly names such as Abid Hasan or Abid Husayn are also improper. S. Abid Husain (1898-1978): "He published forty volumes on Indian culture and Indian nationalism and was a founder of the Islam

4

Male Names

عابد ما عبدتم   "I am not a worshipper of that which you worship." (*surat al-Kaafirun* 109:4).

Abidullah (A) عابد الله (*'aabid allah*): worshipper of Allah.

Abidin (A) عابدين (*'aabideen*) (عبد): pl. of Abid عابد, worshipper. وكانوا لنا عابدين "And they were worshippers of Us (alone)." (*surat al-Anbiyaa'* 21:73).

Zayn-ul-Abidin (A) زين العابدين: ornament of the worshippers (of Allah). See Zayn.

Abrar (A) أبرار (*abraar*) (بَرّ): pl. of Barr بر, pious, kind, righteous. ربنا...وتوفنا مع الابرار "Our Lord,...take to yourself our souls in the company of the righteous." (*surat Aal 'Imraan* 3:193).

Absar (A) أبصار (*absaar*) (بصر): pl. of Basar بصر vision, sight. لا تدركه الابصار وهو يدرك الابصار "Vision comprehends Him (Allah) not, but He comprehends all vision." (*surat al-An'aam* 6:103).

Nur-ul-Absar (A) نور الأبصار: light of vision.

Abu (A) أب: father. Used as a *kunya* (nickname), making a compound whose first part is Abu (father). Comp. Umm أم, mother.

Abu Bakr (A) أبو بكر: father of the young camel.[10]   Abu Bakr

---

and the Modern Age Society." See Donohue, John J. & Esposito, John L., *Islam in Transition*, p. 169.

[10] See Colebrooke, T. E., 'On the Proper Names of the Mohammadans', *Journal of the Royal Asiatic Society of Great Britain and Ireland*, XIII, p. 240 (1881); Paxton, Evelyn, Arabic Names', *Asian Affairs*, LIX, p. 199 (1972).

Male Names

al-Siddiq: the first (632-34) of the 'rightly guided' Khalifas. He was one of the ten *sahaabis* to whom Muhammad (s) gave the good news of entering into paradise.[11] See Siddiq.

Abul Fazl (A) أبو الفضل (*aboo al-fadl*): endowed with bounty, grace. Nickname of Abbas,[12] an uncle of Muhammad (s). Famous historian and author of *'Ain-i-Akbari* and *Akbar Naama* during the reign of Mughal emperor Akbar.[13]

Abu Hanifa (A) أبو حنيفة: founder of the Hanafi School of Law (700-767).

Abu Talib (A) أبو طالب: father of seeker. Abu Talib ibn Abd al-Muttalib: uncle of Muhammad (s) and father of Khalifa Ali. See Talib.

Abyad (A). See Abyaz.

Abyan (A) أبين: clearer, more distinct. Comp. Aban أبان, clear.

Abyaz (A) أبيض (*abyad*): white, bright, brilliant, innocent, pure (see *surat al-Baqarah* 2: 187). See Baiza (*baidaa'*) بيضاء, fem. of Abyaz. Abyad bin Hammal: a *sahaabi*.

Adam (A) آدم (*aadam*): the first man created by Allah (see *surat al-Baqarah* 2:31). قلنا للملائكة اسجدوا لآدم فسجدوا الا ابليس, "We

---

[11] See Lings, Martin, *Muhammad*, p. 329.

[12] See Haykal, M. H., *The Life of Muhammad*, p. 454.

[13] "The most accomplished writer (in Persian) of the reign [of Emperor Akbar] was Abul Fazl, a man of letters, a poet, an essayist, a critic, and a historian." See Majumdar, R. C., *et al.*, *An Advanced History of India*, p. 573.

Male Names

said to the angels: 'Prostrate yourselves to Adam,' and they fell prostrate, all except Iblis." (*surat al-A'raaf* 7:11).

Abul Bashar (A) أبو البشر: father of mankind. An epithet of Adam who was also the first Prophet.

Adib (A) أديب (*adeeb*) (ادب): well-mannered, courteous, polished, man of letters.

Adil (A) عادل (*'aadil*) (عدل): just, honest, upright, righteous.

Adil Khan I (P) عادل خان: Sultan of Khandesh (India) (1437-41).

Adil Shah (P) عادل شاه: King of Iran (1747). Ibrahim Adil Shah II (1580-1627): Sultan of Bijapur (India).[14]

Adli[15] (A) عدلي (*'adlii*): honest.

Adnan (A) عدنان (*'adnaan*): "A descendent of Ismail and traditional ancestor of the North Arabian tribes...who called themselves 'the sons of 'Adnan'."[16] He was "renowned for his eloquence."[17] Adnan Menderis: Prime Minister of Turkey (1950-60).

Affan (A) عفان (*'affaan*): father of Khalifa Usman (*uthmaan*).

---

[14] He was "a talented painter, calligrapher and musician." See Beazley, M., *Who Did What*, p. 162.

[15] See Abd-el-Jawad, Hassan, 'A Linguistic and Socio-cultural Study of Personal Names in Jordan', *Anthropological Linguistics*, XXVIII, p. 83 (1986).

[16] See Glasse, Cyril, *The Concise Encyclopaedia of Islam*, p. 24.

[17] See Steingass, F., *A Comprehensive Persian-English Dictionary*, p. 839.

Male Names

Afif (A) عفيف (*'afeef*) (عفّ): chaste, virtuous, honest, righteous, upright, decent. Fourteenth-century Indian historian.

Afif-ud-Din (A) عفيف الدين: virtuous of the religion (Islam).

Afsar (P) افسر: crown.

Afsar-ud-Din (P+A) افسر الدين: adorning the religion (Islam).

Aftab (P) افتاب (*aftaab*): sun. See Shams شمس; Khurshid خورشيد; Mihr مهر.

Aftab-ud-Din (P+A) افتاب الدين: sun of the religion (Islam).

Afzal (A) أفضل (*afdal*) (فضل): better, best, superior; comp. adj. of فاضل. Al-Malik al-Afdal: son of Sultan Salah-ud-Din Ayyubi.

Aga (T) أغا (*aghaa*): leader, ruler. Aga Khan: title of the Imam of the Ismaili sect of the Shi'ites. Aga Khan Karim (b.1936): 49th Nizari Isma'ili Imam.

Aghlab (A) أغلب (غلب): superior, supreme, stronger, strongest, conqueror, winner; comp. adj. of Ghalib غالب. Ibrahim ibn al-Aghlab: founder (800-12) of the Aghlabid dynasty which ruled Algeria, Tunisia and Sicily from (800-909).[18]

Ahad (A) أحد: one. Al-Ahad الأحد, the One: one of the names of

---

[18] "It was under the Aghlabids that the final transformation of Ifriqiyah from an outwardly Latin-speaking, Christianity-professing land to an Arab-speaking, Islam-professing region took place." See Hitti, Philip K., *History of the Arabs*, p. 452.

8

Male Names

Allah. احد الله هو قل "Say: He is Allah, the One." (*surat al-Ikhlaas* 112:1). See Waahid واحد, one.

Abdul Ahad (A) الأحد عبد: servant of the One.

Ahdaf (A) أهداف (*ahdaaf*) (هدف): pl. of هدف, aim, goal, target.

Ahmad (A) أحمد (حمد): the most praised; comp. adj. of Hamid حميد, praised. One of the names of Muhammad (s) mentioned in the Qur'an. احمد اسمه بعدي من يأتي برسول ومبشرا "I ('Isa) have brought the good news of a Messenger who will come after me whose name will be Ahmad." (*surat al-Saff* 61:6). This name is a favourite among Muslims throughout the world. See Mahmud محمود, praised; Muhammad محمد praised. Ahmad Barelwi: See Sayyid.

> **Ahmadullah** (A) الله أحمد (*ahmad allah*): the most praised (person) of Allah. Ahmad Allah (1808-81): Indian reformist leader.[19]

> **Ahmad Shah** (A+P) شاه أحمد: Ahmad Shah Abd Ali (1722-73): founder of modern Afghanistan. Ahmad Shah Durrani: king of Afghanistan (1747-73) and founder of the Durrani dynasty (1747-1842).

Ahmed (A). See Ahmad.

Ahsab (A) أحسب (حسب): nobler, more respected; comp. adj. of Hasib حسيب, noble.

Ahsan (A) أحسن (حسن): better, superior, more splendid; comp. adj. of

---

Male Names

Hasan حسن, handsome. صبغة الله ومن احسن من الله صبغة "[Our religion] takes its colour from Allah. And who is better than Allah at colouring?" (*surat al-Baqarah* 2:138). See Husna حسنى, fem. of Ahsan.

Aiman (A). See Ayman.

Ain (A). See Ayn.

Ajawid (A) أجاويد (*ajaaweed*): pl. of Jawaad جواد, open-handed, generous, noble.

Ajmal (A) أجمل (جمل): more beautiful; comp. adj. of Jamil جميل, handsome. Hakim Ajmal Khan (1863-1927): Indian physician and politician who was known as 'the uncrowned king of Delhi'.[20]

Ajwad (A) أجود (جود): better, more generous; comp. adj. of Jawad جواد, generous. See Ahsan أحسن; Afzal أفضل (*afdal*).

Akand (P). See Akhund اخوند.

Akbar (A) أكبر (كبر): greater, greatest; comp. adj. of Kabir كبير, great. *Allahu Akbar* الله أكبر "Allah is the Greatest." ولذكر الله اكبر "And remembrance of Allah is the greatest (thing in life)." (*surat al-Ankabut* 29:45). Jalal ud-Din Akbar: the greatest Mughal emperor (1556-1605).[21]

Ali Akbar (A) علي أكبر: son of Imam Husayn who attained

---

[20] See Mujahid, Sharif Al-, *Quaid-i- Azam Jinnah*, p. 692. Also see Ahmad, Aziz, *An Intellectual History of Islam in India*, p. 59.

[21] "[H]e established his dynasty so securely that it lasted for three hundred years and dominated India for two hundred." See Fernandez-Armesto, Felipe, *Millennium*, p. 218.

10

Male Names

martyrdom in the battle of Karbala at the age of twenty-five.[22]

Akhlaq (A) أخلاق (*akhlaaq*) (خلق): good manners, morals; pl. of *Khuluq* خلق, character. وانك لعلى خلق عظيم "Surely you (O Muhammad!) are upon a mighty morality." (*surat al-Qalam* 68:4).

Akhtar (P) اختر: star, good luck. Comp. Ikhtyar اختيار, choice.

> **Akhtar Zamir** (P+A) اختر ضمير (*akhtar dameer*): one possessing an enlightened mind.

Akhund (P) اخوند: honorific title of someone learned in religious matters.[23]

> **Akhund-zada** (P) اخوند زاده: son of a person learned in religious matters.

Akhyar (A) اخيار (*akhyaar*): pl. of Khayr خير, good, better, best, excellent. وانهم عندنا لمن المصطفين الاخيار "In Our sight they [Ibrahim, Ishaq, Ya'qub] are truly of the elect, the excellent." (*surat Saad* 38:47). An epithet of Muhammad (s). See Khayr خير, good.

Akif (A) عاكف ('*aakif*) (عكف): devoted to, dedicated to, persevering in, busily engaged. ثم اتموا الصيام الى الليل ولا تباشروهن وانتم عاكفون في المساجد "Then complete your fast till nightfall and do not touch your wives while you are in *i'tikaaf* (seclusion) in the mosques."

---

[22] See Al-Tabatabai, Allamah Sayyid Muhammad Husayn, *Shi'ite Islam*, p. 201.

[23] See Islam, K. M. Saiful, 'Cataloguing Bengali Muslim Names', *UNESCO Information Science Journal*, II, p. 37 (1980); *The Oxford Encyclopaedia of the Modern Islamic World*, vol. I, pp. 59-60.

11

Male Names

(surat al-Baqarah 2:187).

Akmal (A) أكمل (كمل): more complete, more perfect; comp. adj. of Kamil كامل, perfect." اليوم اكملت لكم دينكم "This day I have perfected your religion." *(surat al-Maa'idah* 5:3).

Akram (A) أكرم (كرم): more generous, most generous, nobler, noblest; comp. adj. of Karim كريم, generous. Al-Akram الأكرم, the most Bountiful: one of the names of Allah. اقرأ وربك الاكرم, "Read: and your Lord is the most Bountiful." *(surat al-'Alaq* 96:3). Mawlana Mohammad Akram Khan (1869-1968): Bengali political leader and editor of *Azad*.

Ala (A) علاء *('alaa')* (علي): exalted, prestige, glory. Comp. Aalaa آلاء, benefits. See Aalaa (f.).

> **Abul 'Alaa'** (A) أبو العلاء: father of glory. Mawlana Sayyid Abul Ala Mawdudi: see Mawdudi.

> **Ala-ud-Din** (A) علاء الدين: glory of religion (Islam). Alauddin Khalji (1296-1316): famous Delhi Sultan.[24]

Alam (A)[25] علم *('alam)*: flag, emblem, banner, sign, a distinguished and outstanding man; sing. of A'laam اعلام (see *surat al-Rahmaan* 55:24). Comp. Aalam عالم, world.

---

[24] He "threatened, briefly, to impose his rule or hegemony throughout the sub-continent...styled himself 'the new Alexander'..." See Fernandez-Armesto, Felipe, *Millennium*, p. 105.

[25] See Madina, Maan Z., *Arabic-English Dictionary of the Modern Literary Language*, p. 450; Steingass, F., *A Comprehensive Persian-English Dictionary*, p. 864.

12

Male Names

Alam-ul-Huda (A) علم الهدى: banner of guidance. An epithet of Muhammad (s).

Al-Amin (A). See Amin.

Alamgir (P). See Aalam.

Aleem (A) عليم (*'aleem*) (علم): learned, expert, scholar. Al-Aleem العليم, the All-knowing: one of the names of Allah. والله عليم حليم "Allah is All-knowing, most Forbearing." (*surat Al-Nisaa'* 4:12). See Aalim عالم, scholar.

Abdul Aleem (A) عبد العليم: servant of the All-knowing.

Ali[26] (A) علي (*'aliyy*): high, lofty, sublime. Al-Aliy العلي, the All-high: one of the names of Allah. وان الله هو العلي الكبير "Because Allah, He is the High, the Great." (*surat al-Hajj* 22:62). Ali ibn Abu Talib: the fourth and the last (656-61) of the 'rightly guided' Khalifas and the first Imam of the Shi'ites. He was a cousin and son-in-law of Muhammad (s) and one of the ten *sahaabis* to whom the Prophet (s) gave the good news of entering into paradise.[27]

Abdul Ali (A) عبد العلي (*'abd al-ali*): servant of the most High.

Alif (A) أليف (*aleef*): friendly, sociable, amicable.

---

[26] Ali should not be combined with such words as *'abid* (worshipper), *bande* (servant), *ghulam* (servant). Such combinations are repugnant to the relationship between man and Allah.

[27] See Lings, Martin, *Muhammad*, p. 329.

Male Names

Alim (A). See Aalim عالم; Aleem عليم.

Allah Bakhsh (P). See Bakhsh.

Allama (A) علاّمة ('allaamah) (علم): very learned. Title given to a very learned scholar, e. g. Ibn Mutahhar al-Hilli (d.1326), Shi'ite theologian;[28] Muhammad Iqbal (d.1938), Indian poet, philosopher and political thinker; Muhammad Husayn Tabataba'i (1903-81): "one of the foremost Qur'anic commentators and traditional Persian philosophers of the twentieth century."[29]

Almas (A) ألماس (almaas): diamond.

Altaaf (A) ألطاف (altaaf): pl. of Lutf لطف, kindness. Comp. ألطف, kinder.

Altaaf Husayn (A) ألطاف حسين: kindness of Husayn. Altaf Husayn Hali (1837-1914): Indian poet.[30]

Altaf (A) ألطف (لطف): kinder, more elegant; com. adj. of Latif لطيف, Kind. Comp. Altaaf ألطاف.

Aluf (A) ألوف (aloof): friendly, faithful, devoted.

Aman (A) أمان (amaan) (امن): trust, safety, protection, tranquillity, peace of mind, calmness. *Fi amaanillah* في أمان الله, in the care of

[28] See Schimmel, Annemarie, *Islamic Names*, p. 58.

[29] See *The Oxford Encyclopaedia of the Modern Islamic World*, vol. IV, p. 161.

[30] "Hali's most outstanding work is his *Musaddas-i-madd-u-jazr-i Islam*, a poem on the decline of Islam in general in modern times, and in India in particular." See Aziz, Ahmad, *An Intellectual History of Islam*, p. 104.

Male Names

Allah: a frequent expression of Muslims placing confidence in Allah.

Amanullah (A) أمان الله (*amaan allah*): Afghan king (1919-29).

Aman-ud-Din (A) أمان الدين: trust of the religion (Islam).

Amanat (A) أمانات (*amaanaat*) (امن): pl. of Amaanah أمانة, trust.
ان الله يامركم ان تؤدوا الامانات الى اهلها "Allah commands you that you restore trusts to their owners." (*surat al-Nisaa'* 4:58).

Amani[31] (A) أماني (*amaani*): pl. of Umniya أمنية, wish, aspiration, hope.[32] See Umniya (f.).

Ambar (A) عنبر (*'anbar*) perfume, ambergris.

Ameer (A) أمير (أمر): prince, commander, chief, lord, leader, master.
Ameer-al-Mu'mineen أمير المؤمنين, Commander of the Faithful: a title of the Khalifa of the Muslim empire. Comp. Aamir آمر, commander.

> **Ameer Ali** (A) أمير علي (1849-1928): Indian jurist, judge and author of *A Short History of the Saracens*; *The Spirit of Islam* and *Mahommedan Law*.

> **Ameer Khusrau** (A+P) أمير خسرو (1253-1325): eminent

---

[31] See Abd-el-Jawad, Hassan, 'A Linguistic and Socio-cultural Study of Personal Names in Jordan', *Anthropological Linguistics*, XXVIII, p. 94 (1986).

[32] In Persian, Amaani أماني means, 'security, trust'. See Steingass, F., *A Comprehensive Persian-English Dictionary*, p. 98.

Male Names

Indian poet who was known as 'the parrot of India'.[33]

Amid (A) عميد (*'ameed*) (عمد): pillar, support, head.

Amid-ud-Dawlah (A) عميد الدولة: support of the state.

Amin (A) أمين (*ameen*) (امن): trustworthy, honest. اني لكم رسول امين "I [Nuh] am a faithful Messenger to you." (*surat al-Shu'araa'* 26:107).

Al-Amin (A) الأمين: an epithet of Muhammad (s) earned in his youth. Abbasid Khalifa (809-813).

Amin-ud-Din (A) أمين الدين: trustworthy in religion (Islam).

Ruhul Amin (A) روح الامين: see Ruh.

Amir (A). See Aamir آمر; Ameer أمير.

Amjaad (A) أمجاد (مجد): pl. of Majd مجد glory, honour. Comp. Amjad أمجد, more glorious.

Amjad (A) أمجد (مجد): more glorious, more distinguished; comp. adj. of Maajid ماجد, glorious. Comp. Amjaad أمجاد, glories. Amjad Ali: ruler of Oudh (India) (1842-7).[34]

Ammar (A) عمار (*'ammaar*): virtuous, pious, devout, religious. See

---

[33] See Mujahid, Sharif Al-, *Quaid-i- Azam Jinnah*, p. 697; Ahmad, Aziz, *An Intellectual History of Islam*, p. 73.

[34] See Ahmad, Aziz, *An Intellectual History of India*, p. 20.

Male Names

Mu'min مؤمن. Ammar ibn Yaasir: a *sahaabi*.[35]

Amr[36] (A) عمرو (*'amr*): life. See Umar عمر.

> **Amr bin al-'Aas** (A) عمرو بن العاص: early Islamic military leader (d.663).[37]

Anan (A) عنان (*'anaan*): clouds.

Anas (A) أنس: friendliness, joy, delight. Comp. Anis أنيس, friendly. Anas ibn Malik: a *sahaabi* known as 'the servant and friend of the Messenger of Allah'[38] and a transmitter of many *hadith*.

Anbar (A). See Ambar.

Anees (A). Anis.

Anis (A) أنيس (*anees*) (أنس): friendly, sociable, intimate friend, kind. See Sadeeq صديق; Rafeeq رفيق; Lateef لطيف. Comp. Anas أنس, friendliness.

Ansar (A) أنصار (*ansaar*) (نصر): pl. of Naasir ناصر, friend, patron, supporter, follower. وما للظالمين من انصار "For wrong-doers there

---

[35] See Lings, Martin, *Muhammad*, p. 329.

[36] See Al-Arnaut, Shafiq, *Qamus al-Asma' al-Arabiyya* [Dictionary of Arabic Names] (in Arabic), p. 68; Colebrooke, T. E., 'On the Proper Names of the Mohammadans', *Journal of the Royal Asiatic Society of Great Britain and Ireland*, XIII, pp. 241-2 (1881).

[37] See Haykal, M. H., *The Life of Muhammad*, p. 98; Glasse, Cyril, *The Concise Encyclopaedia of Islam*, p. 41.

[38] See An-Nawawi, *Forty Hadith*, p. 56.

Male Names

will be no helpers." (*surat Aal 'Imraan* 3:192). Historically, the Ansar were those people of Madina who received and helped Muhammad (s) after the *hijra* in 622 A.D. والمهاجرين والانصار "The Muhajirs and the Ansar" (*surat al-Tawba* 9:117).

Ansari (A) أنصاري (*ansaariyy*): *nisba* (relation) through ancestry to an Ansar. Sa'd ibn Zayd al-Ansari: a *sahaabi*.[39]

Anwaar (A) أنوار (نور): rays of light; pl. of Nur نور, light. Comp. Anwar أنور, brighter.

> **Anwaar-ul-Karim** (A) أنوار الكريم: lights of the Beneficent (Allah).

Anwar (A) أنور (نور): brighter, more brilliant, more luminous; comp. adj. of Nur نور, light. Comp. Anwaar أنوار, rays of light.

> **Anwar as-Sadat** (A) أنور السادات (*anwar al-saadaat*): the most brilliant of the Sayyids. See Saadaat سادات.

Aqdas (A) أقدس (قدس): more or most pure, most holy, more or most sacred. See Qudsi قدسي, holy.

Aqeel (A) عقيل (*'aqeel*): insight, mind, intellect, judiciousness. Aqeel ibn Abu Talib: cousin of Muhammad (s).[40] Comp. Aaqil عاقل, wise.

Aqib (A) عاقب (*'aaqib*) (عقب): successor. Al-'Aaqib العاقب: an

---

[39] See Haykal, M. H., *The Life of Muhammad*, p. 316.

[40] See Lings, Martin, *Muhammad*, p. 285.

epithet of Muhammad (s).[41]

Male Names

Aqil (A). See Aaqil عاقل; Aqeel عقيل.

Aqmar (A) أقمر: bright, brilliant, luminous, moonlit.

Aqqad[42] (A) عقّاد: maker of trimmings,[43] haberdasher. Abbas Mahmud al-Aqqad: Egyptian writer.[44]

Arafat (A) عرفات ('*arafaat*): a plain twelve miles south west of Makkah where pilgrims spend a day performing special worship to Allah during the *Hajj* (see *surat al-Baqarah* 2:198).

Areef (A) عريف ('*areef*) (عرف): learned, expert, authority. See Aarif عارف, learned.

Arib (A) أريب (*areeb*) (أرب): bright, brilliant, clever.

Arif (A). See Aarifعارف; Areef عريف.

---

[41] "[O]ne who comes last (hence an epithet of Muhammad (s), as being styled the last of the Prophets." See Steingass, F., *A Comprehensive Persian-English Dictionary*, p. 830. See Colebrooke, T. E., 'On the Proper Names of the Mohammadans', *Journal of the Royal Asiatic Society of Great Britain and Ireland*, XI, p. 198 (1879).

[42] See Sheniti, Mahmud, 'Treatment of Arabic names', *International Conference on Cataloguing Principles Report*, 1961, p. 276.

[43] See Madina, Maan Z., *Arabic-English Dictionary of the Modern Literary Language*, p. 443.

[44] See *The Oxford Encyclopaedia of the Modern Islamic World*, vol III, p. 400; Choueiri, Youssef, *Islamic Fundamentalism*, p. 133; Mernissi, Fatima, *Beyond the Veil*, p. xxvii.

Male Names

Arkan (A) أركان: pl. of Rukn ركن, support, prop, pillar.

Arshad (A) أرشد (رشد): more rightly guided, more reasonable; comp. adj. of Rashid رشيد, wise. See Rashid.

Arshaq (A) ارشق (رشق): more elegant, more graceful; comp. adj. of رشيق, elegant.

Arslan (T) ارسلان (*arslaan*): lion. Title of the kings of Iran. Alp Arslan: hero-lion.[45] Seljuq Sultan (1063-72) who ended the Byzantine power in Asia Minor.

Arzu (P) آرزو (*aarzu*): wish, hope, love. Siraj-ud-Din Ali Khan Arzu: an eminent Indian poet in Urdu (1689-1756).[46]

As'ad (A) أسعد (سعد): happier, luckier; comp. adj. of Sa'eed سعيد, happy. Comp. Asad أسد, lion. As'ad ibn Zurarah: a *sahaabi*.[47]

Asad (A) أسد: lion. Comp. As'ad أسعد, happier. See Haidar حيدر. Asad ibn Haashim: an ancestor of Muhammad (s).[48]

> **Asadullah** (A) أسد الله (*asad allah*): lion of Allah. Title of Khalifa Ali.[49]

---

[45] See Hitti, Philip K., *History of the Arabs*, p. 475.

[46] Ahmad, Aziz, *An Intellectual History of Islam in India*, p. 97.

[47] See Lings, Martin, *Muhammad*, p. 108.

[48] *Ibid.*, p. 28.

[49] See Steingass, F., *A Comprehensive Persian-English Dictionary*, p. 57; Colebrooke, T. E., 'On the Proper Names of the Mohammadans', *Journal of the Royal Asiatic Society of Great Britain and Ireland*, XI, p. 198 (1879).

20

Male Names

Asaf (P) آصف (*aasaf*): grand vizier of Sulayman.[50] Asaf Khan: prime minister during the reign of Mughal emperor Jahangir. His daughter Mumtaz Mahal was married to Emperor Shah Jahan.

Asaf Jah (P) آصف جاه: as noble and exalted as Asaf.

Asgar (A). See Asghar أصغر.

Asghar (A) أصغر (صغر): younger, smaller; com. adj. of Sagheer صغير, young, small (see *surat Sabaa* 34:3).

Ali Asghar (A) علي أصغر: infant son of Imam Husayn who attained martyrdom in the battle of Karbala when he was a suckling baby.[51]

Ashab (A) أصهب: reddish, blond, fair. Nickname of Asad أسد, lion.

Ashfaq (A) أشفاق (*ashfaaq*) (شفق): pl. of Shafaqa شفقة, compassion, sympathy, pity, mercy, favour.[52] See Ishfaq إشفاق, compassion.

Ashiq (A) عاشق ('*aashiq*): adorer.

Ashiq Ali (A) عاشق علي: adorer of Ali.

Ashiq Muhammad (A) عاشق محمد: adorer of Muhammad (s).

---

[50] See Steingass, F., *A Comprehensive Persian-English Dictionary*, p. 69.

[51] See Al-Tabatabai, Allamah Sayyid Muhammad Husayn, *Shi'ite Islam*, p. 201.

[52] See Wortabet, *Arabic English Dictionary*, p. 316.

Male Names

Ashja (A) أشجع (*ashja'*) (شجع): more courageous, braver; comp. adj. of Shuja' شجاع, courageous.

Ashraf (A) أشرف (شرف): nobler, more honourable; comp. adj. of Sharif شريف, noble. Mawlana Ashraf Ali Thanvi (1864-1943): Indian scholar in the field of Islam and author of *Beheshti Jewar*.

الأشرف صلاح الدين خليل :**Al-Ashraf Salah-ud-Din Khalil** (A) king of Egypt (1290-94).

Asil (A) أصيل (*aseel*) (أصل): of noble origin, highborn, pure, pristine. A *sahaabi*.

Asim (A) عاصم (*'aasim*) (عصم): protector, guardian. والله يعصمك من الناس "Allah will protect you (Muhammad) from mankind." (*surat al-Maa'idah* 5:67). Asim ibn Thabit: a *sahaabi*.[53]

Asir (A) أثير (*atheer*) (اثر): honoured, chosen, preferred. Comp. Aasir آسر, captivating.

Asir-ud-Din (A) أثير الدين: honoured (person) of the religion (Islam).

Askari (A) عسكري (*'askariyy*): soldier.

Hasan Askari (A) حسن عسكري: the eleventh Imam of the Shi'ites (845-72).

Aslam (A) أسلم (سالم): better, more perfect, more complete; comp. adj. of Saalim سالم, safe.

---

[53] See Haykal, M. H. *The Life of Muhammad*, p. 234.

Male Names

Asra (A) أسرى (سري): travel by night. *Asra* refers to the night journey of Muhammad (s) to the seven heavens. See Isra إسراء, the night journey of Muhammad (s).

Asrar (A) أسرار (*asraar*) (سرّ): secrets, mysteries; pl. of Sirr سرّ, secret. See Israr إسرار, secret.

> **Asrar-ul-Haqq** (A) أسرار الحق (*asraar al-haqq*): secrets of the Truth (Allah).

Ata (A) عطاء (*'ataa'*) (عطو): gift, present. وما كان عطاء ربك محظورا "The bounties of your Lord are not closed to anyone." (*surat Bani Israa'il* 17:20). 'Ataa' (d.732): well-known commentator on the Qur'an.

> **Ataullah** (A) عطاء الله (*'ataa' allah*): gift of Allah.

> **Ata-ur-Rahman** (A) عطاء الرحمن (*'ataa' al-rahmaan*): gift of the Merciful (Allah).

Athar (A) أطهر (طهر): purer, more virtuous; comp. adj. of Tahir طاهر, pure (see *surat al-Baqarah* 2:232).

Atif (A) عاطف (*'aatif*) (عطف): compassionate, affectionate, kind-hearted, loving.

Atiq (A) عتيق (*'ateeq*) (عتق): ancient, noble. *Al-Bait al-'Ateeq* البيت العتيق "The ancient House [the Kaaba]" (*surat al-Hajj* 22:29, 33).

Attar (A) عطّار (*'attar*): perfumer.

> **Farid-ud-Din Attar** (A) فريد الدين عطّار: Persian mystic and poet (d.1229).

Male Names

Atuf (A) عطوف (*'atoof*): affectionate, kind hearted, compassionate, loving.

Aulad (A) أولاد (*aulaad*): pl. of walad ولد, son. Aulad Husayn: sons of Husayn.

Averroes (A). See Rushd: Ibn Rushd.

Avicenna (A). See Ibn Sina.

Aurangzeb (P) اورنگزيب: ornament of the throne. Muhyi-id-Din Muhammad Aurangzeb: Mughal emperor, well-known for his piety during whose reign (1658-1707) the Mughal empire reached its farthest limit.

Awrangzeb (P). See Aurangzeb.

Awwab (A) اواب: sincere repentant, one who praises Allah. An epithet of Muhammad (s).

Awwal (A) أول: first. Al-Awwal الأول, the First: one of the names of Allah (see *surat al-Hadeed* 57:3).

    Abdul Awwal (A) عبد الأول (*'abd al-awwal*): servant of the First.

Ayaat (A) آيات (*aayaat*) (آي): pl. of Aayat آية, sign, verse of the Qur'an. See Ayat.

Ayat (A) آية (*aayah*) (آي): sign, revelation, verse of the Qur'an. ومن آياته اليل والنهار والشمس والقمر "Among His signs are the night and the day and the sun and the moon." (*surat Fussilat* 41:37).

24

Male Names

Ayatullah (A) الله آية (*aayat allah*): sign of Allah. It "is an honorific title with hierarchical value in twelver Imamite Shiism, bestowed by popular usage on outstanding *mujtahids*, with reference to the Qur'an 41:53."[54] Ayatullah Ruhullah Khomeini (1902-1989): the architect of revolution in Iran declaring it an Islamic Republic.[55]

Ayatollah (A). See Ayat.

Ayman (A) أيمن (يمن): lucky, blessed, right-hand, right, on the right. وناديناه من جانب الطور الايمن "We called him (Musa) from the right side of the mount." (*surat Maryam* 19:52). See Maimun ميمون; Umm Ayman (f.); Yumnaa يمنى, fem. of Ayman.

Ayn (A) عين (*'ayn*): source, spring (see *surat Aal 'Imraan* 3:13).

> **Ayn-ud-Din** (A) عين الدين: source of the faith (Islam). Ruler of Anatolia (1142).

> **Ayn-ul-Hayat** (A) عين الحياة: fountain of life.

Ayoub (A). See Ayub.

Ayub (A) ايوب (*ayyub*): a Prophet, the biblical Job (see *surat al-Nisaa'* 4:163). Muhammad Ayub Khan: President of Pakistan (1958-69).

---

[54] See *The Oxford Encyclopaedia of the Modern Islamic World*, vol. I, p. 162.

[55] "Khomeini made the revolution of 1979 by means of his almost unaided oratory." See Fernandez-Armesto, Felipe, *Millennium*, p. 559.

Male Names

a اَبو: **Abu Ayyub al-Ansari** (A) ابو ايوب الأنصاري a *sahaabi.*[56]

Ayubi (A) ايوبي (*ayyubiyy*): *nisba* (relation) to Ayub. Ayyubid dynasty: Sultan Salah ud-Din, son of Ayyub is the founder of this dynasty which ruled Egypt, Syria, Diyarbakr and the Yemen from 1169 to the end of the 15th century.

Ayyub (A). See Ayub ايوب.

Azad (P) آزاد (*aazaad*) freedom.

Abul Kalam Azad (A+P) أبو الكلام آزاد (1889-1958): Indian statesman, scholar in the field of Islam and author of *Tarjuman al-Qur'an.*

Azam (A) أعظم (*a'zam*) (عظم): greater, greatest, more important, most important; comp. adj. of Azim عظيم, mighty. الذين آمنوا وهاجروا وجاهدوا في سبيل الله بأموالهم وانفسهم اعظم درجة عند الله "Those who believe, and have left their homes and striven with their wealth and their lives in Allah's way are of the highest rank in the sight of Allah." (*surat al-Tawba* 9:20).

Azamat (A) عظمة ('*azamah*) (عظم): majesty, pride.

Azhaar (A) أزهار (زهر): pl. of Zahrat زهرة, flower, blossom. Comp. Azhar أزهر, shining.

Azhar (A) أزهر (زهر): shining, bright, brilliant, luminous, radiant. Al-

---

[56] He was "the standard-bearer of the Prophet, who had harboured Muhammad in al-Madinah on the occasion of the Hijrah..." See Hitti, Philip K., *History of the Arabs*, p. 201.

Male Names

Azhar: a *sahaabi*. Al-Azhar: a university situated in Cairo.[57] Comp. Azhaar أزهار, flowers.

Azim (A) عظيم (*'azeem*) (عظم): mighty, magnificent, glorious. Al-'Azeem العظيم, the All-glorious: one of the names of Allah (*surat al-Baqarah, aayat al-kursiy* 2:255). والله ذو الفضل العظيم "Allah is of infinite bounty." (*surat al-Baqarah* 2:105). *Al-qur'an al-azeem* القرآن العظيم "The Glorious Qur'an" (*surat al-Hijr* 15:87).

> **Abdul Azim** (A) عبد العظيم (*'abd al-'azeem*): servant of the Mighty.

> **Azim-ush-Shan** (A) عظيم الشأن (*azeem al-Sha'n*): of mighty concern. Mughal emperor (1712).

Azimi (A) عظيمي: of or relating to Azim.

Aziz (A) عزيز (*'azeez*) (عزّ): mighty, strong, illustrious, highly esteemed, dearly loved, beloved. Al-Aziz العزيز, the All-mighty: one of the names of Allah (*surat al-Baqarah* 2:228).

> **Abdul Aziz** (A) عبد العزيز (*'abd al-'azeez*): servant of the All-mighty. Shah Abdul Aziz (1746-1824): son of Shah Wali Allah. Indian religious reformer and author of *Tuhfa*.[58] Ibn Sa'ud Abdul Aziz: founder of modern Saudi Arabia (d.1953).

---

[57] It is "the international university of Islam (and the oldest continuously operating institution of higher learning in the world) founded in 970." See Pipes, Daniel, *In The Path of God: Islam and Political Power*, p. 208.

[58] See *The Oxford Encyclopaedia of the Modern Islamic World*, vol. I, p. 2.

Male Names

Azmi (A) عزمي ('*azmiyy*): one who fulfils his promise.[59]

Azraf (A) أظرف (ظرف): more elegant, more graceful; comp. adj. of Zarif ظريف, elegant.

Azud (A) عضد ('*adud*) upper arm, strength, power.

> **Azud-ud-Dawlah** (A) عضد الدولة (*adud al-dawlah*): the supporting arm of the state. Buwayhid Sultan (949-83).[60] See Dawla.

> **Azud-ud-Din** (A) عضد الدين (*adud al-din*) strength of the religion (Islam).

Azzam (A) عزام ('*azzaam*) (عزم): very determined, resolved, resolute.

---

[59] See Lane, *Arabic-English Lexicon*, p. 2038.

[60] "'Adud was not only the greatest Buwayhid but also the most illustrious ruler of his time." See Hitti, Philip K., *History of the Arabs*, p. 471.

Male Names

B

Baadi (A) البادي (*al-baadii*) (بدو): distinct, evident, plain, clear.

Baahi (A) الباهي (*al-baahii*) (بهو): glorious, magnificent. See Bahi بهي glorious.

Baari' (A) بارئ (برء): originator. Al-Baari' البارئ, the Originator: one of the names of Allah. هو الله الخالق البارئ المصور له الاسماء الحسنى "He is Allah, the Creator, the Originator, the Fashioner. To Him belong the most beautiful names." (*surat al-Hashr* 59:24). Comp. Bari' بريء, innocent.

> **Abdul Baari** (A) عبد البارئ (*'abd al-baari'*): servant of the Creator. Mawlana Abdul Bari (1878-1926): Indian political leader and founder of Madrasa Nizamia, Farangi Mahal.[61]

> **Lutf-ul-Baari** (A) لطف البارئ (*lutf al-baari'*): kindness of the Creator.

> **Sayf-ul-Baari** (A) سيف البارئ (*saif al-baari'*): sword of the Creator.

Baari' (A) بارع (برع): brilliant, superior, outstanding. Comp. Baari'بارئ, originator, Bari'بريء, innocent.

Baariq (A) بارق (برق) shining, lightning, bright, illuminating. Comp.

---

[61] See Hardy, P., *The Muslims of British India*, p. 189. He "wrote over 100 books on religious and other topics..." See Mujahid, Sharif Al-, *Quaid-i- Azam Jinnah*, p. 662.

Male Names

Bareeq بریق, brightness.

Babar (P) ببر (*babr*): tiger.[62] " بابر *baabar*, Name of an emperor of Hindustan, the second of the Mogul race."[63] Zahir-ud-Din Baabar/Baabur: founder (1483-1530) of the Mughal empire.[64] See Zahir.

Badi' (A) بدیع (badee') (بدع): wonderful, marvellous, unique, amazing. Al-Badi' البدیع, the Creator, the Originator: one of the names of Allah. بدیع السماوات والارض "The Creator of the heavens and the earth." (*surat al-Baqarah* 2:117). Comp. Baadi البادی, distinct.

Badi-ul-Aalam (A) بدیع العالم: unique in the world.

Badi-uz-Zaman (A) بدیع الزمان: genius of the age. An outstanding writer of the Abbasid period; a ruler of Khurasan (1506). Bediuzzaman Said Nursi (1876-1960): founder of "[t]he modern Turkish religious movement known as Nurculuk."[65]

Badr (A) بدر: full moon.

Badr-ul-Aalam (A) بدر العالم: full moon of the world.

Badr-ud-Din (A) بدر الدین: full moon of religion (Islam). King of Central Anatolia (d.1278). Badruddin Tyabji (1844-1906): Indian political leader and the first Muslim President

---

[62] See Steingass, F., *A Comprehensive Persian-English Dictionary*, p. 154.

[63] *Ibid.*, p. 135.

[64] "[H]e conquered more of India than any one man had ruled for more than a hundred years." See Fernandez-Armesto, Felipe, *Millennium*, p. 218.

[65] See *The Oxford Encyclopaedia of the Modern Islamic World*, p. 255.

of the Congress (political party).

Badr-ud-Duja (A) بدر الدجى: full moon of the dark (night). An epithet of Muhammad (s).

Badri (A) بدري (*badriyy*): "Of or relating to the full moon."[66]   Abu Mas'ud Badri: a *sahaabi*.[67]

Baha (A) بهاء (*bahaa'*) (بهو): beauty, glory, splendour, magnificence.

> **Baha-ud-Dawlah** (A) بهاء الدولة: glory of the state.   Persian physician (d.*c*.1510) and author of *Khulaasat al-Tajaarib* (*The Quintessence of Experiences*).[68]   Baha-ud-Dawlah Firuz: Buwayhid Sultan (998-1012).

> **Baha-ud-Din** (A) بهاء الدين: glory of the religion (Islam). Biographer of Sultan Salah-ud-Din.

Bahadur (P) بهادر (*bahaadur*): brave, bold, magnanimous.   An honorific title.   See Khan Bahadur.

> **Bahadur Shah II** (P) بهادر شاه: the last Mughal emperor (d.1862).

Bahi (A) بهي (*bahiyy*) (بهو): beautiful, glorious, magnificent, splendid, brilliant.   See Baahi الباهي, glorious.

---

[66] See Steingass, F., *A Comprehensive Persian-English Dictionary*, p. 163.

[67] See *Riyadh-us-Saleheen*, vol. I, p. 409.

[68] See Lewis, Bernard, *The Middle East*, p. 265.

Male Names

Bahiy-id-Din (A) بهيّ الدين: glorious (person) of the religion (Islam).

Bahij (A) بهيج (*baheej*): delightful, cheerful, happy.

Bahir (A) باهر (*baahir*) (بهر): spectacular, brilliant, superb, magnificent, gorgeous.

Bahjat (A) بهجات (*bahjaat*): splendours, pl. of Bahjah بهجة. See Bahja (f.).

Bahram (P) بهرام (*bahraam*): Mars. Iranian royal name.

Baker (A): See Baqir باقر.

Bakhit (P) بخيت (*bakheet*): lucky, fortunate.

Bakhsh[69] (P) بخش: gift, fortune.

    Allah Bakhsh (A+P) الله بخش: gift of Allah.

    Ilaahi Bakhsh (A+P) إلاهي بخش: gift of Allah.

    Khuda Bakhsh[70] (P) خدا بخش: gift of Khuda (Allah).

    Taaj Bakhsh (A+P) تاج بخش: "Distributing crowns; a maker of

---

[69] Names such as Pir Bakhsh or Nabi Bakhsh are improper if it is thought that the child was born because of a favour granted by a Pir or Nabi.

[70] See Colebrooke, T. E., 'On the Proper Names of the Mohammadans', *Journal of the Royal Asiatic Society of Great Britain and Ireland*, XI, p. 214, (1879).

kings (applied to Rustam)."[71]

Bakht (A) بخت: luck, fortune.

Bedar Bakht (P+A). See Bedar.

Bakhtiyar (A+P) بختيار (*bakhtiyaar*): fortunate, lucky. Izz-ud-Dawlah Bakhtiyaar: Buwayhid Sultan in Iraq (967-78). See Izz.

Baki (A). See Baqi باقي.

Bakr (A). See Abu Bakr أبو بكر.

Baktiyar (A+P). See Bakhtiyar.

Bandah[72] (P) بنده: servant.

Baqa (A) بقاء (*baqaa'*): survival, immortality, eternity.

Abul Baqa Khalid (A) أبو البقاء خالد: ruler of Tunisia (1309-1311).

Baqi (A) باقي (*baaqii*): permanent, everlasting, eternal. Al-Baaqi الباقي, the Everlasting: one of the names of Allah. ما عندكم ينفد وما عند الله باق "What is with you wastes away, and what is with Allah remains." (*surat al-Nahl* 16:96). Khwaja Baqi Billah (1563-1603):

---

[71] See Steingass, F., *A Comprehensive Persian-English Dictionary*, p. 273.

[72] A Muslim is a servant only to Allah. Thus names like Bandah Ali (see Colebrooke, T. E., 'On the Proper Names of the Mohammadans', *Journal of the Royal Asiatic Society of Great Britain and Ireland*, XI, p. 213, (1879); Schimmel, Annemarie, *Islamic Names*, p. 35), are considered improper.

Male Names

religious leader and the founder of Naqshbandi order in the Indian subcontinent during the reign of Mughal emperor Akbar.

Abdul Baqi (A) عبد الباقي (*'abd al-baaqii*): servant of the Everlasting.

Baqir (A) باقر (*baaqir*) (بقر): abounding in knowledge, erudite, learned. Muhammad al-Baqir: the fifth Imam of the Shi'ites (d.732).[73] Muhammad al-Baaqir Majlisi: see Majlisi.

Barakat (A) بركات (*barakaat*) (برك): blessings, good fortunes, prosperities; pl. of Barakat بركة, blessing. رحمت الله وبركاته عليكم اهل البيت "The mercy of Allah and His blessings be upon you, O people of the house." (*surat Hud* 11:73). King of Egypt (1277-80).

Abul Barakat (A) ابو البركات: father of blessings.

Barakatullah (A) بركات الله (*barakaat allah*): blessings of Allah.

Bareeq (A) بريق (برق) glitter, lightning flash, lustre, brightness, brilliance, radiance. See Baariq بارق, bright.

Bari (A) بريء (*baree'*): innocent, blameless, guiltless, sound. Comp. Baari' بارع, brilliant; Baari' بارئ, originator.

Barik (A). See Baariq بارق; Bareeq بريق.

[73] See Al-Tabatabai, Allamah Sayyid Muhammad Husayn, *Shi'ite Islam*, p. 202; Fyzee, Asaf, A A., *Outlines of Muhammadan Law*, p. 42; Schimmel, Annemarie, *Islamic Names*, p. 35.

Male Names

Barr (A) ‎بَر: pious, upright, just; sing. of Abraar ‎أبرار. Al-Barr ‎البر, the All-benign: one of the names of Allah (see *surat al-Tur* 52:28). See Salih ‎صالح; Wafiyy ‎وفي.

> **Abdul Barr** (A) ‎عبد البر: servant of the All-benign. Ibn Abd al-Barr al-Qurtubi (d. 463 AH): "one of the greatest *hadith* scholars of his time."[74]

Barraq (A) ‎براق (*barraaq*): flashing, bright, brilliant, glittering.

Bashar (A) ‎بشر: man, mankind. ‎قل انما انا بشر مثلكم يوحى الي ‎انما الهكم اله واحد "Say: (O Muhammad!) I am only a man like you. My Lord inspires in me that your God is only one God." (*surat al-Kahf* 18:110).

> **Abul Bashar** (A) ‎أبو البشر: father of mankind. An epithet of Adam.[75]

> **Khair-ul-Bashar**[76] (A) ‎خير البشر: the greatest man. An epithet of Muhammad (s).

Basharat (A) ‎بشارة (*bashaarah*): good news, glad tidings.[77] See Bishara ‎بشارة, good news.

Bashir (A) ‎بشير (*basheer*) (‎بشر): bringer of good news, Messenger sent

---

[74] See Umari, Akram Diya al, *Madinan Society at the Time of the Prophet*, p. 35.

[75] See *Al-Mawrid: A Modern Arabic-English Dictionary*, p. 18.

[76] Although the name is popular in the Indian sub-continent, it is not used in Arab countries as it is believed that the title belongs exclusively to Muhammad (s).

[77] See *Steingass, F., A Comprehensive Persian-English Dictionary*, p. 188.

Male Names

by Allah. An epithet of Muhammad (s). وما ارسلناك الا كافة للناس بشيرا ونذيرا "And We have not sent you (O Muhammad) except as a bringer of good news and a warner to all mankind." (surat Sabaa 34:28). See Mubashshir مبشر.

Bashshar (A) بشّار (bashshaar): herald of good news.

Basil (A) باسل (baasil) brave, bold, valiant. See Shuja شجاع, brave.

Basim (A) باسم (baasim) (بسم): smiler, smiling.

Basir (A) بصير (baseer) (بصر): sagacious, endowed with insight. Al-Baseer البصير, the All-seeing: one of the names of Allah. ان الله سميع بصير "Allah is All-hearing, All-seeing." (surat Luqmaan 31:28). Abu Basir: a sahaabi.[78]

Basit (A) باسط (baasit) (بسط): one who stretches, enlarges. Al-Baasit الباسط One who stretches out: one of the names of Allah. الله يبسط الرزق لمن يشاء من عباده ويقدر "Allah enlarges rizk (provision) for whom He will of His servants and restricts it (for whom He will)." (surat al-Qasas 28:82).

    Abdul Basit (A) عبد الباسط ('abd al-baasit): servant of the Expander.

Bassam (A) بسّام (bassaam): smiling.

Baten (A). See Batin.

Batin (A) باطن (baatin) (بطن): inward, within, secret, esoteric.

---

78 See Haykal, M.H., The Life of Muhammad, p. 356.

Male Names

Al-Baatin الباطن, the Inward: one of the names of Allah. هو الاول والآخر والظاهر والباطن "He is the First and the Last, and the Outward and the Inward." (see *surat al-Hadeed* 57:3).

Abdul Batin (A) عبد الباطن (*abd al-baatin*): servant of the Inward.

Baz (P) باز: falcon. Shahbaz (P). See Shah.

Bazl (A) بذل (*badhl*): generosity, open-handedness.

Bazl-ur-Rahman (A) بذل الرحمن (*bazl al-rahmaan*): generosity of the All-merciful.

Bedar (P) بيدار (*beedaar*): wakeful, attentive, enlightened.

Bedar-ud-Din (P+A) بيدار الدين: attentive to the religion (Islam).

Bedar Bakht (P+A) بيدار بخت: of wakeful fortune. Mughal emperor (1788).

Beg (T) بيگ: honorific title, lord, prince.

Belal (A). See Bilal.

Ben (A). See Ibn.

Bidar (P). See Bedar.

Male Names

Bilal (A) بلال (*bilaal*): a *sahaabi* who was the first *muezzin*[79] in Islam and a mosque in Medina bears his name. The word Bilal, originates from *ball* بل, moistening, wetting.

Bin (A). See Ibn.

Bishara (A) بشارة (*bishaarah*) (بشر): good news, glad tidings. See Basharat بشارة, good news; Bushra بشرى.

Bishr (A) بشر: joy, happiness, cheerfulness. Bishr ibn Ma'roor: a *sahaabi*.

Borhan (A). See Burhan.

Bukhari (A) بخاري: Muhammad ibn Ismaa'il al-Bukhari (810-70): author of one of the *sahih hadith*.[80] The *nisba* al-Bukhari connects him to his birth place Bukhara near Samarkand.

Bulbul (P) بلبل: nightingale. See Andalib (A) عندليب.

Bundar (P) بندار (*bundaar*): rich, intelligent, firm.

Burhan (A) برهان (*burhaan*) (برهن): proof. يايها الناس قد جاءكم برهان من ربكم "O mankind! A proof has now come to you from your Lord." (*surat al-Nisaa'* 4:174).

Al-Burhan (A) البرهان: the proof. An epithet of

---

[79] Caller to prayer. Traditionally, a *muezzin* calls to prayer from the minaret of a mosque.

[80] "Next to the Koran this is the book that has exerted the greatest influence over the Moslem mind." See Hitti, Philip K., *History of the Arabs*, p. 395.

38

Male Names

Muhammad (s).

Burhan-ud-Din (A) برهان الدين: proof of the religion (Islam). A king of Central Anatolia.

Bux (P). See Bakhsh.

Male Names

C

Chowdhury (Sanskrit/Bengali) چوهدری: chief of four.[81] A hereditary[82] title of honour, awarded by the Mughal emperors to persons of eminence,[83] both Muslims and Hindus.[84]

Chirag (P) چراغ: lamp, light, guide. See Misbah مصباح; Nibras نبراس (f.); Siraaj سراج;

> **Chirag Ali**: Indian scholar on Islamic law and political reformer (1844-95).[85]

---

[81] See Haughton, Graves, C., *Dictionary of Bengali and Sanskrit*, p. 1122.; Mendes, John, *Companion to Johnson's Dictionary, Bengali and English*, p. 130. "Commander of four different fighting forces, the fleet, the cavalry, the infantry, and the elephant corps." See Dil, Afia, 'A Comparative Study of the Personal Names and Nicknames of the Bengali-Speaking Hindus and Muslims' in Gunderson, W. M., *Studies on Bengal*, p. 57. "...Chaudhry (spelled in a dozen different ways). Chaudhry corresponds exactly to the German *Schulze* (the headman of a village)". See Schimmel, Annemarie, *Islamic Names*, p. 56. "Chowdhury (lord of land surrounding the capital)". See Saif-ul-Islam, 'Cataloguing Bengali Muslim Names: problems and possible solutions', *UNESCO J. of Information Science*, II, p. 38 (1980).

[82] See Dogra, R C., 'Cataloguing Urdu Names', *Int. Libr. Rev.* V, p. 358 (1973); Elahi, Fazl; Khurshid, Anis; Kaisar, S Ibne Hasan, 'Cataloguing of Oriental Names', *Quart. J. Pak. Lib. Asso.*, II, p. 7 (1961).

[83] Dil, Afia, 'A Comparative Study of the Personal Names and Nicknames of the Bengali-Speaking Hindus and Muslims' in Gunderson, W. M., *Studies on Bengal*, p. 57

[84] *Ibid.*

[85] See Donohue, John J. & Esposito, John L., *Islam in Transition*, p. 44.

Male Names

Chirag-ud-Din (P+A) چراغ الدین : light of the religion (Islam).

Chishti (P) چشتی : one originating from "Chisht, a village of Khurasan".[86]

Khwaja Mu'in-ud-Din Muhammad Chishti (1142-1236): one of the greatest saints of India. He is known as *Gharibnawaz*, one who cherishes the poor, and is buried in Ajmir. An important *tariqah*, the Chishtiyyah Order bears his name. See Khwaja; Muin.

Shaykh Salim Chishti (d.1571): famous saint buried in Fathpur Sikri (India), a contemporary of Mughal emperor Akbar.

---

[86] See *Shorter Encyclopaedia of Islam*, p. 66.

Male Names

D

Dabir (A) دابر (*daabir*) (دبر): root, origin.

Daabir-ud-Din (A) دابر الدين: root of the religion (Islam).

Dalil (A) دليل (*daleel*) (دلّ): guide, model, leader, example. Daleelan دليلا (see *surat al-Furqaan* 25:45).

    Dalil-ur-Rahman (A) دليل الرحمن (*daleel al-rahmaan*): guide of the Merciful (Allah).

Dana (P) دانا (*daanaa*): wise, learned.

Danesh (P) دانش: knowledge, learning.

Dara (P) دارا (*daaraa*): possessor, sovereign. Comp. Dara (A) (f.). Darius I: king of Persia (521-486 B.C.).[87] Dara Shikoh (1615-59): son of Mughal emperor Shah Jahan.

Darvesh (P). See Darwish.

Darwish (P) درويش: holy man.

Dastgir (P) دستگير (*dastgeer*): patron, protector, saint.[88]

---

[87] See Steingass, F., *A Comprehensive Persian-English Dictionary*, p. 496.

[88] "*Pir-i-dastgir*, 'who takes by the hand' (that is, 'Abdul Qadir Jilani)." See Schimmel, Annemarie, *Islamic Names*, p. 38.

Male Names

Daud (A). See Dawud.

Dawla[89] (A) دولة (*dawlah*): wealth, empire, state, power. Siraj-ud-Dawlah: see Siraj.

Dawlat (A) دولة. See Dawla.

Dawlat Qazi (*qadi*) (A): Bengali poet (1600-38).[90]

Dawlat Khan (A+P) دولت خان. See Khan.

Dawud (A) داود (*daawud*): a Prophet and father of Prophet Sulayman. In the Bible, he is known as David. وآتينا داود زبورا "We gave Daud Zabur (Psalms)." (*surat Bani Israa'il* 17:55).

Abu Dawud (A) ابو داود: author of one of the *sahih hadith* (d.875).

Dawud Shah (A+P) داود شاه: Bengal Sultan (1572-76).

Deen (A). See Din.

Dewan (A). See Diwan.

Dhul Fiqar (A). See Zul Fiqar ذو الفقار.

Didar (P) ديدار (*didaar*): vision, sight.

---

[89] Originally, a title of honour, e. g. Dabir al-Dawlah. See Dogra, R C., 'Cataloguing Urdu Names', *Int. Libr. Rev.*, v, p. 358 (1973).

[90] "His scholarship in Arabic, Persian and also Sanskrit raised Bengali in his hands to a high literary standard." See Aziz, Ahmad, *An Intellectual History of Islam*, p. 114-5.

Male Names

Dil (P) دل: heart, mind.

Dil Nawaz (P) دلنواز: soothing heart, mind.

Dil-awar (P) دلاور (*dil-aawar*): bold, brave. Dilawar Khan Husayn Ghuri: Sultan of Malwa (India) (1401-05).

Dilwar (P) دلوار (*dilwaar*): bold, courageous.

Din (A) دين (*deen*): religion, faith, belief, *diyaana* ديانة. Originally, a *khitab*, i.e. an honorific title of which the last part is al-Din. ان الدين عند الله الاسلام "The religion with Allah is Islam." (*surat Aal 'Imraan* 3:19).

> **Sayf-ud-Din** (A) سيف الدين: sword of the religion (Islam). See Sayf.

Diwan (A+P) ديوان (*diwaan*): royal court, tribunal of justice. See Majlis مجلس.

> **Diwan Muhammad** (A) ديوان محمد: court of Muhammad (s).

Dost (P) دوسة: friend.

> **Dost Muhammad** (P+A) دوسة محمد: friend of Muhammad (s). Afghan king (1819-63).

Dudu Miyan: See Mia.

Duha (A) ضحى (*duhaa*): forenoon. *Al-Duhaa* الضحى: title of the 93rd *sura* of the Qur'an. See Zuha.

44

E

Ebrahim (A). See Ibrahim.

Ehsan (A). See Ihsan.

Ehtesham (A). See Ihtisham.

Ejaz (A). See Ijaz.

Elias (A). See Ilyas.

Emad (A). See Imad.

Emir (A). See Ameer.

Enam (A). See Inam.

Enayat (A). See Inayat.

Male Names

F

Faaid (A). See Faid فائد.

Faaiz (A) فائز (فوز): victorious, triumphant, successful. اصحاب الجنة هم الفائزون "The inheritors of paradise, they are the victorious." (*surat al-Hashr* 59:20). Comp. Fayz فيض (*fayd*), superabundance.

Al-Faiz (A) الفائز: Fatimid Khalifa (1154-60).

Faarih (A) فارح: happy, delighted. See Farih فرح, happy.

Faaruq (A). See Faruq.

Fadi (A) الفادي (*al-faadii*) (فدى): redeemer, ransomer.

Fadil (A). See Fazil.

Fadl (A). See Fazl.

Fahd (A) فهد: leopard.

Faheem (A) فهيم (فهم): intelligent, judicious, learned erudite. Comp. Fahim فهم, quick-witted.

Fahim (A) فهم: quick-witted, sharp-witted. Comp. Faheem فهيم, intelligent.

Fahmi (A) فهمي: intelligent, intellectual.

46

Male Names

Faid (A) فائد (*faa'id*) (فيد): benefit, advantage, gain, worth, welfare.

Faiq (A) فائق (*faa'iq*) (فوق): excellent, outstanding, distinguished, superior, ascendant.

Fairuz[91] (A). See Firuz.

Faisal (A). See Faysal.

Faiz (A). See Fayz.

Fajr (A) فجر: dawn, rise, beginning, start. صلوة الفجر "The dawn prayer." (*surat al-Nur* 24:58). ان قرآن الفجر كان مشهودا "The recital of the Qur'an at dawn is ever witnessed." (*surat Bani Israa'il* 17:78).

Fakhar (A) فخار (*fakhaar*): honour, pride, glory.

Fakhir (A) فاخر (*faakhir*) (فخر): excellent, superior, magnificent. See Mumtaz ممتاز.

Fakhr (A) فخر: glory, pride, honour.

> **Fakhr-ud-Din** (A) فخر الدين: pride of the religion (Islam). Persian theologian-philosopher (1149-1209). Fakhr al-Din al-Ma'ni II (1590-1635): Amir of Lebanon.

> **Fakhr-ud-Dawlah** (A) فخر الدولة: glory of the kingdom. King of Iran (983-97).

---

[91] See Madina, Maan Z., *Arabic-English Dictionary of the Modern Literary Language*, p. 516; Cowan, J Milton (ed.) Hans Wehr, *A Dictionary of Modern Written Arabic*, p. 735; Abd-el-Jawad, Hassan, 'A Linguistic and Socio-cultural Study of Personal Names in Jordan', *Anthropological Linguistics*, XXVIII, p. 89 (1986).

47

Male Names

Fakhri (A) ‫فـخـري‬ (*fakhriyy*): proud (for noble cause), honorary.

Falah (A) ‫فلاح‬ (*falaah*): success, prosperity.

Falih (A) ‫فالح‬ (*faalih*): fortunate, lucky, successful, prosperous.

Faqih (A) ‫فقيه‬ (*faqeeh*) (‫فقه‬): jurist, scholar in *fiqh* (Islamic jurisprudence). Ruler of Granada (Spain) (1272-1302).

Faqir (A) ‫فقير‬ (*faqeer*) (‫فقر‬): poor, needy. ‫يايها الناس انتم‬ ‫الفقراء الى الله‬ "O mankind! You are the needy for Allah." (*surat Faatir* 35:15). See Gharib ‫غريب‬, poor. Faqir-Allah: seventeenth-century Indian musician.[92]

Farah (A) ‫فرح‬: joy, happiness, delight. See Bishr ‫بشر‬; Farhat ‫فرحة‬, happiness.

    Abul Farah (A) ‫أبو الفرح‬: father of joy. A Persian poet.[93]

Faraj (A) ‫فرج‬: comfort, relief, ease, repose.

    Abul Faraj (A) ‫أبو الفرج‬: father of comfort. Abu al-Faraj al-Isfahani (d.10th century): one of the most famous Arab men of letters, author of *The Book of Songs*.[94]

---

[92] "Faqir-Allah compiled his famous *Rag Durpan*, partly a translation from Sanskrit, and one of the most authoritative works on Indian music in Persian." See Ahmad, Aziz, *An Intellectual History of India*, p. 148.

[93] See Colebrooke, T. E., 'On the Proper Names of the Mohammadans', *Journal of the Royal Asiatic Society of Great Britain and Ireland*, XI, p. 188 (1879).

[94] *Ibid.*

48

Male Names

Faraman (A) فرمان (*faramaan*): order, decree.

Faramanullah (A) فرمان الله (*faramaan allah*): order of Allah.

Farhad (P) فرهاد (*farhaad*): "Mas. pr. name";[95] "lover of Shirin"[96] (Persian literature).

Farhan (A) فرحان (*farhaan*): glad, happy, cheerful, delighted.

Farhat (A) فرحات (*farhatt*) joys, delights; pl. of Farha فرحة, joy. See Farha فرحة (f.).

Fari (A) فارع (*faari'*): tall, towering, lofty.

Farid (A) فريد (*fareed*) (فرد): unique, matchless.

    Farid-ud-Din (A) فريد الدين: unique of the religion (Islam). Farid-ud-Din Attar: see Attar.

Farih (A) فرح: happy, delighted. See فارح, happy.

Farman (A). See Faraman.

Farouk (A). See Faruq.

Farrukh (P) فرخ (for فر رخ): beautiful-faced, happy, auspicious, fortunate. Comp. Faruq فاروق.

    Farrukh Siyar (P) فرخ سير: Mughal emperor (1713-19).

---

[95] See Haim, S., *The Shorter Persian-English Dictionary*, p. 525.

[96] See Steingass, F., *A Comprehensive Persian-English Dictionary*, p. 925.

49

Male Names

Farrukh-zaad (P) فرخ زاد: of happy birth.

Faruq (A) فاروق *(faaruq)*: one who distinguishes truth from falsehood, just. Title of Khalifa Umar, the second of the 'rightly guided' Khalifas (634-44).[97] Comp. Farrukh فرخ, beautiful-faced.

Faruqi (A) فاروقي *(faaruqiyy)*: *nisba* (related) through ancestry to the second Khalifa Umar al-Faruq. Malik Raja Faruqi: Sultan of Khandesh (India) (1370-99).[98]

Fasih (A) فصيح *(faseeh)* (فصح): eloquent, fluent, well-spoken. واخي هارون هو افصح مني "(Musa said:) My brother Harun is more eloquent than me." *(surat al-Qasas* 28:34).

Fasih-ur-Rahman[99] (A) فصيح الرحمن *(faseeh al-Rahmaan)*: eloquent (by grace of the Merciful).

Fateh (A). See Fatih فاتح.

Fath (A) فتح: victory, conquest, triumph. *Al-Fath* الفتح: title of the 48th *sura* of the Qur'an. اذا جاء نصر الله والفتح "When help and the victory from Allah comes." *(surat al-Nasr* 110:1).

Abul Fath (A) أبو الفتح: father of victory. A *sahaabi*. Name of Mughal emperor Akbar. Abu al-Fath Nasr: eleventh-century

---

[97] See Steingass, F., *A Comprehensive Persian-English Dictionary*, p. 903.

[98] Since [Malik Raja Faruqi] claimed descent from the caliph 'Umar b. al-Khattab, his successors called themselves the Faaruqis (al-Faaruq 'the just' being a name given to that caliph). See Bosworth, C. E., *The Islamic Dynasties*, p. 208.

[99] See Colebrooke, T. E., 'On the Proper Names of the Mohammadans', *Journal of the Royal Asiatic Society of Great Britain and Ireland*, XI, p. 203 (1879).

Male Names

jurist of Andalus.[100]

Fath Shah (A+P) فتح شاه: victorious King. Afghan King (1842). Jalal ud-Din Fath Shah: Bengal Sultan (1481-87).

Fath Allah (A) فتح الله: victory granted by Allah. Fath-Allah Shirazi (d.1588): minister of Mughal emperor Akbar.[101]

Fathi[102] (A) فتحيّ (*fathiyy*): one who wins victory after victory.

Fathy (A). See Fathi. Hasan Fathy: see Hasan.

Fatih (A) فاتح (*faatih*) (فتح): conqueror, victor, originator. وانت خير الفاتحين "You (Allah) are the best of those who make decision." (*surat al-A'raaf* 7:89). Muhammad II Fatih: king of Anatolia (1444-51).

Fatin (A) فطين, فطن (*fateen*): intelligent, sagacious. Comp. Faatin (f.) فاتن, beautiful.

Fattah (A) فتّاح (*fattaah*) (فتح): conqueror, victor. Al-Fattaah الفتّاح, the Deliverer: one of the names of Allah. وهو الفتاح العليم "He is the All-knowing Judge." (*surat Sabaa* 34:26).

   Abdul Fattah (A) عبد الفتّاح (*'abd al-fattaah*): servant of the Conqueror.

---

[100] See Armstrong, Karen, *Jerusalem: One City Three faiths*, p. 269.

[101] He was "well-versed in Arabic literature and theological studies." See Ahmad, Aziz, *An Intellectual History of India*, p. 54.

[102] See Paxton, Evelyn, 'Arabic Names', *Asian Affairs*, LIX, p. 199 (1972).

51

Male Names

Fattuh (A) فتّوح (فتح): the little conqueror; diminutive of Fattah فتّاح, conqueror. See Fattah.

Fauzi (A). See Fawzi.

Fawwaz[103] (A) فوّاز (fawwaaz): winner of victory after victory.

Fawz (A) فوز: victory, triumph, success. ومن يطع الله ورسوله فقد فاز فوزا عظيما "He that obeys Allah and His Messenger, has already gained a great victory." (surat al-Ahzaab 33:71).

Fawzi[104] (A). See Fawziy.

Fawziy (A) فوزي (fauziyy) (فوز): triumphant, victorious.

Faysal (A). فيصل (فصل): umpire, arbitrator, sword. King of Oman (1888-1913); king of Saudi Arabia (ruled 1964-75). See Hakam حكم, umpire.

Fayyaad (A). See Fayyaz.

Fayyaz (A) فيّاض (fayyaad) (فيض): generous, munificent, bountiful, liberal. See Karim كريم, generous.

Fayz (A) فيض (faid): superabundance, effluence, liberality. See Nayif نيف; Ziyada زيادة. Comp. Faaiz فائز, victorious.

---

[103] See Abd-el-Jawad, Hassan, 'A Linguistic and Socio-cultural Study of Personal Names in Jordan', *Anthropological Linguistics*, XXVIII, p. 82, 84 (1986).

[104] *Ibid.*, p. 84.

Male Names

Fayzullah[105] (A) فيض الله: *(fayd allah)*: abundance from Allah.

Fayz-ul-Anwar[106] (A) فيض الانوار: distributor of light or graces. An epithet of Khalifa Ali.

Fayz-ud-Din (A) فيض الدين: abundance of religion (Islam).

Fayz-ul-Haqq (A) فيض الـحق: *(fayd al-haqq)*: abundance from the Truth (Allah).

Fayz-i-Rabbaani (P) فيض ربّاني: possessing divine surplus.

Fayzi (A) فيضي *(faidiyy)*: endowed with superabundance. Eminent poet (1574-95) at the court of Mughal emperor Akbar, who wrote commentaries on the Qur'an.[107]

Fazil (A) فاضل *(faadil)* (فضل): virtuous, superior, outstanding, eminent.

Fazl (A) فضل *(fadl)*: favour, grace, kindness, gift, present, bounty. قل ان الفضل بيد الله يؤتيه من يشاء "Say (O Muhammad): Lo! the bounty is in the hands of Allah. He bestows it on whom he wishes." *(surat Aal 'Imraan* 3:73). Fazl-i-Hussain (1877-1936): Indian politician who promoted Muslim interests.[108]

---

[105] See Colebrooke, T. E., 'On the Proper Names of the Mohammadans', *Journal of the Royal Asiatic Society of Great Britain and Ireland*, XI, p. 212 (1879).

[106] *Ibid.*, p. 199.

[107] "'Urfi, Faydi and Naziri made the age of Akbar the golden age of Persian poetry in India." See Ahmad, Aziz, *An Intellectual History of India*, p. 76.

[108] See Hardy, P., *The Muslims of British India*, p. 200.

Male Names

Abul Fazl (A). See Abu.

Al-Fadl ibn 'Abbas (A): cousin of Muhammad (s).[109]

Fazle Ilahi[110] (A) فضل إلاهي: bounty of Allah.

Fazlullah[111] (A) فضل الله (*fadl allah*): bounty of Allah (see *surat al-Nisaa'* 4:83).

Fazl-ul-Haqq (A) فضل الـحق (*fadl al-haqq*): bounty of the Truth (Allah). A.K. Fazlul Haqq (1873-1962): Bengali statesman who "moved the historic Lahore Resolution, 23 March 1940"[112] for the establishment of Pakistan.

Fazle Rabbi (A) فضل ربي: bounty of my Lord. قال هذا من فضل ربي "[Sulayman] said: This is of the bounty of my Lord." (*surat al-Naml* 27:40).

Fazli (A) فضلي (*fadliyy*): kind, bountiful, graceful, virtuous. Eminent eighteenth-century Indian writer in Urdu.[113]

Ferdaus (A). See Firdaus.

---

[109] See Haykal, M.H., *The Life of Muhammad*, p. 454.

[110] See Steingass, F., *A Comprehensive Persian-English Dictionary*, p. 932.

[111] See Colebrooke, T. E., 'On the Proper Names of the Mohammadans', *Journal of the Royal Asiatic Society of Great Britain and Ireland*, XI, p. 212 (1879).

[112] See Mujahid, Sharif Al-, *Quaid-i- Azam Jinnah*, p. 683.

[113] See Aziz, Ahmad, *An Intellectual History of Islam in India*, p. 106.

Male Names

Fida (A) فداء (*fidaa'*): sacrifice (see *surat Muhammad* 47:4).

Fikri (A) فكري (*fikriyy*): intellectual.

Firdaus (A) فردوس: paradise, heaven. ان الذين آمنوا وعملوا الصالحات كانت لهم جنات الفردوس نزلا "Those who believe and do good works, the gardens of paradise are waiting for their welcome." (*surat al-Kahf* 18:107).

Firdausi (A) فردوسي (*firdausiyy*): heavenly.

> **Abul Qaasim Mansur Firdausi** (A) ابو القاسم منصور فردوسي (940-1020): Persian poet and author of great epic *Shahnama* (The Book of Kings) who also composed *Yusuf* and *Zuklaykha*.

Firuz (P) فيروز: victorious. Firoz Shah Tughlaq: Delhi sultan (1351-88).

> **Firuz Akhtar** (P) فيروز اختر: fortunate.

> **Firuz Bakht** (P+A) فيورز بخت: fortunate.

Fuad (A) فؤاد (*fu'aad*) (فءد): heart. ان السمع والبصر والفؤاد كل اولئك كان عنه مسئولا "Surely, the hearing, the sight, the heart all of those shall be questioned." (*surat Bani Israa'il* 17:36). Fu'aad: King of Egypt.[114] Nimat Fuad: See Ni'mat (f.).

---

[114] He "was proclaimed *malik* (king) in February 1922...Egypt was declared independent...The constitution made Islam the religion of the state and Arabic the official language." See Hitti, Philip K., *History of the Arabs*, p. 750-1.

55

Male Names

Furogh (P) فروغ: splendour, light, brightness.

Furqan (A) فرقان (*furqaan*): criterion (between right and wrong), proof, evidence. Al-Furqaan الفرقان: an attribute of the Qur'an and title of the 25th *sura*. تبارك الذي نزل الفرقان على عبده ليكون للعالمين نذيرا "Blessed is He Who has revealed to His servant the Criterion (of right and wrong) that he may be a warner to the peoples." (*surat al-Furqaan* 25:1)

Futuh (A) فتوح (فتح): victories, conquests; pl. of فتح, victory.

Abul Futuh (A) ابو الفتوح: father of victories.

G

Gaffar (A). See Ghaffar.

Gafur (A). See Ghafur.

Galib (A). See Ghalib.

Gamal (A). See Jamal.

Gani (A). See Ghani.

Gauhar (P) گوهر: gem, jewel, noble.

    Gauharzay (P) گوهر زای: born of a noble family, benevolent, generous.

Ghaffar (A) غفار (*ghaffaar*) (غفر): pardoner, merciful. Al-Ghaffaar الغفار, the All-forgiving: one of the names of Allah. رب السماوات والارض وما بينهما العزيز الغفار "Lord of the heavens and the earth and all that is between them, the All-mighty, the All-forgiving." (*surat Saad* 38:66). See Ghafur غفور.

    Abdul Ghaffar (A) عبد الغفار (*'abd al-ghaffaar*): servant of the All-forgiving. Khan Abdul Ghaffar Khan: Indian political leader and founder of the *khuda'i khidmatgar* (Servant of God) Red-shirt Movement in India.[115]

---

[115] See Martin, Gilbert, *A History of the Twentieth Century*, vol. I, p. 800.

Male Names

Ghafur (A) غَفُر (غَفْر) (*ghafoor*): pardoner, merciful.   Al-Ghafur الغفور, the All-forgiving: one of the names of Allah.   ان الله غفور رحيم "Allah is All-forgiving and Most Merciful." (*surat al-Baqarah* 2:173).   See Ghaffaar غفار.

Abdul Ghafur (A) عبد الغفور (*'abd al-ghafoor*): servant of the All-forgiving.

Ghais (A) غيث (*ghaith*): rain.   وينزل الغيث "He [Allah] sends rain". (*surat Luqmaan* 31:34).

Ghaiyyas (A) غَيَّاث (*ghaiyyath*): helper, reliever.   See Ghiyas غياث.

Ghalib (A) غالب (*ghaalib*) (غلب): conqueror, victor, winner.   ومن يتول الله ورسوله والذين آمنوا فان حزب الله هم الغالبون "And whoso turns (for friendship) to Allah, His Rasul and the believers (will know that) the party of Allah shall be victorious." (*surat al-Maa'idah* 5:56).   See Mansur منصور; Muntasir منتصر.   Ghalib ibn 'Abd Allah: a *sahaabi*.[116]   Mirza Asad-Allah Khan Ghalib: Indian poet in Persian and Urdu (1797-1869).[117]   Muhammad al-Ghalib: ruler of Granada (Spain) (1230-1272).

Ghallab[118] (A) غلاب (غلب) ever victorious, triumphant.

Ghani (A) غَنِي (*ghaniyy*): rich, wealthy, prosperous.   Al-Ghaniyy

---

[116] See Lings, Martin, *Muhammad*, p. 274.

[117] He "is generally regarded as the greatest of Urdu poets." See Ahmad, Aziz, *An Intellectual History of Islam in India*, p. 77.

[118] See Abd-el-Jawad, Hassan, 'A Linguistic and Socio-cultural Study of Personal Names in Jordan', *Anthropological Linguistics*, XXVIII, p. 84 (1986).

Male Names

الغني, the All-sufficient: one of the names of Allah. والله الغني
وانتم الفقراء "Allah is rich and you are poor." (*surat Muhammad* 47:38).

Abdul Ghani (A) عبد الغني (*'abd al-ghani*): servant of the All-sufficient.

Ghanim (A) غانم (*ghaanim*): successful.

Gharib[119] (A) غريب (*ghareeb*): "poor, needy, humble, gentle".[120] *Gharibnawaaz*:[121] who cherishes the poor. See Faqir فقير, poor.

Ghassan[122] (A) غسَّان: prime, vigour (of youth).

Ghaus (A) غوث (*ghauth*): help, aid, rescue, succour. See Ghiyas (*ghiyath*) غياث.

Ghays (A). See Ghais.

Ghazanfar (A) غضنفر (*ghadanfar*): lion. Title of Khalifa Ali. Raja Ghaznafar Ali Khan (1895-1963): Pakistani political leader.

Ghazi (A) الغازي (*al-ghaazii*) (غزو): "conqueror, hero, gallant soldier

---

[119] See Colebrooke, T. E., 'On the Proper Names of the Mohammadans', *Journal of the Royal Asiatic Society of Great Britain and Ireland*, XI, p. 236 (1879).

[120] See Steingass, F., *A Comprehensive Persian-English Dictionary*, p. 886.

[121] Nickname of Muinuddin Chishti, the great saint of India.

[122] See Abd-el-Jawad, Hassan, 'A Linguistic and Socio-cultural Study of Personal Names in Jordan', *Anthropological Linguistics*, XXVIII, p. 93 (1986). The name of a tribe in Arabia. See Haykal M.H., *The Life of Muhammad*, p. 626.

Male Names

(especially combating infidels)".[123]   Title of Mughal emperor Aurangzeb (1658-1707).

Ghazzali (A) غزالي (*ghazzaali*): Abu Haamid Muhammad al-Ghazzali أبو حامد محمد الغزالي: outstanding theologian and scholar on Islam (1058-1111).

Ghiyas (A) غياث (*ghiyaath*) (غيث): help, relief, aid.

> **Ghiyas-ud-Din** (A) غياث الدين: helper of the religion (Islam). Ghiyasuddin Tughluq: Delhi Sultan (d.1325).

Ghofran (A). See Ghufran.

Ghufran (A) غفران (*ghufraan*) (غفر): pardon, forgiveness. وقالوا سمعنا واطعنا غفرانك ربنا واليك المصير "They say: We have heard, and we obey. Grant us your forgiveness, O our Lord, and to you the end of the journey." (*surat al-Baqarah* 2:285).

Ghulam[124] (A) غلام (*ghulaam*): servant, boy, youth. فبشرناه بغلام حليم "So, We gave him [Ibrahim] good news of a gentle son." (*surat al-Saffat* 37:101).

Golam (A). See Ghulam.

---

[123] See Steingass, F., *A Comprehensive Persian-English Dictionary*, p. 878.

[124] Just as 'Abd عبد, servant may form personal names in combination with the names of Allah, so too may Ghulam. The following should however be avoided: Ghulam Ahmad, Ghulam Ali, Ghulam Haydar, Ghulam Hasan, Ghulam Husayn, Ghulam Muhammad; Ghulam Mustafa, Ghulam Rasul, Ghulam Nabi. (see Colebrooke, T. E., 'On the Proper Names of the Mohammadans', *Journal of the Royal Asiatic Society of Great Britain and Ireland*, XI, p. 183 (1879)).

H

Haafiz (A) حافظ (حفظ): title of a man who has memorised the whole Qur'an; guardian, protector. Al-Haafiz الحافظ, the Guardian: one of the names of Allah. ان كل نفس لما عليها حافظ "There is no human soul but has a guardian over it." (*surat al-Taariq* 86:4). فالله خير حافظا "Allah is the best to take care." (*surat Yusuf* 12:64). Shams ud-Din Muhammad Haafiz (d.1391): Persian poet famous for composing *ghazal* (lyrical poem) and author of *Diwan* (collection of poems).

> **Abdul Haafiz** (A) عبد الحافظ (*'abd al-haafiz*): servant of the Guardian.

Haakim (A) حاكم (حكم): judge, ruler, governor, leader, chief. Al-Haakim الحاكم, the Judge: one of the names of Allah. أليس الله باحكم الحاكمين "Is not Allah the wisest of all judges?" (*surat al-Teen* 95:8). Abbasid Khalifa (1261-1302). See Qazi (*qadi*) قاضي.

> **Abdul Haakim** (A) عبد الحاكم (*'abd al-haakim*): servant of the Judge.

Haamed (A). See Haamid.

Haamid (A) حامد (حمد): praiser (of Allah). الحامدون "Those who praise (Allah)" (*surat al-Tawba* 9:112). Haamid b. Sa'id: Sultan of Oman (1786-92). Abu Haamid Muhammad al-Ghazzali: See Ghazzali.

Male Names

Haaris[125] (A) حارث (*haarith*) (حرث): ploughman, cultivator. Al-Haarith: uncle of Muhammad (s).[126]

Haashim (A) هاشم: great-grandfather of Muhammad (s), ancestor of the *Banu* Hashim, an important tribe in early Islam. 'Haashim' has been derived from hashama هشم, he breaks.[127]

Haashimi (A) هاشمي: Hashimite, a *nisba* (relation) through ancestry to the Banu Haashim.[128] "The name Hashimite is sometimes taken as a family name by descendants of the clan, as for example the royal family of Jordan, who are...descendants of the Prophet."[129] The official name of Jordan is, 'The Hashimite Kingdom of Jordan'.

Habib (A) حبيب (*habeeb*) (حب): beloved, dear one, friend. See Mahbub محبوب. Habib ibn Zayd ibn 'Asim al-Ansari: a *sahaabi*.

Habibullah (A) حبيب الله (*habeeb allah*): friend of Allah. An

---

[125] "A very common name in olden times." See Colebrooke, T. E., 'On the Proper Names of the Mohammadans', *Journal of the Royal Asiatic Society of Great Britain and Ireland*, XIII, p. 246 (1881).

[126] See Haykal, M.H., *The Life of Muhammad*, p. 45.

[127] "The name is said to have been applied to the ancestors of Mahomet...from an incident in his life related by Tabari. He fed the poor during a season of scarcity, and 'broke the bread in the soup.'" See Colebrooke, T. E., 'On the Proper Names of the Mohammadans', *Journal of the Royal Asiatic Society of Great Britain and Ireland*, XIII, p. 241 (1881).

[128] "Al-Hashimi, related to Hashim". See Sheniti, Mahmud, 'Treatment of Arabic names', *International Conference on Cataloguing Principles Report*, 1961, p. 275. Also see Colebrooke, T. E., 'On the Proper Names of the Mohammadans', *Journal of the Royal Asiatic Society of Great Britain and Ireland*, XI, p. 222 (1879).

[129] See Glasse, Cyril, *The Concise Encyclopaedia of Islam*, p. 150.

Male Names

epithet of Muhammad (s).[130]

Hadaya (A) هدايا (*hadaayaa*): gifts, presents; pl. of Hadiyya هديَّة, gift.

Hadi (A) هادي (*haadi*) (هدي): leader, guide. Al-Haadi الهادي, the Guide: one of the names of Allah. وكفى بربك هاديا ونصيرا "But your Lord is enough as a Guide and a Helper." (*surat al-Furqaan* 25:31). Title of Imam Ali ibn Muhammad Naqi, the tenth Imam of the Shi'ites (d.868). See Murshid مرشد.

> **Abdul Hadi** (A) عبد الهادي (*'abd al-haadi*): servant of the Guide.

Hafez (A). See Haafiz.

Hafeez (A). See Hafiz.

Hafi (A) حفي (*hafiyy*) (حفو): welcoming, greeting.[131]

Hafiz (A) حفيظ (*hafeez*) (حفظ): guardian, protector. Al-Hafeez الحفيظ, the Guardian: one of the names of Allah. وربك على كل شيء حفيظ "And your Lord (O Muhammad) takes note of all things." (*surat Sabaa* 34:21).

> **Abdul Hafiz** (A) عبد الحفيظ (*'abd al-hafeez*): servant of the Guardian.

---

[130] See Glasse, Cyril, *The Concise Encyclopaedia of Islam*, p. 279; Colebrooke, T. E., 'On the Proper Names of the Mohammadans', *Journal of the Royal Asiatic Society of Great Britain and Ireland*, XI, p. 198 (1879).

[131] See *Al-Mawrid: A Modern Arabic-English Dictionary*, p. 479.

Male Names

Hafs (A) حفص: collecting, gathering.[132] Name given to Khalifa Umar by Muhammad (s).[133]

Abu Hafs 'Umar (A) أبو حفص عمر: ruler of Tunisia (1284-85).

Hai (A). See Hayy.

Haidar[134] (A) حيدر: lion. Title of Khalifa Ali. See Asad أسد. Haidar Ali (1722-82): ruler of Mysore (India).

Haider (A). See Haidar.

Haisam (A). See Haysam.

Haji (A) حاج (*haajj*): title of someone who has performed *Hajj*. الحاج "the pilgrims" (see *surat al-Tawbah* 9:19).

Hakam (A) حكم (*hakam*): arbitrator, judge. Al-Hakam الحكم, the Judge: one of the names of Allah. افغير الله ابتغي حكما "Shall I seek for judge other than Allah?" (*surat al-An'aam* 6:114). See Faysal فيصل. al-Hakam II al-Mustansir: Spanish Umayyad Khalifa (961-76).[135]

Abdul Hakam (A) عبد الحكم (*'abd al-hakam*): servant of the

---

[132] See Steingass, F., *A Comprehensive Persian-English Dictionary*, p. 424.

[133] *Ibid.*; Colebrooke, T. E., 'On the Proper Names of the Mohammadans', *Journal of the Royal Asiatic Society of Great Britain and Ireland*, XI, p. 188 (1879).

[134] A Muslim is a servant only to Allah. So, names like Ghulam Haidar, meaning 'servant of Ali' are improper.

[135] "Under him the university of Cordova...rose to a place of pre-eminence among the educational institutions of the world." See Hitti, Philip K., *History of the Arabs*, p. 530.

Male Names

Arbitrator.

Hakeem (A) حكيم (حكم): wise, sage, judicious, prudent. Al-Hakeem الحكيم, the All-Wise: one of the names of Allah. ان الله عزيز حكيم, "Allah is All-mighty, All-wise." (*surat al-Baqarah* 2:220).

Abdul Hakeem (A) عبد الحكيم (*'abd al-hakeem*): servant of the All-wise.

Hakim (A). See Haakim حاكم; Hakeem حكيم.

Halim (A) حليم (*haleem*) (حلم): patient, tolerant. Al-Haleem الحليم, the All-clement: one of the names of Allah. والله غفور حليم "Allah is All-forgiving, All-clement." (*surat al-Baqarah* 2:225). See Saabir صابر; Sabur صبور.

Abdul Halim (A) عبد الحليم (*'abd al-haleem*): servant of the All-clement. Sultan of Morocco (1361).

Hamad (A) حمّاد (*hammaad*): much praising.

Hamd (A) حمد: praise, laudation of Allah. الحمد لله رب العالمين "Praise be to Allah, Lord of the worlds." (*surat al-Faatihah* 1:2).

Hamdani (A). See Hamdan (f.).

Hamdi[136] (A) حمدي (*hamdiyy*): engaged in praising Allah.

---

[136] See Abd-el-Jawad, Hassan, 'A Linguistic and Socio-cultural Study of Personal Names in Jordan', *Anthropological Linguistics*, XXVIII, p. 84 (1986); Paxton, Evelyn, 'Arabic Names', *Asian Affairs*, LIX, p. 199 (1972).

Male Names

Hamed (A). See Haamid حامد.

Hamid (A) حميد (*hameed*) (حمد): praised, commended, praiseworthy, commendable. Al-Hameed الحميد, the All-laudable: one of the names of Allah. واعلموا ان الله غني حميد "And know that Allah is free of all wants and worthy of all praise." (*surat al-Baqarah* 2:267). See Mahmud محمود.

Abdul Hamid (A) عبد الحميد ('*abd al-hameed*): servant of the All-laudable. Abdul Hamid I: Ottoman Khalifa (1774-89); Abdul Hamid II: Ottoman Khalifa (1876-1909).

Hamidullah (A) حميد الله (*hameed allah*): praised by Allah.

Hammad (A). See Hamad.

Hammam (A) همّام: energetic, active. Hammam bin Harith: a *sahaabi*.

Hammud (A) حمّود (*hammood*): much praise to Allah.

Hamud (A) حمود (حمد): praised, commended, praiseworthy, commendable. See Hamid حميد; Mahmud محمود.

Hamza (A) حمزة (*hamzah*): lion.[137] Uncle (d.625) of Muhammad (s) who was known as 'Lion of Allah and His Prophet'[138] on account of his bravery in battles.

Hanai (A) هنائي (*hanaa'i*): associated with happiness, bliss. See Hani.

---

[137] See Steingass, F., *A Comprehensive Persian-English Dictionary*, p. 430.

[138] See *Shorter Encyclopaedia of Islam*, p. 131.

Male Names

Hanbal (A) حنبل: Ahmad ibn Muhammad ibn Hanbal (780-855): founder of the Hanbali School of Law.

Hani (A) هانئ (*haani'*): happy, glad, delighted. A *sahaabi*. See Hania (f.).

Hanif (A) حنيف (*haneef*) (حنف): true, one of true faith, upright. ما كان ابراهيم يهوديا ولا نصرانيا ولكن كان حنيفا مسلما "Ibrahim was not a Jew nor yet a Christian but he was an upright man who had surrendered to Allah accepting Islam." (*surat Aal 'Imraan* 3:67).

  Hanif-ud-Din (A) حنيف الدين: true of religion (Islam).

Hanifa (A) حنيفة (*haneefah*): fem. of Hanif. See Hanif. See Abu.

Hanin (A) حنين (*haneen*): yearning, desire.

Hannan (A) حنّان (*hannaan*) (حن): compassionate, merciful, affectionate, tender-hearted. See Hanaan حنان, compassion (f.).

Hanun (A) حنون (*hanoon*): compassionate, merciful, affectionate, tender-hearted, soft hearted.

Haqq (A) حقّ: true, truth, real, right, just. Al-Haqq الحقّ, the Truth: one of the names of Allah. *Al-Haaqqah* الحاقة, the Reality: title of the 69th *sura* of the Qur'an. قل الله يهدي للحقّ "Say: Allah leads to the truth." (*surat Yunus* 10:35). Fazlul Haqq: See Fazl.

  Abdul Haqq (A) عبد الحقّ (*'abd al-haqq*): servant of the Truth. Sultan of Morocco (1196-1217).

Haqqi (A) حقّي (*haqqiyy*): a person who upholds the truth, just.

Male Names

Haque (A). See Haqq.

Haris (A). See Haaris حارث (*haarith*).

Hariz (A) حريز (*hareez*): strong, secure, guarded.

Harun (A) هارون (*haarun*): a Prophet, known as Aaron in the Bible and brother of Prophet Musa. ووهبنا له من رحمتنا اخاه هارون نبيا "We bestowed upon him (Musa) of Our mercy his brother Harun, (also) a Prophet." (*surat Maryam* 19:53).

> **Harun-ur-Rashid** (A) هارون الرشيد (*haaroon al-rasheed*): Celebrated Abbasid Khalifa (786-809).[139]

Hasan (A) حسن: handsome, beautiful, good-looking. See Jamil جميل, handsome. Hasan al-Banna (1906-49): Egyptian political thinker and founder of the Muslim Brotherhood. Hasan Fathy (1900-89): Egyptian architect of international repute.

> **Abul Hasan** (A) أبو الحسن: father of Hasan. *Kunya* of Khalifa Ali.

> **Hasan Mujtaba** (A) حسن مجتبى (625-670): son of Khalifa Ali and the second Imam of the Shi'ites.[140]

---

[139] "The ninth century opened with two imperial names standing supreme in world affairs: Charlemagne in the West and Harun al-Rashid in the East. Of the two Harun was undoubtedly the more powerful and represented the higher culture." See Hitti, Philip K., *History of the Arabs*, p. 298. "Music, art and learning flourished under Harun, and his capital became the cultural centre of the Islamic world." *Who Did What: The Mitchell Beazley Illustrated Biographical Dictionary*, p. 145.

[140] See Al-Tabatabai, Allamah Sayyid Muhammad Husayn, *Shi'ite Islam*, p. 194.

Male Names

Nur-ul-Hasan (A) نور الحسن: light of Hasan.

Hasanat (A) حسنات (*hasanaaat*) (حسن): good deeds, kind acts, favours; pl. of حسنة Hasanah. ربنا آتنا في الدنيا حسنة وفي الآخرة حسنة "Our Lord! Give us in this world that which is good and in the Hereafter that which is good." (*surat al-Baqarah* 2:201). See Fazilat فضيلة (*fadeelat*), virtue (f.).

Hasanayn (A) حسنين: the two Hasans, i.e. Hasan and Husayn, the two sons of Khalifa Ali.

> **Hasanayn Nawaz** (A+P) حسنين نواز: cherished by the two Hasans.

Hasani (A) حسني (*hasaniyy*): of Hasan; *nisba* (relation) through ancestry to Hasan, grandson of Muhammad (s).

Hashamat (A) حشمت: pomp, magnificence.

Hashem (A). See Haashim.

Hasher (A) حاشر: collector. Al-Hasher الحاشر: an epithet of Muhammad (s).[141]

Hashimi (A). See Haashimi.

---

[141] See Steingass, F., *A Comprehensive Persian-English Dictionary*, p. 407, Colebrooke, T. E., 'On the Proper Names of the Mohammadans', *Journal of the Royal Asiatic Society of Great Britain and Ireland*, XI, p. 198 (1879).

Male Names

Hasib (A) حسيب (*haseeb*) (حسب): noble, respected, highborn.[142] Al-Hasseb الحسيب, the Reckoner: one of the names of Allah. ان الله كان على كل شيء حسيبا "Allah keeps a watchful account over everything." (*surat al-Nisaa'* 4:86). See Nabeel نبيل, noble.

Abdul Hasib (A) عبد الحسيب (*'abd al-haseeb*): servant of the Reckoner.

Hasif (A) حصيف (*haseef*) (حصف): judicious, wise, prudent, sagacious. See Hakeem حكيم.

Hasim (A) حاسم (*haasim*): decisive, definite.

Hasin (A) حصين (*haseen*): strong, secure, guarded.

Hassan (A) حسّان: beautifier.

Hassan bin Sabit (*thaabit*) (A) حسّان بن ثابت: a *sahaabi* well-known as a poet.[143]

Hatem (A) حاتم (*haatim*): judge, justice. Haatim al-Taa'iy: a legendary figure of Arabia noted for his hospitality in the sixth century before the spread of Islam.[144]

Hatif (A) هاتف (*haatif*): "praiser; a voice from heaven, or from an

---

[142] "الحسيب, of an old or noble family." See Colebrooke, T. E., 'On the Proper Names of the Mohammadans', *Journal of the Royal Asiatic Society of Great Britain and Ireland*, XI, p. 177 (1879).

[143] See Haykal, M.H., *The Life of Muhammad*, p. 275.

[144] *Ibid.*, p. 431.

Male Names

invisible speaker;...guardian angel."[145]

Hatim (A). See Hatem.

Hayat (A) حياة (*hayaah*) (حي): life. In the Qur'an, Allah addresses mankind: اعلموا انما الحياة الدنيا لعب "Know that the life of the world is but a sport." (*surat al-Hadeed* 57:20).

Haydar (A). See Haidar.

Haysam (A) هيثم (*haytham*): lion.

Haytham (A). See Haysam.

Hayy (A) حيّ: alive, living. Al-Hayy الحيّ, the Living: one of the names of Allah. الله لا اله الا هو الحي القيوم "Allah! There is no God save Him, the Alive, the Eternal." (*surat al-Baqarah, Aayat al-Kursiy* 2:255).

> **Abdul Hayy** (A) عبد الحي (*'abd al-hayy*): servant of the Living.

Hazrat (A) حضرة (*hadrat*): an honorific title, used at the beginning of a name, e.g. Hazrat Muhammad (s). Your (His) Excellency.

Hazim (A) حازم (*haazim*): firm, resolute, energetic, judicious. Hazim ibn Harmalah: a *sahaabi*.

Hedayat (A). See Hidayat.

---

[145] See Steingass, F., *A Comprehensive Persian-English Dictionary*, p. 1485. It should be noted that Haatif also means 'telephone'.

Male Names

Helal (A). See Hilal.

Hemayat (A). See Himayat.

Hena (A). See Hinna (f.).

Hiba (A) هبة (*hibah*): gift.

Hibatullah (A) هبة الله (*hibat allah*): gift of Allah.

Hidayat (A) هداية (*hidaayah*) (هدي): guidance. See Irshaad إرشاد.
Hidayat Rasul: nineteenth-century Indian politician.[146]

Hidayatullah (A) هداية الله (*hidaayat allah*): guidance of Allah.

Hidayat-ul-Haqq (A) هداية الحق (*hidaayat al-haqq*):
guidance of the Truth (Allah).

Hikmat (A) حكمة (*hikmah*): wisdom. يؤتي الحكمة من يشاء ومن يؤت
الحكمة فقد اوتي خيرا كثيرا "He gives wisdom to whom He pleases,
and he to whom wisdom is given, he truly has received abundant good."
(*surat al-Baqarah* 2:269).

Hilal (A) هلال (*hilaal*): crescent, new moon. يسئلونك عن الاهلة قل هي
مواقيت للناس والحج "They ask you, (O Muhammad), of new moons.
Say: They are but signs to mark fixed periods of time for mankind and
for the Hajj." (*surat al-Baqarah* 2:189). Hilal bin Harith: a *sahaabi*.

Hilali (A) هلالي (*hilaaliyy*): crescent-like.

---

146 See Hardy, P., *The Muslims of British India*, p. 177.

72

Male Names

Hilmi (A) حلمي (*hilmii*): patient, tolerant, lenient, clement.

Himayat (A) حماية (*himaayah*) (حمي): protection, safeguarding, sheltering.

Himmat (A) همة (هم): ambition, endeavour, resolution, determination.

Hisham (A) هشام (*hishaam*): beneficence, liberality. Umayyad Khalifa (724-43).

Hoque (A). See Haqq.

Hosain (A). See Husayn.

Hosni (A). See Husni.

Hud (A) هود: a Prophet (*sura Hud* 11:50). *Hud*: title of the 11th *sura* of the Qur'an.

Huda (A) هدى: right guidance, right path. قل ان هدى‌الله هو الهدى "Say: The guidance of Allah, that is the (only) guidance." (*surat al-Baqarah* 2:120). See Irshad إرشاد.

> **Nur-ul-Huda** (A) نور الهدى: light of the right guidance (of Allah).

Humam (A) همام (*humaam*) (هم): brave and noble, magnanimous, generous. See Shuja' شجاع, brave.

> **Humam-ud-Din** (A) همام الدين: brave (person) of the religion (Islam), generous.

73

Male Names

Humayd (A) حـمـيـد: diminutive of Ahmad أحـمـد, praised.

Humayun (P) هـمـايـون (*humaayun*): auspicious, fortunate. Muhammad Humayun (d.1556): Mughal emperor, father of Akbar the Great.

Husain (A). See Husayn.

Husam (A) حـسـام (*husaam*): sword. See Saif سـيـف.

> **Husam-ud-Dawlah** (A) حـسـام الـدولة: sword of the state. King of Iran (1074-1110).

> **Husam-ud-Din** (A) حـسـام الـدين: sword of religion (Islam).

Husayn (A) حـسـيـن: diminutive of Hasan حـسـن, beautiful. Imam Husayn: son of Khalifa Ali and the third Imam of the Shi'ites, who attained martyrdom in the battle of Karbala.[147]

> **Abul Husayn** (A) أبو الـحـسـيـن: father of Husayn, i.e. Khalifa Ali. Abul Husayn Muslim (d.875): author of one of the *sahih hadith* .

Husayni (A) حـسـيـنـي (*husainiyy*): of Husayn; *nisba* (relation) through ancestry to Husayn, grandson of Muhammad (s).

Husni (A) حـسـنـي (*husnii*): possessing beauty.

---

[147] He is known as *Sayyid al-Shuhada* (the lord among martyrs). See Al-Tabatabai, Allamah Sayyid Muhammad Husayn, *Shi'ite Islam*, p. 196.

Male Names

I

Iba (A) إباء (*ibaa'*): sense of honour, self-esteem, magnanimity, generosity.

Ibn (A) ابن: son. Ibn Abbas (d. 687): a *sahaabi*, well-known as a commentator on the Qur'an.[148] Ibn Batuta (1304-68): famous Moroccan traveller and historian. Ibn Kasir (*katheer*): Ismaa'il bin 'Amr bin Kathir (d. 1372): well-known commentator on the Qur'an, *Tafsir al-Qur'an al-Azim*.[149]   Ibn Khaldun (1332-1406): Arab historian and author of *Muqaddamah*.[150] Ibn Rushd: see Rushd. Ibn Taymiyah (1263-1328): Taqi ud-Din Ahmad ibn Taymiyah: religious reformer and political thinker.[151]

Isa ibn Maryam (A) عيسى ابن مريم: 'Isa (Jesus) son of Maryam (Mary). انما المسيح عيسى ابن مريم رسول الله وكلمته" "Christ Jesus the son of Mary was (no more than) a Messenger of Allah,

---

[148] He "is considered to be the most knowledgeable of the Companions in *tafsir*. He has been called '*tarjuman al-quran*', the interpreter of the Qur'an." See Denffer, Ahmad Von, '*Ulum Al-Qur'an*, 128.

[149] In the area of the commentaries on the Qur'an, this book is "perhaps second to Tabari." See Denffer, Ahmad Von, '*Ulum Al-Qur'an*, p. 138.

[150] It was described by Arnold Toynbee as 'the greatest work of its kind that has ever yet been created by any mind in any time or place'. See Beazley, M., *Who Did What*, p. 162. "By the consensus of critical opinion ibn-Khaldun was the greatest philosopher Islam produced and one of the greatest of all time." See Hitti, Philip K., *History of the Arabs*, p. 568.

[151] "He bowed to no authority other than the Koran, tradition and the practice of the community and lifted his voice high against innovation, saint-worship, vows and pilgrimage to shrines." See Hitti, Philip K., *History of the Arabs*, p. 689.

Male Names

and His word." (*surat al-Nisaa'* 4:171).

Ibn Sina[152] (A) ابن سـينا: Sina was "the father of Abu Ali ibn Sina, the celebrated physician Avicenna".[153] Ibn Sina (980-1037): "one of the renowned intellectual figures of the Middle Ages...His lofty reputation in Europe earned him the title of 'Prince of Physicians'."[154]

Ibrahim (A) إبراهـيم (*ibraaheem*): kind father[155] (combination of Abu أب, father and Rahim رحيم, kind). A Prophet, the biblical Abraham and father of Ismail and Ishaq, both were also Prophets. *Ibrahim*: title of the 14th *sura* of the Qur'an. An epithet of Prophet Ibrahim is *Khalilullah* خليل الله, 'friend of Allah' (see Khalil). The sacred Kaaba in Makkah to which Muslims turn their faces (*qibla*) during prayer, was built by Ibrahim at the command of Allah with the help of his son Ismail. See Khalil. One of the sons of Muhammad (s) was called Ibrahim.

Ibtisam (A) ابتسـام (*ibtisaam*) (بسم): smiling, smile. See Tabassum تبسُّم, smile (f.).

Idrak (A) إدراك: intellect, perception, achievement, attainment.

---

[152] In Arabic, Sina refers to mount Sinai. See Steingass, F., *A Comprehensive Persian-English Dictionary*, p. 718; Haim, S., *The Shorter Persian-English Dictionary*, p. 422; Schimmel, Annmarie, *Islamic Names*, p. 8.

[153] See Steingass, F., *A Comprehensive Persian-English Dictionary*, p. 718.

[154] See Glasse, Cyril, *The Concise Encyclopaedia of Islam*, pp. 175-6.

[155] According to Colebrooke, the biblical name Abraham means, 'father of nations'. See Colebrooke, T. E., 'On the Proper Names of the Mohammadans', *Journal of the Royal Asiatic Society of Great Britain and Ireland*, XI, p. 187 (1879).

Male Names

Idris (A) إدريس: a Prophet, the biblical Enoch. واذكر في الكتاب إدريس انه كان صديقا نبيا "And make mention in the Book of Idris. He was a man of truth, [and] a *Nabi* [Prophet]." (*surat Maryam* 19: 56). Idris ibn-Abdullah: great-grandson of Imam Hasan and the founder (789-93) of the Idrisid dynasty which ruled Morocco from 789-926.

Idrisi (A) إدريسي: *nisba* (relation) to Idris. Al-Idrisi (d.1166): Arabian geographer.[156]

Iftikhar (A) افتخار (*iftikhaar*) (فخر): pride.

> **Iftikhar-ud-Din** (A) افتخار الدين: pride of the religion (Islam). Mian Muhammad Iftikharuddin (1907-62): Pakistani political leader.

Ihsan (A) إحسان (*ihsaan*) (حسن): benevolence, charity, kindness, kind act, performance of good deeds. ان الله يامر بالعدل والاحسان وايتائ ذي القربى "Allah enjoins justice and kindness, and giving to kinsfolk." (*surat al-Nahl* 16:90). See Ma'ruf معروف.

> **Ihsan-ul-Haqq** (A) إحسان الحق: (*ihsaan al-haqq*): kindness of the Truth (Allah).

Ihtisham (A) احتشام (*ihtishaam*) (حشم): chastity, modesty, decency, decorum.

Ijaz (A) إعجاز (*i'jaaz*) (عجز): miracle, inimitability, wondrous nature (of the Qur'an). Comp. I'zaaz إعزاز, honour.

---

[156] "The chief ornament of Roger II's court was al-Idrisi, the most distinguished geographer and cartographer of the Middle Ages." See Hitti, Philip K., *History of the Arabs*, p. 609.

77

Male Names

Ijaz-ul-Haqq (A) إعجاز الـحق (*i'jaaz al-haqq*): inimitability of the Truth (Allah).

Ijlal (A) إجلال (*ijlaal*) (جلّ): glorification, exaltation, honour, reverence respect.

Ikhlas (A) إخلاص (*ikhlaas*) (خلص): sincerity, honesty, integrity, fidelity, faithfulness. *Al-Ikhlaas* الإخلاص: title of the 112th *sura* of the Qur'an. See Wafa وفاء, faithfulness (f.).

Ikhtiyar (A) اختيار (*ikhtiyaar*) (خير): choice, preference, selection.

Ikhtiyar-ud-Din Ghazi Shah (A+P) اختيار الدين غازي شاه Bengal Sultan (1349-52).

Iklil (A) إكليل (*ikleel*): crown.

Ikram (A) إكرام (*ikraam*) (كرم): honour, glory, respect. تبارك اسم ربك ذي الـجلال والإكرام "Blessed be the name of your Lord, Mighty and Glorious." (*surat al-Rahmaan* 55:78).

Ikramullah (A) إكرام الله (*ikraam allah*): glory of Allah.

Ikram-ul-Haqq (A) إكرام الـحق (*ikraam al-haqq*): glory of the Truth (Allah).

Iksir (A) إكسير (*ikseer*): elixir.

Ilahi (A) إلاهي: divine.

Ilahi Bakhsh (A+P) إلاهي بخش: gift of Allah.

78

Male Names

Ilham (A) إلهام (*ilhaam*) (لهم): inspiration, revelation.

Ilias (A). See Ilyas.

Ilyas (A) إلياس (*ilyaas*): a Prophet, the biblical Elias. وان إلياس لمن المرسلين "So was Ilyas among those sent (by Us)." (*surat al-Saffat* 37:123).

> **Iliyas Shah** (A+P) إلياس شاه: Bengal Sultan (1345-58).

> **Muhammad Ilyas** (A) محمد إلياس: Indian religious reformer and founder of the *Tablighi Jamaat* (1885-1944).[157]

Imad (A) عماد (*'imaad*) (عمد): pillar, post, support. الله الذي رفع السماوات بغير عمد "Allah is He Who raised the heavens without any pillars." (*surat al-Ra'd* 13:2).

> **Imaad-ud-Dawlah**[158] (A) عماد الدولة: prop of the state. Buwayhid Ameer (934-49).

> **Imad-ud-Din** (A) عماد الدين: pillar of the faith (Islam). Imad ud-Din Zangi: founder (1127-46) of the Zangid dynasty (1127-

---

[157] See Ahmad, Mumtaz, 'Islamic Fundamentalism in South Asia: The Jamaat-i-Islami and the Tablighi Jamaat of South Asia', in Marty & Appleby, *Fundamentals Observed*, p. 512. "[T]he Tabligh has become one of the most important re-Islamizing movements in the world." See Kepel, Gilles, *Allah in the West*, p. 92.

[158] See Colebrooke, T. E., 'On the Proper Names of the Mohammadans', *Journal of the Royal Asiatic Society of Great Britain and Ireland*, XI, p. 207 (1879).

Male Names

62).[159]

Imam (A) إمام (*imaam*) (امّ): one who leads communal prayer; leader, chief, model, example. واجعلنا للمتقين اماما "And make us models for the God-fearing people." (*surat al-Furqaan* 25:74). The founders of the schools of law are known as Imams, e.g. Imaam Abu Hanifa of the Hanafi *madhhab*. For the Shi'ites, Imams occupy the special spiritual position accorded to the descendants of Khalifa Ali and Fatima, daughter of Muhammad (s). *Imam ul-Muttaqin*, 'leader of the God-fearing': an epithet of Muhammad (s).

Iman (A) إيمان (*imaan*) (أمن): belief, faith in Allah. والله اعلم بايمانكم "Allah knows best concerning your faith." (*surat al-Nisaa'* 4:25).

Imdad (A) إمداد (*imdaad*) (مدّ): help, aid, support.

Imran[160] (A) عمران (*'imraan*): father of Maryam (mother of Prophet 'Isa). *Aal 'Imraan* آل عمران, 'The Family of 'Imraan': title of the 3rd *sura* of the Qur'an. ومريم ابنت عمران "Maryam, daughter of Imran." (*surat al-Tahreem* 66:12).

Imtiyaz (A) امتياز (*imtiyaaz*) (ميز): distinction, mark of honour.

Inam (A) إنعام (*in'aam*) (نعم): gift, present. See Atia عطية (f.), gift.

---

[159] He "was a great man of the twelfth century, and he is rated as a hero of Muslim history. He was the first Muslim ruler to break the power of the crusaders." See Hasan, Masudul, *History of Islam*, vol. I, p. 452. "The rise of Imad al-Din...marks the turning of the tide in favour of Islam." See Hitti, Philip K., *History of the Arabs*, p. 644.

[160] Note: 'Umraan عمران: culture, civilisation, prosperity.

Male Names

Inam-ul-Haqq (A) إنعام الـحق (*in'aam al-Haqq*): gift of the Truth (Allah).

Inayat (A) عناية ('*inaayah*) (عني): care, concern. *Al-inaayat al-ilaahiyya* العناية الالاهية, divine providence.

Inayatullah (A) عناية الله ('*inayaat allah*): care of Allah. Allama Inayatullah Khan Mashriqi (1888-1963): Indian politician and founder of the *Khaksar* (humble) movement in India.[161]

Inayat-ur-Rahman (A) عناية الرحمن ('*inaayat al-Rahmaan*): care of the most Gracious.

Inayat-ud-Din (A) عناية الدين: (taking) care of religion (Islam).

Insaf (A) إنصاف (*insaaf*) (نصف): justice, impartiality, fairness, equity.

Inshirah (A) إنشراح (*inshiraah*) (شرح): joy, delight, happiness, cheerfulness.

Intisar (A) انتصار (*intisaar*) (نصر): victory, triumph. See Nasr نصر; Zafar ظفر.

Iqbal (A) إقبال (*iqbaal*) (قبل): good-luck, prosperity, welfare.

Muhammad Iqbal (A) محمد إقبال (1873-1938): Indian poet, philosopher, religious and political thinker. He is the author of *Asrar-i-khudi* (*Secrets of the Self*) and *Reconstruction of Religious Thought in Islam*.

---

161 See Hardy, P., *The Muslims of British India*, p. 216.

Male Names

Irfan (A) عرفان (*'irfaan*) (عرف): knowledge, learning, erudition.

Irshad (A) إرشاد (*irshaad*) (رشد): guidance. See Hidayat هداية.

Irtida (A). See Irtiza.

Irtiza (A) ارتضاء (*irtidaa'*): contentment, approval.

Irtiza Husayn (A) ارتضاء حسين: approval of Husayn.

Isa (A) عيسى (*'isa*): a Prophet, the biblical Jesus. انما المسيح عيسى ابن مريم رسول الله و كلمته "The Messiah (Masih), Jesus ('Isa), son of Maryam was only a Messenger of Allah and his word." (*surat al-Nisaa'* 4:171). In the Qur'an, Jesus proclaims to his people: آتاني الكتاب وجعلني نبيا "He (Allah) has given me the Book and established me as a Prophet (*surat Maryam* 19:30).

Abu Isa (A) أبو عيسى: father of Isa. Abu Isa Muhammad al-Tirmidhi: see Tirmizi (*tirmidhi*).

Is'ad (A) إسعاد (*is'aad*) (سعد): making happy or prosperous, blessing, favouring.

Ishaq (A) إسحاق (*ishaaq*): a Prophet, the biblical Isaac and son of Prophet Ibrahim. وبشرناه بإسحاق نبيا من الصالحين. "We gave him the good news of Ishaq, a Prophet of the righteous." (*surat al-Saffat* 37:112).

Ishfaq (A) إشفاق (*ishfaaq*) (شفق): compassion, sympathy, pity.[162] See Shafaqat شفقة; Rahmat رحمة; Ashfaq أشفاق compassion.

---

[162] See *Al-Mawrid: A Modern Arabic-English Dictionary*, p. 114.

Male Names

Ishtiyaq (A) اشتـيـاق (*ishtiyaaq*) (شـوق): wish, desire, yearning.

Iskandar (P) اسكندر: Alexander. Iskander Mirza: President of Pakistan (1956-58).

Islah (A) إصلاح (*islaah*) (صـلـح): reform, improvement, betterment.

Islam (A) إسلام (*islaam*) (سـلـم): submission, surrender (to the will of Allah). Name of the religion of the Muslims. ان الدين عند الله الاسلام "Religion with Allah is Islam." (*surat Aal 'Imraan* 3:19). ورضيت لكم الإسلام دينا "I have chosen for you Islam as religion." (*surat al-Maa'idah* 5:3).

    Islam Shah (A+P) إسلام شاه: Delhi Sultan (d.1554).

Ismail (A) إسماعيل (*ismaa'eel*): a Prophet, the biblical Ishmael and son of Prophet Ibrahim. واذكر في الكتاب إسماعيل انه كان صادق الوعد وكان رسولا نبيا "And make mention in the Book of Ismail. He was a keeper of his promise and he was a *Rasul* (Messenger) and a *Nabi* (Prophet)." (*surat Maryam* 19:54). In pursuance of a dream, Ibrahim, was prepared to sacrifice his son Ismail who was also willing to fulfil the command of Allah (see *surat al-Saffat* 37:102). This is commemorated by Muslims in the offering of sacrifice on the tenth of *Dhu Al-Hijjah*, which is known as *'Eid al-Adha*, the Feast of the Sacrifice. Ismaa'il I: founder (1501-24) of the Safawid dynasty (1501-1732), "the most glorious of the native dynasties of Moslem Persia."[163]

Ismat (A) عصمة (عصـم): purity, chastity, modesty. See Ismet.

Ismet (A). See Ismat. Ismet Pasha (Inonu): President of Turkey (1938-

---

[163] See Hitti, Philip K., *History of the Arabs*, p. 703.

Male Names

50) who "[l]ike Kemal...had fought against the British at Gallipolli."[164]

Isra (A) إسراء (*israa'*) (سرى): travel by night. *Al-Israa'* الإسراء: the night journey of Muhammad (s) to the seven heavens which happened on the 27th night of the month of Rajab in the year before the *hijra*. *Al-Israa'* أإسراء: title of the 17th *sura* of the Qur'an. سبحان الذي اسرى بعبده ليلا من المسجد الحرام الى المسجد الاقصا "Glory be to Him, Who carried His servant by night from the Sacred Mosque (at Makkah) to the Farthest Mosque (at Jerusalem)." (*surat al-Israa'* 17:1). See Asra أسرى.

Israr (A) إسرار (*israar*) (سر): secret, mystery.[165] See Asrar أسرار, secrets.

Itidal (A) اعتدال (*i'tidaal*) (عدل): moderation, moderateness, golden mean, clemency.

Itimad (A) اعتماد (*i'timaad*) (عمد): reliance, dependence, confidence.

Iyad (A) إياد (*iyaad*): support, might, strength.

Izaz (A) إعزاز (*i'zaaz*) (عز): honour, esteem, regard, affection. Comp. I'jaz إعجاز, miracle.

Izaz-ud-Dawlah[166] (A) إعزاز الدولة: honour of the state.

---

[164] See Martin, Gilbert, *A History of the Twentieth Century*, vol. I, p. 642.

[165] See *Steingass, F., A Comprehensive Persian-English Dictionary*, p. 57.

[166] See Colebrooke, T. E., 'On the Proper Names of the Mohammadans', *Journal of the Royal Asiatic Society of Great Britain and Ireland*, XI, p. 207 (1879).

Male Names

Izz (A) عزّ: power, might, honour.

Izz-ud-Din (A) عزّ الدين (*izz al-Din*): honour of the religion (Islam). Saffarid king in Iran (1362-82).

Izz-ud-Dawlah Bakhtiyar[167] (A+P) عزّ الدولة بختيار: glory of the state. Buwayhid Sultan in Iraq (967-78).

Izzat (A) عزة: honour, fame, power. سبحان ربك رب العزة عما يصفون "Glory to your Lord, the lord of Honour. He is free from what they ascribe to Him." (*surat al-Saaffaat* 37:180).

---

[167] *Ibid.*

Male Names

J

Jaabir (A). See Jabir جابر.

Jaasir (A). See Jasir.

Jabbar (A) جبار (*jabbaar*): powerful, mighty. Al-Jabbaar الجبار, the All-compeller: one of the names of Allah (see *surat al-Hashr* 59:23).

> **Abdul Jabbar** (A) عبد الجبار (*'abd al-jabbar*): servant of the All-compeller.

Jaber (A). See Jabir جابر.

Jabir[168] (A) جابر (*jaabir*): bonesetter, restorer. Jaabir ibn 'Abd Allah: a *sahaabi*.[169] Jaabir ibn-Hayyan: Arabian alchemist, known as the father of Arabic alchemy.[170]

Jadwal (A) جدول: brook, rivulet.

---

[168] "There are Kuwaiti personal names for the Sheikhs or ruling class in Kuwait, as ... Jaabir." See Yassin, M. Aziz F., 'Personal Names Address in Kuwaiti Arabic', *Anthropological Linguistics*, XX, p. 54. Also see Bland, N., 'On the Muhammadan Science of Tabir, or Interpretation of Dreams', *Journal of the Royal Asiatic society*, XVI, p. 154.

[169] See An-Nawawi, *Forty Hadith*, p. 76; Lings, Martin, *Muhammad*, p. 208.

[170] "Western tradition credits him with the discovery of several chemical compounds not mentioned in the twenty-two surviving Arabic works that bear his name." See Hitti, Philip K., *History of the Arabs*, p. 380.

Male Names

Jafar (A) جعفر (*ja'far*): spring, rivulet. Comp. Zafar ظفر, victory.
Ja'far ibn Abu Taalib: a *sahaabi*. Abu Ja'far Muhammad ibn-Jarir al-
Tabari: see Tabari.

Jafar as-Sadiq جعفر الصادق (699-765): the sixth Imam of
the Shi'ites and the founder of the Ja'fari School of Law.[171]

Jafnat[172] (A) جفنة: generous, liberal.

Jahan (P) جهان (*jahaan*): world. See Dunya (A) دنيا (f.).

Shah Jahan (P) شاه جهان: king of the world. See Shah.

Jahangir (P) جهانگير: world conqueror.

Nur-ud-Din Muhammad Jahangir (A+P) نور الدين جهانگير:
Mughal emperor (1605-27) during whose reign the Indian miniature
painting reached its climax.

Jahid (A) جاهد (*jaahid*) (جهد): diligent, hardworking, striving.

Jalal (A) جلال (*jalaal*) (جلّ): majesty, grandeur, glory. Dhul Jalal ذو
الجلال, full of Majesty: one of the names of Allah (*surat al-Rahmaan*
55:27).

Jalal-ud-Din (A) جلال الدين: the majesty of religion. Jalal-ud-Din

---

[171] See Al-Tabatabai, Allamah Sayyid Muhammad Husayn, *Shi'ite Islam*, p. 203.

[172] See Steingass, F., *A Comprehensive Persian-English Dictionary*, p. 366.

Male Names

Akbar: Mughal emperor (1556-1605). Jalal ud-Din Rumi (1207-1273): one of the great mystic poets of Islam.[173]

Jalil (A) جليل (*jaleel*) (جلَ): great, exalted, magnificent. Al-Jalil الجليل, the Exalted: one of the names of Allah.

Abdul Jalil (A) عبد الجليل (*'abd al-jaleel*): servant of the Exalted.

Jamal (A) جمال (*jamaal*) (جمل): beauty, grace (see *surat al-Nahl* 16:6). Prophet Yusuf is deemed to be the embodiment of *jamal* (beauty). In the Qur'anic story, Zulaykha (wife of Aziz) invites her women friends to a party. When they see Prophet Yusuf, his beauty captivates them and they cut their hands with their serving knives (see *surat Yusuf* 12:31). See Malak (f.); Yusuf (m.); Zulaykha (f.).

Jamal-ud-Din (A) جمال الدين: beauty of the religion (Islam). Sayyid Jamal ud-Din al-Afghani (1838-1897): celebrated political reformer.[174]

Jamali (A) جمالي (*jamaaliyy*): divine beauty. Haamid ibn Fadl-Allah Jamali (d.1536): eminent Indian poet.[175]

Jami (A) جامع (*jaami'*): gatherer, collector, author, writer. Nur-ud-Din

---

[173] See Glasse, Cyril, *The Concise Encyclopaedia of Islam*, p. 204; Schimmel, Annemarie, *Islamic Names*, p. 38.

[174] He was "one of the great founding figures of the Muslim awakening of the late millennium...He advocated parliamentary democracy but would not admit the insufficiency of the political lessons of the Koran." See Fernandez-Armesto, Felipe, *Millennium*, p. 567-8.

[175] See Ahmad, Aziz, *An Intellectual History of India*, p. 75.

Male Names

Abdur Rahman Jami'(1414-1492): Persian Sufi poet.

Jamil (A) جميل (*jameel*) (جمل): handsome, attractive, impressive (see *surat Yusuf* 12:18). A *sahaabi*. See Hasan حسن.

Abdul Jamil[176] (A) عبد الجميل (*'abd al-jameel*): servant of the Beautiful.

Jamshed (P) جمشيد: the sun in Pisces.[177] "Mas. pr. name."[178] A king of Iran.

Jan (P) جان (*jaan*): life; sing. of Jaanaan جانان.

Jan-e-Alam (P+A) جان عالم (*jaan-i-'aalam*): life of the world. An epithet of Muhammad (s).

Jan Muhammad (P+A) جان محمد: life of Muhammad (s).

Janab (A) جناب (*janaab*): an honorific title, Your (His) Excellency.

Jar Allah (A) جار الله: neighbour of Allah. Epithet of Al-Zamakhshari, the famous commentator on the Qur'an.

Jasim (A) جسيم (*jaseem*): great and famous.

---

[176] "Sometimes Divine names which are not given in the generally accepted lists printed at the beginning of modern copies of the Qur'an can be found, for example 'Abdul Jamil, relating to hadith that 'God is beautiful, Jamil, and loves beauty'..." See Schimmel, Annemarie, *Islamic Names*, p. 26.

[177] See Steingass, F., *A Comprehensive Persian-English Dictionary*, p. 371.

[178] See Haim, S., *The Shorter Persian-English Dictionary*, p. 210.

Male Names

Jasim-ud-Din (A) جسيم الدين: great (man) of the religion (Islam). Eminent Bengali poet (1902-76), author of *The Field of Embroidered Quilt* (Eng. trans.).[179]

Jasir (A) جاسر (*jaasir*): brave, bold, courageous, valiant. See Jasur جسور, brave.

Jasur (A) جسور (*jasoor*): brave, bold, courageous, valiant. See Jasir جاسر, brave.

Jauhar (A). See Jawhar.

Javed (P) جاود (*jaawid*): eternal, perpetual.

Jawad (A) جواد (*jawwaad*) (جود): generous, liberal, open-handed. Nickname of Imam Taqi, the ninth Imam of the Shi'ites.[180] See Karim كريم, generous.

Jawahir (A) جواهر (*jawaahir*) jewels; pl. of Jawhar جوهر, jewel.

Jawhar (A) جوهر (جوهر): jewel, essence.

Jalal-ud-Din Ali Jawhar Shah 'Alam (A+P) جلال الدين علي جوهر شاه عالم: Mughal emperor (1760-88).

Jawwad (A) جواد (*jawwaad*). See Jawad.

Jihad (A) جهاد (*jihaad*) (جهد): striving, holy war. فلا تطع الكافرين وجاهدهم به جهادا كبيرا "So obey not the *kafirs* (disbelievers) but

---

[179] Ahmad, Aziz, *An Intellectual History of Islam in India*, p. 116.

[180] See Al-Tabatabai, Allamah Sayyid Muhammad Husayn, *Shi'ite Islam*, p. 207.

Male Names

strive against them with a great endeavour." (*surat al-Furqaan* 25:52).

Jilani. See Qaadir.

Juma (A) جمعة (*jum'ah*): assembly. *Al-Jumu'ah* الجمعة: obligatory (*fard*) prayer for Muslims to perform in congregation at midday on Fridays *yaum al-jum'ah*. *Al-Jumu'ah* الجمعة: title of the 62nd *sura* of the Qur'an. اذا نودى للصلوة من يوم الجمعة فاسعوا الى ذكر الله وذروا البيع "When the call is heard for the prayer of the day of congregation, haste to remembrance of Allah and leave off business." (*surat al-Jum'ah* 62:9). Parents may wish to name a male child born on this auspicious day of the week 'Jum'a'.

Jumayyil (A) جميّل: diminutive of Jamil جميل, handsome. See Jamil.

Junayd (A) جنيد: diminutive of Jund جند, army, soldiers. An Ameer of Khurasan.[181]

---

[181] See Al-Arnaut, Shafiq, *Qamus al-Asma' al-Arabiyya* [Dictionary of Arabic Names] (in Arabic), p. 38.

Male Names

K

Kab (A) كعب (*ka'b*): fame, glory, honour, high rank. Ka'b ibn Malik al-Ansari: a *sahaabi*.

Kabir (A) كبير (*kabeer*) (كبر): great, grand, magnificent. Al-Kabeer الكبير, the All-great: one of the names of Allah. وان الله هو العلي الكبير "And because Allah, He is the most High, the most Great." (*surat al-Hajj* 22:62).

Kabil (A). See Qabil.

Kader (A). See Qadir.

Kadir (A). See Qadir.

Kafi (A) كافي (*kaafi*): sufficient. Al-Kafi الكافي, the All-sufficient: one of the names of Allah. أليس الله بكاف عبده "Is not Allah sufficient for His servant?" (*surat al-Zumar* 39:36).

> **Abdul Kafi** (A) عبد الكافي (*'abd al-kaafi*): servant of the All-sufficient.

Kafil (A) كفيل (*kafeel*) (كفل): guarantor, surety, sponsor. ولا تنقضوا الايمان بعد توكيدها وقد جعلتم الله عليكم كفيلا "And break not your oaths after you have confirmed them, and after you have made Allah surety over you." (*surat al-Nahl* 16:91).

> **Kafil-ud-Din** (A) كفيل الدين: surety of the religion (Islam).

Male Names

Kaikaus (P). See Kaykaus.

Kaikobad (P). See Kayqobad.

Kaisar (A). See Qaisar.

Kalam (A) كلام (*kalaam*): speech, conversation.

> **Abul Kalam Azad** (A+P) أبو الكلام آزاد: father of free speech. See Azad.

Kalim (A) كليم (*kaleem*) (كلم): interlocutor, speaker.

> **Kalimullah** (A) كليم الله (*kaleem allah*): one who conversed with Allah. An epithet of Prophet Musa. وكلم الله موسى تكليما "Allah spoke directly to Musa." (*surat al-Nisaa'* 4:164). Bahmanid Sultan in Northern Deccan (India) (1525-27).

Kamal (A) كمال (*kamaal*) (كمل): perfection, completion, integrity.

> **Kamal-ud-Din** (A) كمال الدين: perfection of religion (Islam). Thirteenth-century Arab historian.[182] Kamal ud-Din Bihzad (d.1536): Persian painter.

> **Mustafa Kamal** (A) مصطفى كمال: founder of modern Turkey (1881-1938).

Kamel (A). See Kamil.

---

[182] See Tate, Georges, *The Crusades and the Holy Land* (Translated from the French), p. 59, quoting an extract from his book, *Chronicle of Alleppo*.

Male Names

Kamil (A) كامل (*kaamil*), كميل (*kameel*) (كمل): perfect, complete, genuine. Al-Kamil الكامل, the perfect: an epithet of Muhammad (s). Al-Kamil Ayyubi (1218-38): ruler of Egypt.[183] Mustafa Kamil (1874-1908): Egyptian nationalist leader who fought for independence of Egypt.

Kamr (A). See Qamar قمر.

Kamran (P) كامران (*kaamraan*): lucky, happy, success.   Son of Mughal emperor Babur.

Karam[184] (A) كرم: generosity, bounty.

Karamullah (A) كرم الله (*karam allah*): bounty of Allah.

Karamat (A) كرامات (*karaamaat*) (كرم): acts of generosity. "Gifts or powers of a spiritual...nature acquired by a saint, short of miracle working."[185]

Karamat Ali (A) كرامات علي (1800-73): Indian religious reformer.[186]

Kardar (P) كاردار: prime minister.

---

[183] "He was so favourably disposed toward his Christian subjects that the Coptic church still recognises him as the most beneficent sovereign it ever had." See Hitti, Philip K., *History of the Arabs*, p. 654.

[184] See Abd-el-Jawad, Hassan, 'A Linguistic and Socio-cultural Study of Personal Names in Jordan', *Anthropological Linguistics*, XXVIII, p. 83 (1986). It is also a well known Christian Lebanese family name. "Certain families, mainly Christian Lebanese, such as the Karam..." See Hitti, Philip K., *History of the Arabs*, p. 670.

[185] See Glasse, Cyril, *The Concise Encyclopaedia of Islam*, p. 219.

[186] See Hardy, P., *The Muslims of British India*, p. 110.

94

Male Names

Karim (A) كريم (*kareem*) (كرم): kind, generous, benevolent, noble.
Al-Kareem الكريم, the most Generous: one of the names of Allah.
يايها الانسان ما غرك بربك الكريم "O man! What has made you
careless concerning your Lord, the Bountiful...?" (*surat al-Infitaar* 82:6).
See Jawad جواد; Mannan منان.

> **Abdul Karim** (A) عبد الكريم (*'abd al-karim*): servant of
> the most Generous. Moroccan political leader (1882-1963).

> **Aga Khan Karim** (T+P+A). See Aga.

Kasim (A). See Qasim.

Kasir (A) كثير (*katheer*) (كثر): much, abundant, plenty. يايها الذين
آمنوا اذكروا الله ذكرا كثيرا "O believers, remember Allah often."
(*surat al-Ahzaab* 33:41). Ibn Kasir (*katheer*): see Ibn.

Kausar (A) كوثر (*kawthar*): abundance. *Al-Kauthar* الكوثر: title of
the 108th *sura* of the Qur'an. A spring in paradise mentioned in the
Qur'an. انا اعطيناك الكوثر "We have given you abundance." (*surat
al-Kauthar* 108:1).

Kaykaus (P) كيكاوس (*kaykaawus*): just, noble. King of Iran (d.1058).

Kayqobad (P) كيقباد (*kayqubaad*): king of Iran.[187] Mi'izz ud-Din
Kayqobadh: Delhi Sultan (1287-90).

Kazi (A). See Qazi.

Kazim (A) كاظم (*kaazim*) (كظم): one who controls or suppresses his

---

[187] See Steingass, F., *A Comprehensive Persian-English Dictionary*, p. 1070.

Male Names

anger. الذين ينفقون في السراء والضراء والكاظمين الغيظ والعافين عن الناس والله يحب المحسنين "Those who spend (of that which Allah has given them) in prosperity or in adversity; those who restrain their anger and are forgiving toward (all) men; for Allah loves those who do good." (*surat Aal 'Imraan* 3:134).

Musa al-Kazim موسى الكاظم: the seventh Imam of the Shi'ites (d.799).[188]

Keramat (A). See Karamat.

Khaaliq (A) خالق (خلق): creator. Al-Khaaliq الخالق, the Creator: one of the names of Allah. قل الله خالق كل شيء "Say: Allah is the Creator of all things." (*surat al-Ra'd* 13:16). Comp. Khaliq خليق, most qualified.

> **Abdul Khaaliq** (A) عبد الخالق ('abd al-khaaliq): servant of the Creator.

Khaatib (A) خاطب: suitor, matchmaker.

Khabir (A) خبير (khabeer) (خبر): learned, expert, authority. Al-Khabeer الخبير, One Who is aware: one of the names of Allah. ان الله خبير بما تعملون "Allah is well-informed of what you do." (*surat al-Hashr* 59:18).

Khadem (A). See Khadim.

Khadim (A) خادم (khaadim) (خدم): servant.

---

[188] See Al-Tabatabai, Allamah Sayyid Muhammad Husayn, *Shi'ite Islam*, p. 205.

Khair (A). See Khayr.

Khaja (A). See Khwaja.

Khalaf (A) خلف: successor.

Khalaf Hasan (A) خلف حسن: successor of Hasan.

Khaled (A). See Khalid.

Khaleq (A). See Khaliq.

Khalid (A) خالد (*khaalid*) (خلد): immortal, eternal. جزاؤهم عند ربهم جنات عدن تجري من تحتها الانهار خالدين فيها ابدا "Their reward is with their Lord: Gardens of Eden, underneath which rivers flow, wherein they will dwell forever." (*surat al-Bayyinah* 98:8).

> **Khalid ibn al-Walid** (A) خالد بن الوليد: general to whom Muhammad (s) awarded the title of honour 'Sword of Allah' (d.642).

Khalifa (A) خليفة (*khaleefah*) (خلف): successor, viceroy, vicegerent; a title of the head of the Muslim empire. وهو الذي جعلكم خلائف الارض "It is He who has appointed you as viceroys in the earth." (*surat al-An'aam* 6:165). After the death of Muhammad (s), Abu Bakr was elected by the Muslim community as the Khalifa of the new Muslim territory. He was followed successively by three other elected Khalifas: Umar, Usman (*uthmaan*) and Ali. These four are known collectively as *al-khulafaa' al-raashidun* الخلفاء الراشدون, the 'rightly guided' Khalifas. The title of the Khalifa of the Muslim empire was *ameer al-mu'mineen* أمير المؤمنين, Commander of the Faithful. The title 'Khalifa' was abolished in 1924 when the Ottoman sultanate came to an

97

Male Names

end and Turkey became a secular republic.

Khalil (A) خليل (*khaleel*) (خـل): friend. واتخذ الله ابراهيم خليلا "Allah took Ibrahim as His friend." (*surat al-Nisaa'* 4:125). Khalil al-Ashraf: Mamluk Sultan (1290-93).

Khalilullah (A) خليل الله (*khaleel allah*): friend of Allah, an epithet of Prophet Ibrahim. واتخذ الله إبراهيم خليلا "Allah chose Ibrahim for a friend." (*surat al-Nisaa'* 4:125).

Khalil-ur-Rahman (A) خليل الرحمن (*khaleel al-rahmaan*): friend of the most Gracious, an epithet of Muhammad (s).

Khaliq[189] (A) خليق (*khaleeq*) (خلق): most qualified, suitable (for), worthy (of). Comp. Khaaliq الخالق, the Creator.

Khaliq-uz-Zaman (A) خليق الزمان: the most qualified (person) of the era. Choudhry Khaliquzzaman (1889-1973): Pakistani political leader, author of *Pathway to Pakistan*.

Khaliq-us-Subhan (A) خليق السبحان: worthy of the Glory (Allah).

Khalis (A) خالص (*khaalis*): pure, true, real.

Khaluq (A) خلوق (*khalooq*): noble-minded, courteous, polite, good-natured.

---

[189] See Colebrooke, T. E., 'On the Proper Names of the Mohammadans', *Journal of the Royal Asiatic Society of Great Britain and Ireland*, XI, p. 203 (1879).

Male Names

Khan[190] (P) خان: prince, *ameer*, nobleman. One of the titles of the Khalifa.[191]

Khan Bahadur (P) خان بهادر: honorific title awarded to Muslims during the British rule in the Indian sub-continent. See Bahadur.

Khandakar (P) خوندکار: emperor.

Khandkar (P). See Khandakar.

Khashi (A) خاشع (*khaashi'*): pious, devout.

Khasib (A) خصیب (*khaseeb*): fruitful, prolific.

Khasru (P). See Khusrau.

Khastagir (P). See Khwastagar.

Khatib (A) خطیب (*khateeb*): title of someone who delivers *khutba* (sermon) during the Friday *Jum'a* prayers; orator, speaker. Comp. Khaatib خاطب, suitor.

Khayr (A) خیر: good, blessing, boon, wealth, fortune. والله خیر وابقی

---

[190] See Steingass, F., *A Comprehensive Persian-English Dictionary*, p. 443; "Of Mongolian origin". See Haim, S., *The Shorter Persian-English Dictionary*, p. 257.

[191] See Glasse, Cyril, *The Concise Encyclopaedia of Islam*, p. 222. "Originally, 'Khan' is a hereditary title of the chief of the tribe which is now used very much as part of a name. It is surname when it is preceded by two names; and an honorific title when preceding other names..." See Elahi, Fazal *et al.*, 'Cataloguing of Oriental Names', *Quart. J. Pak Lib Asso.* II, p. 7.

Male Names

"Allah is best and most lasting." (*surat Taa Haa* 20:73). See Akhyar اخيار pl. of Khayr خير.

Abul Khayr (A) أبو الخير: father of good work.

Khayr-ud-Din (A) خير الدين: boon of religion (Islam). Ruler of Algeria (1517-99).

Khayr-ul-Bashar[192] (A) خير البشر: the greatest man, an epithet of Muhammad (s).

Khayrat (A) خيرات (*khayraat*) (خير): blessings, good works, good deeds; pl. of Khayrah خيرة, blessing. ويسارعون في الخيرات واولئك من الصالحين "Those who compete with one another in performing good works are pious." (*surat Aal 'Imraan* 3:114).

Khayri (A) خيري (*khayriyy*): benevolent, charitable.

Khayyam (A) خيَّام: tent-maker. Umar Khayyam: see Umar.

Khidr (A). See Khizr.

Khizr (A) خضر (*khidr*): green. In *sura al-Kahf* (no.18), the Qur'an mentions a person whom Allah endowed with special knowledge. The tradition identifies him as Khizr (*khidr*) who allowed Prophet Musa to accompany him in the course of his journey and later explained his apparently strange conduct which had not been understood by Prophet Musa due to his lack of relevant knowledge (see *sura Al-Kahf* 18:65-82).

---

[192] Although the name is popular in the sub-continent, it is not used in the Arab countries as it is believed that the title belongs exclusively to Muhammad (s).

Male Names

Khizr Khan (A+P) خضر خان: Delhi Sultan (1414-21).

Khomeini. See Ayatullah.

Khorshed (P). See Khurshid.

Khosrau[193] (P). See Khusrau.

Khuda (P) خدا: Allah.

> **Khuda Banda** (P) خدا بنده: servant of Khuda. "Name of the Persian king Muhammad Sikandar Shah, father of 'Abbas the Great."[194]
>
> **Khuda Dad** (P) خدا داد: gift of Khuda
>
> **Khudawand** (P) خدا وند: king, prince, lord.

Khulud (A) خلود (خلد) (*khulood*): immortality, eternity. ذلك يوم الخلود "This is the day of immortality." (*surat Qaaf* 50:34).

Khurram (P) خرم: cheerful, glad, fresh. Son of Mughal emperor Jahangir who ascended the throne of Delhi as Shah Jahan.

Khurshid (P) خورشید (*khursheed*): sun. See Aftaab افتاب; Mihr مهر; Shams شمس.

Khusrau (P) خسرو: "a celebrated Persian king; a royal surname in

---

[193] See Haykal, Muhammad Husayn, *The Life of Muhammad*, p. 363.

[194] See Steingass, F., *A Comprehensive Persian-English Dictionary*, p. 449.

Persia."[195] Son of Mughal emperor Jahangir. Ameer Khusrau: see Ameer.

Khusrau Firuz (P) خسرو فيروز: Buwayhid Sultan in Iraq (1048-55).

Khwaja (P) خواجه (*khwaaja*): lord, master, a man of distinction, a high ranking person. Title of a minister or important dignitary. Khwaja Abdus Samad: see Samad. Khwaja Muin ud-Din Chishti: see Chishti. Khwaja Nazimuddin: see Nazim.

Khwaja Abdul Ghani (P+A) خواجه عبد الغني: Bengali Nawab known for his social work.

Khwastagar (P) خواستگر: petitioner, candidate.

Kibria (A) كبرياء (*kibriyaa'*) (كبر): divine majesty, divine grandeur. وله الكبرياء في السماوات والارض "To Him (Allah) belongs majesty in the heavens and the earth." (*surat al-Jaathiah* 45:37).

Ghulam Kibria (A) غلام كبرياء: servant of the Divine Grandeur.

Kidwa (A). See Qidwa.

Kifah[196] (A) كفاح: struggle, fight.

Kohinur (P+A) كوه نور (*kohinoor*): the mountain of light. A 109 carat

---

[195] *Ibid.*, p. 460.

[196] This name "appeared in Egypt during the Arab-Israeli war." See Schimmel, Annemarie, *Islamic Names*, p. 17.

diamond removed in 1849 from the Mughal jewels in India and added to the British crown jewels in London.

Korban (A). See Qurban.

Kudsi (A). See Qudsi.

Kutb (A). See Qutb.

Male Names

L

Labib (A) لبيب (*labeeb*) (لَبّ): intelligent, reasonable, rational, wise.

Lashkar (P) لشكر: soldier, army. See Askari; Junayid.

Muhammad Lashkari (A+P) محمد لشكري: Indian king (1463-82).

Latif (A) لطيف (*lateef*) (لطف): kind, gracious, courteous, gentle friendly. Al-Lateef اللطيف, the All-gentle: one of the names of Allah. ان الله لطيف خبير "Allah is the All-gentle and the All-aware." (*surat al-Hajj 22:63*).

> **Abdul Latif** (A) عبد اللطيف (*'abd al-lateef*): servant of the All-gentle. Ruler in Samarqand (1449-50). Shah Abd al-Latif (1689-1752): eminent Indian poet in Sindhi.[197] Nawab Abdul Latif (1828-93): founder of the Muhammadan Literary and Scientific Society of Calcutta to uplift the position of Muslims in the field of education.[198]

Liakat (A). See Liaqat لياقة.

Liaqat (A) لياقة (*liyaaqah*): decorum, decency. Nawabzada Liaqat Ali Khan (1895-1951): the first prime minister of Pakistan.

Lisan (A) لسان (*lisaan*) (لسن): tongue, language. قال رب اشرح لي صدري ويسر لي امري واحلل عقدة من لساني "[Musa] said: My Lord!

---

[197] See Aziz, Ahmad, *An Intellectual History of Islam*, p. 124.

[198] See Hardy, P., *The Muslims of British India*, p. 104.

Male Names

Relieve my mind, ease my task for me and loose the knot from my tongue." (*surat Ta Ha* 20:25-27). وهذا كتاب مصدق لسانا عربيا "And this Book confirms it in the Arabic language." (*surat al-Ahqaaf* 46:12).

Lisan-ud-Din (A) لسان الدين: language of religion (Islam). Arab author who lived in Spain (1313-74).

Lokman (A). See Luqman لقمان.

Luqman (A) لقمان (*luqmaan*): "The sage Luqman...is the type of perfect wisdom. Many instructive apologues are credited to him, similar to Aesop's Fables in Greek tradition."[199] *Luqmaan* لقمان: title of the 31st *sura* of the Qur'an. ولقد أتينا لقمان الحكمة ان اشكر لله "We bestowed wisdom on Luqmaan, saying: Give thanks to Allah." (*surat Luqmaan* 31:12).

Lutf (A) لطف: kindness, friendliness, grace, favour from Allah.

Lutfullah (A) لطف الله (*lutf allah*): kindness of Allah.

Lutf-ur-Rahman (A) لطف الرحمن (*lutf al-rahmaan*): favour of the All-merciful.

Lutf-ul-Baari' (A). See Baari', the Creator.

Lutfi[200] (A) لطفي (*lutfiyy*): kind, friendly, courteous. Lutfi Pasha: grand vizier of Ottoman Khalifa Sulayman the Magnificent. Ahmad

---

[199] See Ali, Yusuf, *The Holy Qur'an*, n. 3593.

[200] See Paxton, Evelyn, 'Arabic Names', *Asian Affairs*, LIX, p. 199 (1972).

105

Male Names

Lutfi al-Sayyid (1872-1963): Egyptian political thinker and educationist.[201]

---

[201] See Choueiri, Youssef, *Islamic Fundamentalism*, p. 42; Ahmed, Leila, *Women and Gender in Islam*, p. 149; Donohue, John J. & Esposito, John L., *Islam in Transition*, p. 70.

M

Maajid (A) ماجد (مجد): glorious, noble. Al-Maajid الماجد, the All-glorious: one of the names of Allah. See Majeed مجيد, glorious.

> **Abdul Maajid** (A) عبد الماجد (*'abd al-maajid*): servant of the All-glorious.

Maalik (A) مالك (ملك): owner, proprietor, master. Al-Maalik المالك, the Owner: one of the names of Allah. مالك الملك "Owner of the sovereignty" (*surat Aal 'Imraan* 3:26). مالك يوم الدين "Master of the Day of Judgment." (*surat al-Faatihah* 1:3). Name of an angel (see *surat al-Zukhruf* 43:77). See Malik ملك, king. Maalik ibn Anas: founder of the Maaliki School of Law (716-795), author of *Al-Muwatta*.

> **Abdul Maalik** (A) عبد المالك (*'abd al-maalik*): servant of the Owner.

Mabruk (A) مبروك (*mabrook*) (برك): blessed, prosperous.

Mafiz (A). See Mufiz (*mufid*).

Mahasin (A) محاسن (*mahaasin*): pl. of Mahsanah محسنة, beauty, attraction, virtue, merit.

> **Abul Mahasin** (A) ابو المحاسن: father of virtues, merits.

Mahbub (A) محبوب (حبّ) (*mahboob*): dear, beloved.

> **Mahbubullah** (A) محبوب الله (*mahboob allah*): beloved of

107

Allah.

Mahdi (A) مهدي (*mahdiyy*) (هدي): rightly guided. See Rasheed رشيد; Muhtadi مهتدي.

Al-Mahdi المهدي (A): the rightly guided. An epithet of Muhammad (s). Abbasid Khalifa (775-85).

Muhammad al-Muntazar al-Mahdi محمد المنتظر المهدي: the twelfth Īmam of the Shi'ites, who disappeared in 939.[202]

Mahfuz (A) محفوظ (*mahfooz*) (حفظ): safeguarded, well-protected. بل هو قرآن مجيد في لوح محفوظ "Nay, it is a glorious Qur'an in a guarded tablet." (*surat al-Buruz* 85:21-22). See Masun مصون.

Mahib (A) مهيب (*maheeb*) (هيب): majestic, dignified, magnificent.

Mahir (A) ماهر (*maahir*) (مهر): skilled, skilful, proficient.

Mahjub (A) محجوب (*mahjoob*) (حجب): hidden, covered, screened.

Mahmood (A). See Mahmud.

Mahmud (A) محمود (*mahmood*) (حمد): praised, praiseworthy, lauded, laudable. عسى ان يبعثك ربك مقاما محمودا "It may be that your Lord

---

[202] See Al-Tabatabai, Allamah Sayyid Muhammad Husayn, *Shi'ite Islam*, p. 211. "Mahdi will appear again, filling with justice the world that has been corrupted by injustice and inequity." *Ibid.*, p. 212. "[His] sudden disappearance has favoured the hopes of his followers that he is still living, and will appear again on the earth to unite the faithful." See Colebrooke, T. E., 'On the Proper Names of the Mohammadans', *Journal of the Royal Asiatic Society of Great Britain and Ireland*, XI, p. 202 (1879).

Male Names

will raise you (O Muhammad!) to a praised station." (*surat Bani 'Israa'il* 17:79). See Muhammad محمد praised; Ahmad احمد more laudable. Mahmud ibn Maslamah al-Ansari: a *sahaabi* who was "martyred in the siege of the stronghold of Naim."[203] Mahmud of Gaznah (971-1030): founder of Ghaznavid dynasty (977-1186), ruler of Afghanistan.[204] Mahmud Shaltut (1893-1963): "one of a celebrated number of Azhari shaykhs...[d]uring [whose] tenure, al-Azhar began to take its modern shape."[205] He is author of ten-volume *Tafsir al-Qur'an* and *Al-Fatawah*. Mahmudul Hasan (1851-1920):[206] Indian religious and political leader who was known as *Shaykh al-Hind*.

Mahmud-un-Nabi (A) محمود النبيّ : praised by the *Nabi* (Prophet) (s).

Mahrus (A) محروس (*mahroos*) (حرس): safeguarded, protected, secured.

Mahtab (P) ماهتاب (*maahtaab*): moonlight.

Maimun (A) ميمون (*maimoon*) (يمن): auspicious, prosperous, lucky, fortunate, blessed. See Ayman أيمن, blessed.

Ma'in (A) معين (*ma'een*) (عين): fountain, spring (*surat al-Waaqi'ah*

---

[203] See Umari, Akram Diya al, *Madinan Society at the Time of the Prophet*, p. 146.

[204] "Mahmud's empire at his death was...the most extensive and imposing edifice since the heyday of the early 'Abbasid caliphate, and the military machine which made it possible was the most effective army of its age." See Bosworth, C. E., *The Islamic Dynasties*, p. 182. Due to invasion of India by Mahmud, "Indian History enters on a new epoch." See Majumdar, R. C., *An Advanced History of India*, p. 170.

[205] See *The Oxford Encyclopaedia of the Modern Islamic World*, vol. IV, p. 42.

[206] See Hardy, P., *The Muslims of British India*, p. 186; Mujahid, Sharif Al-, *Quaid-i-Azam Jinnah*, p. 700.

56:18). Comp. Muin معين (عون), helper.

Maisur (A) ميسور (*maisoor*) (يسر): easy, successful, fortunate, lucky, prosperous.

Majd (A) مجد: glory, honour.

Majdi (A) مجدي (*majdiyy*): glorious, praiseworthy.

Majeed (A) مجيد (مجد): glorious, noble. Al-Majeed المجيد, the All-glorious: one of the names of Allah. ذو العرش المجيد "Lord of the throne, full of all glory." (*surat al-Buruz* 85:15). القرآن المجيد "The glorious Qur'an." (*surat Qaaf* 50:1). See Maajid ماجد, glorious.

> **Abdul Majeed** (A) عبد المجيد (*'abd al-majeed*): servant of the All-glorious. King of Anatolia (1839-61).

Majid (A). See Maajid ماجد; Majeed مجيد.

Majlis (A) مجلس (جلس): gathering, assembly. يايها الذين آمنوا اذا قيل لكم تفسحوا في المجالس فافسحوا يفسح الله لكم "O you who believe! When you are told to make room in the assemblies, (spread out and) make room; Allah will make room for you." (*surat al-Mujaadilah* 58:11).

Majlisi (A) مجلسي: of or relating to Majlis. Muhammad al-Baaqir Majlisi (1628-1700): Iranian scholar who "is said to have written as many as thirteen books in Arabic and fifty-three in Persian."[207]

Majmudar (A+P) مجموع دار (جمع): an officer responsible for auditing

---

[207] See *The Oxford Encyclopaedia of the Modern Islamic World*, vol. III, pp. 27-8.

the accounts of the revenue-collector during the Muslim rule in the Indian sub-continent, now a family title.

Majumdar (A). See Majmudar.

Majzub (A) مجذوب (*majdhoob*) (جذب): "Drawn, attracted by Divine grace and renouncing all worldly concerns, to give oneself entirely over to piety and contemplation."[208]

Makbul (A). See Maqbul مقبول.

Makram (A) مكرم (كرم): noble trait, excellent quality. Comp. Mukram مكرم, honoured.

Malih (A) مليح (*maleeh*) (ملح): handsome.

Malik (A) ملك (ملك): king, sovereign. Al-Malik الملك, the King: one of the names of Allah. ملك الناس "King of mankind." (*surat al-Naas* 114:2). See Maalik مالك, master.

> **Abdul Malik** (A) عبد الملك (*'abd al-malik*): servant of the King. Abd al-Malik ibn Marwan: the greatest Umayyad Khalifa (685-705), known as 'father of kings', who built the magnificent Dome of the Rock on the Temple Mount in Jerusalem.[209]

> **Malik Shah** (A+P) ملك شاه: Seljuq Sultan in Iraq and Persia

---

[208] See Steingass, F., *A Comprehensive Persian-English Dictionary*, p. 1176.

[209] It is "[t]he first great religious building in the history of Islam." See Lewis, Bernard, *The Middle East*, p. 82. Abd al-Malik "made Arabic the official language of his empire, and minted a new Islamic gold coin." See *Who Did What*, The Mitchell Beazley Illustrated Biographical Dictionary, p. 6.

Male Names

(1072-92).²¹⁰

Maluf (A) مألوف (*ma'loof*) (الف): familiar, popular.

Mamduh (A) ممدوح (*mamdooh*) (مدح): praised, celebrated, famous, laudable.

Mamtaz (A). See Mumtaz ممتاز.

Mamun (A) مأمون (*ma'moon*) (امن): trustworthy, honest, faithful, reliable, something about which one feels secure. ان عذاب ربهم غير مأمون "The punishment of their Lord is that before which none can feel secure." (*surat al-Ma'aarij* 70:28).

Al-Mamun المأمون (A): Abbasid Khalifa (813-33).

Manaf (A) مناف (*manaaf*): Abd Manaaf:²¹¹ an ancestor of Muhammad (s).²¹²

Manal (A) منال (*manaal*) (نيل): attainment, acquisition.

Manar (A) منار (*manaar*) (نور): lighthouse.

Manhal (A) منهل: fountain, spring.

---

²¹⁰ He reformed the Persian calendar which led to the production of Jalali calendar which "in the judgment of a modern scholar, is 'somewhat more accurate than ours'". See Hitti, Philip K., *History of the Arabs*, p. 477.

²¹¹ Manaaf is not one of the names of Allah. In that sense, Abdul Manaaf is improper.

²¹² See Haykal, Muhammad Husayn, *The Life of Muhammad*, p. 45.

Male Names

Mannan (A) مـنان (*mannaan*) (مـن): benevolent, bountiful, generous. Al-Mannaan المـنان, the Benevolent: one of the names of Allah. See Karim كريم, benevolent.

Abdul Mannan (A) عبد المـنان (*'abd al-mannan*): servant of the Benevolent.

Mansur (A) مـنصور (*mansoor*) (نصر): assisted, victorious, triumphant. انه كان مـنصورا "Verily, he is helped." (*surat Bani Israa'il* 17:33). Al-Mansur المـنصور: Abbasid Khalifa (754-75). See Muntasir مـنتصر; Ghalib غالب.

Mansur-ud-Din (A) مـنصور الدين: victorious in religion (Islam).

Manus (A) مـأنوس (*ma'noos*) (أنس): friendly, sociable, polite. See Anis أنيس, friendly.

Manzur (A) مـنظور (*manzoor*) (نظر): approved of, chosen, promising.

Manzur-e-Khuda (A+P) مـنظور خدا: approved by Khuda (Allah).

Maqbul (A) مـقبول (*maqbool*) (قبل): accepted, admitted, granted, approved.

Maqsud (A) مـقصود (*maqsood*) (قصد): intended, aimed at. See Murad مراد, intended.

Maram (A) مـرام (*maraam*) (روم): wish, desire, aspiration.

Maruf (A) مـعروف (*ma'roof*) (عرف): favour, kindness, kind act, famous. تامرون بالمعروف وتنهون عن المنكر "You enjoin the doing of what

113

is right and forbid the doing of what is wrong." (*surat Aal 'Imraan* 3:110). See Ihsan إحسان.

Marwa (A) مروة (*marwah*): a flint-stone. A hill near the sacred Kaaba in Makkah. Hajar, wife of Prophet Ibrahim, ran between the two hills of Safa and Marwa in search of water for her infant son Ismail. In commemoration, Muslim pilgrims walk briskly between these two hills ritually seven times during the *Hajj.* ان الصفا والمروة من شعائر الله فمن حج البيت او اعتمر فلا جناح عليه ان يطوف بهما "Behold! Safa and Marwa are among the symbols of Allah. It is therefore no sin for him who is on pilgrimage to the House (of Allah) or visits it, to go round them." (*surat al-Baqarah* 2:158).

Marzuq (A) مرزوق (رزق) (*marzooq*): blessed (by God), fortunate, prosperous, successful.

Mashhud (A) مشهود (*mashhood*) (شهد): witnessed. ان قرءان الفجر كان مشهودا "The recital of the Qur'an at dawn is ever witnessed. (*surat Bani Israa'il* 17:78).

Masih (A) مسيح (*maseeh*): the Messiah, 'Isa (Jesus), a Prophet. انما المسيح عيسى ابن مريم رسول الله وكلمته "The Masih (Messiah), 'Isa (Jesus), son of Maryam was only a Messenger of Allah and His word." (*surat al-Nisaa'* 4:171).

Masih-uz-Zaman (A) مسيح الزمان: Masih (Messiah) of the age.

Masir (A) مصير (*maseer*) (صير): destiny, goal. والى الله المصير "For the final goal is to Allah." (*surat Aal 'Imraan* 3:28).

Male Names

Masud (A) مسعود (*mas'ood*) (سعد): fortunate, happy, lucky. See Sa'eed سعيد, happy. Masud III (1099-1115): Sultan of Ghaznah.[213] Masud Sa'd Salman (d.1121): Indian poet in Persian, Arabic and Hindi.[214]

Abdullah ibn Mas'ud (A) عبد الله ابن مسعود: a *sahaabi* well-known for his knowledge on commentary on the Qur'an.[215]

Masud Khan (A+P) مسعود خان: Sultan of Malwa (India) (1436).

Masum (A) معصوم (عصم) (*ma'soom*): innocent, sinless) infallible, protected. Al-Masum المعصوم, the innocent: an epithet of Muhammad (s). See Mahfuz محفوظ, protected.

Masun (A) مصون (*masoon*): safeguarded, well-protected.

Matin (A) متين (*mateen*) (متن): strong, powerful. Al-Mateen المتين the Strong: one of the names of Allah. ان الله هو الرزاق ذو القوة المتين "For Allah is He Who is the All-provider, the Possessor of Strength, the Strong." (*surat al-Dhaariyaat* 51:58).

Abdul Matin (A) عبد المتين (*'abd al-mateen*): servant of the Strong.

Maudud (A). See Mawdud.

---

[213] The monumental 'Tower of Victory' was built in his name in Ghazni, to celebrate his victory over the Hindu rulers of Kanauj. See Lewis, Bernard, *The Middle East*, p. 82.

[214] "His Persian works, published in Iran, cover nearly eight hundred pages, and [a] modern Iranian critic has included him among the ten greatest poets of the Persian language." See Ikram, S. M., *History of Muslim Civilization in India and Pakistan*, p. 45.

[215] See An-Nawawi, *Forty Hadith*, p. 59. He "had attached himself to the Prophet so closely as to be almost one of the household." See Lings, Martin, *Muhammad*, p. 168.

Maududi (A). See Mawdudi.

Maulvi (A) مولوي (*Maulawi*): title of a person learned in the field of Islam and Shari'a. In the Indian subcontinent, it is still used as a title for Muslim gentry.

Mausuf (A) موصوف (*mawsoof*) (وصف): worthy of description, endowed with laudable qualities.

Mawahib (A) مواهب (*mawaahib*) (وهب): pl. of Mauhiba موهبة, gift, talent.

Mawdud (A) مودود (*mawdood*) (ودّ): beloved.

Mawdudi (A) مودودي: more beloved. Mawlana Sayyid Abul Ala Mawdudi (1903-79): outstanding scholar and thinker in the field of Islam of the twentieth century. He is founder of the Jamaati-i-Islami and author of a large number of books including the well known commentatory on the Qur'an, *The Meaning of the Qur'an*.

Mawhub (A) موهوب (*mawhoob*) (وهب): gifted, talented, endowed, favoured.

Mawla (A) مولى (ولي) (*mawlaa*): helper, protector. Al-Mawla المولى, the Lord Supreme: one of the names of Allah. انت مولانا فانصرنا على القوم الكافرين "You (Allah) are our Lord Supreme, give us victory over the disbelieving people." (*surat al-Baqarah* 2:286). See Nasir نصير; Sadiq صديق.

Fazle Mawla (A) فضل مولى: bounty of the Lord (Allah).

Mazhar (A) مظهر (ظهر): manifestation, expression. See Dalil دليل.

Male Names

Mazhar-ud-Din (A) مظهر الدین: manifestation of the religion (Islam).

Mazhar-ul-Haqq (A) مظهر الحق (*mazhar al-haqq*): manifestation of the Truth (Allah). Indian political leader (1866-1929).[216]

Mazid (A) مزید (*mazeed*) (زِید): increase, excess, maximum.

Mazumdar (A). See Majmudar.

Mehbub (A). See Mahbub.

Mehdi (A). See Mahdi.

Mehmed (A). See Muhammad.

Mehmet (A). See Muhammad.

Mesbah (A). See Misbah.

Mia[217] (P) میان (*miyan*): honorific title, form of polite address, sir, master. It is used either as a prefix or suffix to a name. Dudu Miyan (1819-62): son of Shariatullah. Bengali political and religious reformer.[218]

---

[216] See Hardy, P., *The Muslims of British India*, p. 190.

[217] "In the subcontinent *miyan* is a respectful but loving way to address a venerable elderly man." See Schimmel, Annemarie, *Islamic Names*, p. 68.

[218] "The militancy of Saiyid Ahmad Bareilly's and Dudu Miyan's followers was to have profound long-term effects on British political strategy in India." Hardy, P., *The Muslims of British India*, p. 60; He "formed almost a parallel government in some villages of

117

Male Names

Miad (A) ميعاد (*mee'aad*) (وعد): appointed time, time, promise. وعد
الله لا يخلف الله الميعاد "(It is) a promise of Allah. Allah does not fail in His promise." (*surat al-Zumar* 39:20).

Mibsam (A) مبسام (*mibsaam*) (بسم): much smiling.

Mimrah (A) ممراح (*mimraah*) (مرح): cheerful, lively.

Minah (A) منح (*minah*): gifts, favours; pl. of Minhah منحة.

Minhaj (A) منهاج (*minhaaj*) (نهج): method, system, order, way. لكل
جعلنا منكم شرعة ومنهاجا "For each We have appointed a (divine) law and a way of life." (*surat al-Maa'idah* 5:48). Minhaj al-Siraj: thirteenth-century historian of India.

Minnat (A) مِنَّة (مِنْ): grace, kindness, favour, gift. See Fazl فضل
(*fadl*); Jamil جميل; Ihsan إحسان.

> **Minnatullah** (A) منة الله (*minnat allah*): gratitude owed to Allah.

Miqdam (A) مقدام (*miqdaam*) (قدم): in the forefront of battle, very bold, undaunted. A ruler of Morocco. Al-Miqdaam ibn Ma'd: a *sahaabi*.

Mir (P) مير (*meer*): prince, governor, leader. Abbreviation of Ameer أمير (A). Titu Mir (1782-1831): Bengali political leader.[219]

Bengal." See Ahmad, Aziz, *An Intellectual History of Islam in India*, p. 10. Also See Choueiri, Youssef, *Islamic Fundamentalism*, p. 22.

[219] "[By] 1827 he was campaigning in favour of a purified Islam, in an idiom similar to that of Saiyid Ahmad Bareilly and Haji Shari'at-Allah...In November 1831 they [British authorities] destroyed the insurgents' stockade...[and] killed Titu Mir..."See Hardy, P., *The*

Male Names

Miraj (A) معراج (*mi'raaj*): place of ascent. Al-mi'raaj المعراج: ascension of Muhammad (s) to the seven heavens. "The Mi'raj is usually dated to the 27th night of the month of Rajab."[220] Parents may wish to name a child born on this sacred date 'Miraj'.

Miran (P) ميران (*meeraan*): princes; pl. of Mir مير.

> **Miraan Mubaarak Khan** (P+A) ميران مبارك خان: Sultan of Khandesh (India) (1441-57).

Mirjahaan (P) مير جهان: king of the world.

Mirza (P) ميرزا (*mirzaa*): son of a prince. Honorific title.

> **Abdullah Mirza** (A+P) عبد الله ميرزا: ruler of Samarqand (1450-51).

Misaq (A) ميثاق (*meethaaq*) (وثق): agreement, covenant, contract, compact. واذكروا نعمة الله عليكم وميثاقه الذي واثقكم به اذ قلتم سمعنا واطعنا "Remember Allah's grace upon you and His covenant by which He bound you when you said: We hear and we obey." (*surat al-Maa'idah* 5:7).

Misbah (A) مصباح (صبح): lamp. مثل نوره كمشكاة فيها مصباح المصباح قي زجاجة "The similitude of His light is as a niche wherein is a lamp. The lamp is in a glass." (*surat al-Nur* 24:35). Al-Misbah المصباح, the Lamp: an epithet of Muhammad (s). See Chirag (P) جراغ; Nibras نبراس (f.); Siraj سراج.

Muslims of British India, pp. 57-8.

[220] See Ali, Yusuf, *The Holy Qur'an*, p. 691.

Male Names

Misbah-ud-Din (A) مصباح الدين: lamp of the religion (Islam).

Miyan (P). See Mia.

Mizan (A) ميزان (*meezaan*) (وزن): balance, scales. واقيموا الوزن بالقسط ولا تخسروا الميزان "Establish the measure with justness and cut not the measure short." (*surat al-Rahmaan* 55:9).

Mizan-ur-Rahman (A) ميزان الرحمن (*meezaan al-rahmaan*): balance of the most Merciful.

Mobarak (A). See Mubarak.

Mofazzal (A). See Mufazzal.

Mofiz (A). See Mufiz.

Mohaimen (A). See Muhaymin.

Mohamed (A). See Muhammad.

Mohammad (A). See Muhammad.

Mohiuddin (A). See Muhyiddin.

Mohr (P). See Muhr.

Mohsen (A). See Muhsin.

Mohsin (A). See Muhsin.

Male Names

Moin (A). See Muin.

Mojammel (A). See Mujammil.

Mokammel (A). See Mukammil.

Mokhles (A). See Mukhlis.

Moktader (A). See Muqtadir.

Molla (A). See Mulla.

Momen (A). See Mumin.

Monaem (A). See Munaim.

Monowar (A). See Munawwar.

Moosa (A). See Musa.

Morshed (A). See Murshid.

Mosaddeq (A). See Musaddiq.

Mosharraf (A). See Musharraf.

Moshtaq (A). See Mushtaq.

Mosleh (A). See Muslih.

Moslem (A). See Muslim.

Male Names

Motahhar (A). See Mutahhar.

Moti (A). See Mu'ti, Muti'.

Mottaleb (A). See Muttalib.

Mozaffar (A). See Muzaffar.

Mozahir (A). See Muzahir.

Muammar (A) معمر (mu'ammar) (عمر): long-lived, one given long life; title of Luqman.[221] وما يعمر من معمر ولا ينقص من عمره الا في كتاب "No one grows old or has his life cut short but in accordance with His decree." (surat Faatir 35:11). Mu'ammar ibn Raashid (d.153 AH): hadith scholar.[222]

Muawin (A) معاون (mu'aawin) (عون): assistant, helper, supporter. See Muin معين, helper.

Muayyad (A) مؤيّد (ايد): supported, championed, approved, victorious. Hisham II al-Muayyad: Spanish Umayyad Khalifa (976-1009, 1010-13).

Muaz (A) معاذ (mu'aadh) (عوذ): protected.

Mu'aadh bin Jabal (A) معاذ بن جبل: a sahaabi whom Muhammad (s) sent as a judge to Yemen.[223] It is reported

---

221 See Ali, Yusuf, The Holy Qur'an, n. 3593.

222 See Umari, Akram Diya al, Madinan Society at the Time of the Prophet, p. 31.

223 An-Nawawi, Forty Hadith, p. 98.

Male Names

in hadith that Muhammad (s) allowed him to exercise *ijtihaad* in deciding cases if he did not find clear guidance in either the Qur'an or the *sunnah*.

Muazzam (A) معظّم (*mu'azzam*) (عظم): exalted, glorified. Muazzam Shah Alam I Bahadur Shah I: Mughal emperor (1707-12).

Muazzaz (A) معزّز (*mu'azzaz*) (عز): strengthened, supported, promoted, advanced.

Mubajjal (A) مبجل (بجل): glorified, exalted, honourable, greatly respected.

Mubarak[224] (A) مبارك (*mubaarak*) (برك): blessed, fortunate, lucky, auspicious. فاذا دخلتم بيوتا فسلموا على انفسكم تحية من عند الله مباركة طيبة "When you enter houses, give salaam one another with a greeting from Allah, blessed and good." (*surat al-Nur* 24:61). Qutb ud-Din Mubarak Shah: Delhi Sultan (1316-20).

Mubashsher (A) مبشّر (*mubashshir*) (بشر): bringer of good news, a Prophet. An epithet of Muhammad (s). يايها النبي انا ارسلناك شاهدا ومبشرا ونذيرا "O Nabi! Truly We have sent you as a witness, a bringer of good news and a warner." (*surat al-Ahzaab* 33:45). See Basheer بشير.

Mubin (A) مبين (*mubeen*) (بين): clear, plain, distinct. قرآن مبين "Clear Qur'an" (*surat Ya Sin* 36:69). يايها الناس قد جاءكم برهان من ربكم وانزلنا اليكم نورا مبينا "O mankind! Now has come

---

This name is prevalent in all Muslim countries but note that "[t]here are Kuwaiti personal names for the Sheikhs or ruling class in Kuwait, as Mubaarak." See Yassin, M. Aziz F., 'Personal Names Address in Kuwaiti Arabic', *Anthropological Linguistics*, XX, p. 54.

Male Names

to you a proof from your Lord and We have sent down to you a clear Light." (*surat al-Nisaa'* 4:174).

Mubtasim (A) مبتسم (بسم): smiling, smiler.

Mudabber (A) مدبّر (*mudabbir*) (دبر): planner, designer, author, director. فالمدبرات امرا "And those who govern the event." (*surat al-Naazi'aat* 79:5).

Muddassir (A) مدّثر (*muddaththir*) (دثر): wrapped in, enveloped. Al-Muddaththir المدثر, 'The enveloped': title of the 74th *sura* of the Qur'an. In this *sura*, Allah addresses Muhammad (s): يايها المدثر "O You wrapped in your cloak!" (*surat al-Muddaththir* 74:1).

Mudrik (A) مدرك (درك): perceptive, intelligent, reasonable, endowed with reason.

Mufakhkhar (A) مفخّر (فخر): glorious, exalted.

Mufazzal (A) مفضّل (*mufaddal*) (فضل): preferred, chosen, favoured. See Mukhtar مختار; Mustafa مصطفى.

Mufid (A) مفيد (mufeed) (فيد) beneficial, advantageous, favourable, profitable. Shaikh al-Mufid (d.1022): Shi'ite jurist.

Mufiz (A) مفيض (*mufeed*) (فيض): a giver.[225]

Mufti (A) المفتي (*al-Muftii*) (فتو): interpreter or expounder of *Shari'a* (Islamic law).

---

[225] See Steingass, F., *A Comprehensive Persian-English Dictionary*, p. 1287.

Male Names

Mughis (A) مغيث (*mugheeth*) (غيث): helper, assistant. A *sahaabi*.

Muhafiz (A) محافظ (حفظ): preserver, custodian, guardian.

Muhafiz-ud-Din (A) محافظ الدين: preserver of the religion (Islam).

Muhaimen (A). See Muhaymin.

Muhajir (A) مهاجر (*muhaajir*) (هجر): emigrant. Historically, the Makkans who emigrated to Madina with Muhammad (s) are called Muhajir. ومن يخرج من بيته مهاجرا الى الله ورسوله ثم يدركه الموت فقد وقع اجره على الله "Whoso leaves his home as an emigrant to Allah and His Messenger, and death overtakes him, his reward is then incumbent upon Allah." (*surat al-Nisaa'* 4:100).

Muhammad (A) محمَّد (حمد): praised, lauded, commended, praiseworthy. Muhammad ibn Abdullah (570-632): Messenger of Allah who preached the faith of Islam. محمد رسول الله "Muhammad is the Messenger of Allah." (*surat al-Fath* 48:29). *Muhammad*: title of the 47th *sura* of the Qur'an. The Qur'an, the Holy Book of Muslims was revealed to Muhammad (s) through angel Jibreel (Gabriel). The Qur'an mentions that Muhammad was the last Prophet sent by Allah for the guidance of mankind. ما كان محمد ابا احد من رجالكم ولكن رسول الله وخاتم النبين "Muhammad is not the father of any man among you, but he is the Messenger of Allah and the Seal of the Prophets." (*surat al-Ahzaab* 33:40). See Mahmud محمود, praised; Ahmad احمد, more laudable. Muhammad Zaman: seventeenth-century Persian artist. Muhammad Ali (d.1849): founder of modern Egypt whose dynasty ruled Egypt from 1805 to 1953. Muhammad Ali (1878-1931): Indian political leader who

Male Names

championed the cause of Muslims in pre-independent India.[226]

Abu Muhammad (A) أبو محمَّد: father of Muhammad. Name of Khalifa Harun al-Rashid. See Harun.

Muhannad (A) مهنَّد (هند): sword made of Indian steel. Comp. Sayf سيف, sword.

Muhaymin (A) مهيمن (هيمن): ruler, overlord. Al-Muhaimin المهيمن, the All-preserver: one of the names of Allah. (*surat al-Hashr* 59:23).

Abdul Muhaimin عبد المهيمن (*'abd al-muhaimin*): servant of the All-preserver.

Muhayya' (A) مهيَّأ (هي): prepared, ready. Comp. Muhayya محيَّا (f.) face.

Muhazzab (A) مهذَّب (*muhadhdhab*) (هذب): polite, courteous, purified.

Muhib (A) محبّ (*muhibb*) (حب): loving, affectionate, friend.

Muhibuddin (A) محبّ الدين (*muhibb al-din*): friend of the religion (Islam).

Muhibullah (A) محبّ الله (*muhibb allah*): friend of Allah.

Muhit (A) محيط (*muheet*) (حوط): encompassing, ocean. و كان الله بكل شيء محيطا "Allah encompasses everything." (*surat al-Nisaa'* 4:126).

---

[226] See Afzal Iqbal (ed.), *Selected Writings and Speeches of Mohomed Ali*, quoted in Hardy, P., *The Muslims of British India*, p. 218.

Male Names

Muhiuddin (A). See Muhyi.

Muhr (P) مهر: seal, seal-ring.[227]

Muhriz (A) محرز (حرز): winner, gainer, possessor, holder. A *sahaabi*.

Muhsin (A) محسن (حسن): benevolent, beneficent, charitable, humanitarian. ان الله يحب المحسنين "Allah loves those who do good." (*surat al-Baqarah* 2:195). Son of Khalifa Ali who died in childhood. Haji Muhsin: nineteenth-century Bengali philanthropist.[228]

Muhtadi (A) المهتدي (*al-Muhtadii*) (هدي): rightly guided, following the right path, on the right way. من يهد الله فهو المهتدي "Whom Allah guides, he is rightly guided." (*surat al-A'raaf* 7:178). Al-Muhtadi المهتدي: Abbasid Khalifa (869-70). See Rasheed رشيد; Mahdi مهدي.

Muhtasham (A) محتشم (حشم): great, powerful, attended by many followers.

Muhtashim (A) محتشم (حشم): decent, modest, chaste, shy.

Muhyi (A) محيي[229] (*muhyii*) (حي): one who gives life, reviver. Al-Muhyi المحيي, the Quickener: one of the names of Allah. ان الذي احياها لمحيي الموتى "Verily, He who brings it to life can surely give life to the dead. (*surat Fussilat* 41:39).

---

[227] See Steingass, F., *A Comprehensive Persian-English Dictionary*, p. 1353.

[228] He "gave a substantial grant to the East India Company in the early nineteenth century, for the general advancement of Muslim education." See Ahmad, Aziz, *An Intellectual History of Islam in India*, pp. 59-60.

[229] See Steingass, F., *A Comprehensive Persian-English Dictionary*, p. 1191.

127

Male Names

Muhyi-id-Din[230] (A) محيي الدين: reviver of the religion (Islam).[231] A sobriquet of Sheikh Abdul Qader Jilani (1077-1166),[232] scholar of spiritual knowledge. Muhy id-Din Muhammad Aurangzeb Alamgir (1658-1707): pious Mughal emperor.

Muid (A) معيد (*mu'eed*) (عود): teacher. Al-Mu'eed المعيد, "(God) the restorer or bringer again."[233]

> **Abdul Muid** (A) عبد المعيد (*'abd al-muid*): servant of the Restorer.

Muin (A) معين (*mu'een*) (عون): helper, patron, supporter. See Mujir مجير, protector.

> **Muin-ud-Din** (A) معين الدين: helper of the religion (Islam). Khwaja Muin-ud-Din Muhammad Chishti (1142-1236): see Chishti.

> **Muin-ul-Islam** (A) معين الإسلام: supporter of Islam.

---

[230] See Al-Arnaut, Shafiq, *Qamus al-Asma' al-Arabiyya* [Dictionary of Arabic Names] (in Arabic), p. 28, Keller, *Reliance of the Traveller* (Translation of *'Umdat al-Salik* in Arabic by Ahmad ibn Naqib al-misri), p. 1082.

[231] See Steingass, F., *A Comprehensive Persian-English Dictionary*, p. 1191.

[232] See Lewis, Bernard, *The Middle East*, p. 240; Glasse, Cyril, *The Concise Encyclopaedia of Islam*, p. 15. "Sometimes saints are referred to by nicknames that express their kindness towards their poor followers, such as *Pir-i-dastgir*, 'who takes by the hand' (that is, 'Abdul Qaadir Jilani)...he is *ghauth-i-a'zam* [the great saint] as well as Muhyiddin 'the reviver of the faith." See Schimmel, Annemarie, *Islamic Names*, p. 38.

[233] See Steingass, F., *A Comprehensive Persian-English Dictionary*, p. 1277.

Male Names

Muin-ud-Dawlah[234] (A) معين الدولة: defender of the state.

Muizz (A) مُعِز (Mu'izz) (عِز): one who honours, strengthens.

Muizz-ud-Din (A) معز الدين: one who strengthens the religion (Islam). Muiz ud-Din Jahandar Shah (d.1713): Mughal emperor.

Muizz-ud-Dawlah (A) معز الدولة: he who renders the state mighty. Muizz ud-Dawlah: Buwayhid *Ameer al-Umara* (936-49).

Mujahid (A) مجاهد (*mujaahid*) (جهد): one who struggles, strives, or fights for the cause of Islam, soldier of jihad. فضل الله المجاهدين باموالهم وانفسهم على القاعدين درجة "Allah has conferred on those who fight with their wealth and lives a higher rank than those who stay at home." (*surat al-Nisaa'* 4:95). Mujahid (d.722): well-known commentator on the Qur'an (*Tafsir Mujahid*).

Ala-ud-Din Mujahid (A) علاء الدين مجاهد: Bahmanid Sultan in Northern Deccan (India) (1375-78).

Mujammil (A) مجمّل (جمل): adorner, beautifier.

Mujib (A) مجيب (*mujeeb*) (جوب): replier, answerer. Al-Mujib المجيب, the Answerer: one of the names of Allah. ان ربي قريب مجيب "My Lord is near and answers prayer." (*surat Hud* 11:61). Sheikh Mujibur Rahman (d.1975): founder of Bangladesh.

Abdul Mujib (A) عبد المجيب (*'abd al-mujeeb*): servant of the

---

234 See Colebrooke, T. E., 'On the Proper Names of the Mohammadans', *Journal of the Royal Asiatic Society of Great Britain and Ireland*, XI, p. 209 (1879).

Male Names

Answerer.

Mujid (A) موجد (وجد): creator, originator, author.

Mujir (A) مجير (mujeer) (جور): protector, defender, helper, supporter.

Mujtaba (A) مجتبى (mujtabaa) (جبى): chosen, selected. An epithet of Muhammad (s). Hasan Mujtaba: son of Khalifa Ali and the second Imam of the Shi'ites. See Hasan.

Mujtahid (A) مجتهد (جهد): diligent, industrious, hardworking. A jurist in Shari'a who formulates an independent opinion based on the fundamental sources of law.

Mukafih (A) مكافح (mukaafih) (كفح): freedom fighter. See Mujahid مجاهد.

Mukammil (A) مكمّل (كمل): perfecting, completing.

Mukarram (A) مكرّم (كرم): honoured, revered, honourable. See Mukram مكرم, honoured. See Mukarrama (f.).

Al-Mukarram Ahmad (A) المكرّم احمد: ruler in Yemen (1067-84).

Mukhallad (A) مخلّد (خلد): immortal. ويطوف عليهم ولدان مخلدون اذا رايتهم حسبتهم لؤلؤا منثورا "There serve them youths of everlasting youth, whom, when you see them, you would think them scattered pearls." (surat al-Dahr 76:19).

Mukhles (A). See Mukhlis.

Male Names

Mukhlis (A) مخلص (خلص): sincere, honest, true, faithful. فادعوا الله مخلصين له الدين ولو كره الكافرون "Pray, then, to Allah, making religion pure for Him (only), however much the disbelievers dislike it." (*surat al-Mu'min* 40:14).

Mukhtar (A) مختار (*mukhtaar*) (خير): selected, chosen, preferred, favourite. See Mufazzal مفضل (*mufaddal*); Mustafa مصطفى. Umar al-Mukhtar (1858-1931): Libyan resistance leader.

> **Mukhtarul Haqq** (A) مختار الحق (*mukhtaar al-haqq*): chosen by the Truth (Allah). An epithet of Muhammad (s).

Mukit (A). See Muqit.

Mukram (A) مكرم (كرم): one who is honoured. بما غفر لي ربي وجعلني من المكرمين "That my Lord has forgiven me and that He has placed me among the honoured." (*surat Ya Sin* 36:27). See Mukarram مكرَّم, honoured. Comp. Makram مكرم, noble trait.

Muktafi (A) مكتفي (Muktafii) (كفى): satisfied, contended. Al-Muktafi المكتفي: Abbasid Khalifa (902-08).

Muktasid (A). See Muqtasid.

Mulham (A) ملهم (لهم): inspired.

Mulk (A) ملك: kingdom, sovereignty, supreme power or authority. Originally a title of honour, e.g. Muhsin al-Mulk, Waqar al-Mulk. قل اللهم مالك الملك تؤتي الملك من تشاء وتنزع الملك ممن تشاء "Say: O Allah! Owner of sovereignty! You give sovereignty to whom You please, and You strip sovereignty from whom You please." (*surat Aal 'Imraan* 3:26).

131

Male Names

Nizam-ul-Mulk (A). See Nizam.

Sayf-ul-Mulk (A) سيف الملك: sword of the kingdom.

Mulla (A). See Mullah.

Mullah (A) ملّا: "A Persian construction probably from the Arabic *mawla* ('master', 'leader', 'lord'), *mullah* is the title used to identify a religious functionary [...] a learned man, or someone with religious education."[235]

Mumin (A) مؤمن (*mu'min*) (امن): believer (in Islam), pious. Al-Mumin المؤمن, the All-faithful: one of the names of Allah. (*surat al-Hashr* 59:23). *Al-mu'min* المؤمن, 'the Believer': title of the 40th *sura* of the Qur'an. *Al-Mu'minun* المؤمنون, 'the Believers': title of the 23rd *sura* of the Qur'an. و الله ولي المؤمنين "And Allah is the protecting friend of the believers" (*surat Aal 'Imraan* 3:68)

> **Abdul Mu'min** (A) عبد المؤمن ('*abd al-mu'min*): servant of the All-faithful. Almohad ruler in North Africa and Spain (1130-63); ruler in Tunisia (1489-90).

Mumtaz (A) ممتاز (*mumtaaz*) (ميز): distinguished, superior, outstanding. See Mumtaz Mahal (f.).

Munadil (A) مناضل (*munaadil*) (نضل): freedom fighter, defender.

Munaim (A) مناعم (*munaa'im*) (نعم): "benevolent, kind."[236] Al-Munaa'im المناعم, the Benevolent: one of the names of Allah.

---

[235] See *The Oxford Encyclopaedia of the Modern Islamic World*, vol. III, p. 177.

[236] See Steingass, F., *A Comprehensive Persian-English Dictionary*, p. 1319.

Male Names

See Munim منعم, benefactor.

Munasir (A) مناصر (نصر): helper, protector, friend. See Naasir ناصر; Nasir نصير, helper.

Munawar (A). See Munawwar.

Munawwar (A) منوّر (نور): illuminated, brilliant.

Muni (A) منيع (*munee'*) (منع): strong, secure, well-fortified, unconquerable.

Munif (A) منيف (*muneef*) (نيف): eminent, exalted, superior, high, lofty.

Munim (A) منعم (*mun'im*) (نعم): benefactor, donor, grantor. Al-Mun'im المنعم, the Benefactor: one of the names of Allah. See Munaim مناعم, kind.

> **Abdul Munim** (A) عبد المنعم (*'abd al-mun'im*): servant of the Benefactor.

Munir (A) منير (*muneer*) (نور): bright, brilliant, radiant, luminous. In the following verse of the Qur'an, Muhammad (s) is described as *Siraj Munir*, i.e. a shining lamp: يايها النبي انا ارسلناك شاهدا ومبشرا ونذيرا وداعيا الى الله باذنه وسراجا منيرا "O Nabi (Prophet), We have sent you as a witness and a bringer of good news and a warner, and as a summoner to Allah by His permission and as a shining lamp." (*surat al-Ahzaab* 33:45-46). Al-Munir المنير, the Illuminator: an epithet of Muhammad (s).

> **Munir-uz-Zamaan** (A) منير الزمان: brilliant of the age.

133

Male Names

Munis (A) مؤنس (*mu'nis*) (انس): sociable, friendly, kind, gentle. See Anis أنيس; Latif لطيف. Mu'nis ibn Fadaalah: a *sahaabi*.[237]

Munjid (A) منجد (نجد): helper, supporter, rescuer.

Munna (A) مُنّة (*munnah*): strength, power.

Munqiz (A) منقذ (*munqidh*) (نقذ): saviour, rescuer, deliverer.

Munsif (A) منصف (نصف): just, fair, righteous.

Muntasir (A) منتصر (نصر): victorious, triumphant (see *surat al-Qamar* 54:44). Al-Muntasir المنتصر: Abbasid Khalifa (861-862). See Ghalib غالب; Mansur منصور.

Muntazar (A) منتظر (نظر): expected, prospective, anticipated. Muhammad al-Muntazar: the twelfth Imam of the Shi'ites.[238]

Munzir (A) منذر (*mundhir*) (نذر): warner, cautioner, forerunner, Messenger sent by Allah to warn mankind. قل انما انا منذر "Say (O Muhammad!): I am only a warner." (*surat Saad* 38:65). See Bashir بشير; Nazir نذير. Mundhir ibn 'Amr: a *sahaabi*.[239] Al-Mundhir: Spanish Umayyad Khalifa (886-88).

Muqarrab (A) مقرب (قرب): intimate companion, friend, one who is brought near the throne of Allah, one who is nearest to Allah. اولئك المقربون "These will be those nearest to Allah" (*surat al-Waaqi'ah* 56:11).

---

[237] See Haykal, Muhammad Husayn, *The Life of Muhammad*, p. 632.

[238] He "is called the 'awaited *Mahdî* (*al-Mahdi-l-muntazar*)". See Glasse, Cyril, *The Concise Encyclopaedia of Islam*, p. 367.

[239] See Haykal, Muhammad Husayn, *The Life of Muhammad*, p. 275.

Male Names

Muqit (A) مقيت (*muqeet*) (قوت): Al-Muqeet المقيت, the Nourisher: one of the names of Allah. وكان الله على كل شيء مقيتا "Allah nourishes everything." (*surat al-Nisaa' 4:85*).

Muqla (A) مقلة: eye, eyeball, the middle of anything. Ibn Muqlah (886-940): Abbasid vizier and "founder of Arabic calligraphy".[240]

Muqtadi (A) مقتدي (*Muqtadii*) (قدى): follower, one who follows an imam during ritual prayer. Abbasid Khalifa (1075-94).

Muqtadir (A) مقتدر (قدر): able, powerful, mighty. Al-Muqtadir المقتدر, the Omnipotent: one of the names of Allah. و كان الله على كل شيء مقتدرا "Allah is able to do all things." (*surat al-Kahf 18:45*). See Qaadir قادر; Qadir قدير. Abbasid Khalifa (908-32).

> **Abdul Muqtadir** (A) عبد المقتدر (*'abd al-muqtadir*): servant of the Omnipotent.

Muqtafi (A) مقتفي (*muqtafii*) (قفو): one who follows (another). Al-Muqtafi (1136-60): Abbasid Khalifa.

Muqtasid (A) مقتصد (قصد): frugal, thrifty, provident, moderate. امة مقتصدة "Moderate *ummah* (people)." (*surat al-Maa'idah 5:66*). See Mudabbir مدبر.

Murad (A) مراد (*muraad*) (رود): will, intended, aimed at. Son of Mughal emperor Akbar.[241] Murad I-IV: Ottoman Sultans. See Arzu آرزو (f.); Maqsud مقصود; Munya منية (f.).

---

[240] See Hitti, Philip K., *History of the Arabs*, p. 468.

[241] See Majumdar, R. C., et al., *An Advanced History of India*, p. 359.

Male Names

Murshid (A) مرشد (رشد): leader, guide, adviser, counsellor. من يهد الله فهو المهتد ومن يضلل فلن تجد له وليا مرشدا "He whom Allah guides, is rightly guided; but he whom Allah sends astray, for him you will not find a guiding friend." (*surat al-Kahf* 18:17). See Nasih ناصح, adviser.

Murtada (A). See Murtaza.

Murtaza (A) مرتضى (*murtadaa*) (رضي): chosen, approved. An epithet of Muhammad (s). Name of Imam Husayn, grandson of Muhammad (s). Sayyid al-Murtaza: a great-great-grandson of Shi'ite Imam Musa Kazim (d.1044). Murtada Zabidi: Indian scholar, a pupil of Shah Wali Allah.[242]

Musa (A) موسى (*moosaa*): a Prophet, the biblical Moses. واذكر في الكتاب موسى انه كان مخلصا وكان رسولا نبيا "And make mention in the Book of Musa. He was specially chosen, and he was a *Rasul* (Messenger) and a *Nabi* (Prophet)." (*surat Maryam* 19:51). An epithet of Musa is *Kalimullah*, 'Interlocutor with Allah' (see Kalim). Abu Musa al-Ash'ari: a *sahaabi* and a well-known commentator on the Qur'an.

Musad (A) مسعد (*mus'ad*): fortunate, lucky.

Musaddiq (A) مصدّق (صدق): one who confirms. An epithet of Muhammad (s). واذ اخذ الله ميثاق النبيين لما آتيتكم من كتاب وحكمة ثم جاءكم رسول مصدق لما معكم لتؤمنن به ولتنصرنه "When Allah made (His) covenant with the Prophets, (He said): Behold that I have given you a Book and wisdom. Afterward a Messenger will come

---

[242] He went to live in Yemen and later in Cairo. "His ten volume commentary on the *Qamus* was the main foundation of Lane's Arabic Lexicon." See Ikram, S. M., *History of Muslim Civilization in India and Pakistan*, p. 666.

to you, confirming what you possess. You shall believe in him and you shall help him." (surat Aal 'Imraan 3:81). Muhammad Musaddiq (1881-1967): prime minister of Iran who wanted to nationalise its oil industry.[243]

Musaid (A) مساعد (musaa'id) (سعد): helper, assistant, supporter.

Musawwir (A) مصوّر: shaper, fashioner. Al-Musawwir المصور, the Shaper: one of the names of Allah. هو الله الخالق البارئ المصور له الاسماء الحسنى "He is Allah, the Creator, the Maker, the Fashioner. To Him belong the most beautiful names." (surat al-Hashr 59:24).

> **Abdul Musawwir** (A) عبد المصور ('abd al-musawwir): servant of the Fashioner.

Musharraf (A) مشرّف (شرف): honoured, exalted. Mir Musharraf Husayn (1848-1911): Bengali "novelist, playwright, essayist and poet."[244]

Musharrif (A) مشرّف (شرف): one who exalts.

> **Musharrif-ud-Dawlah** (A) مشرّف الدولة: one who exalts the kingdom. Musharrif-ud-Dawlah Hasan (1021-25): Buwayhid Sultan in Iraq.

Mushfiq (A) مشفق (شفق): kind, tender, fearful. ولا يشفعون الا لمن ارتضى وهم من خشيته مشفقون "They intercede for none except those whom He accepts, and they tremble in awe of Him." (surat al-Anbiyaa' 21:28). See Shafiq شفيق.

---

[243] See Fernandez-Armesto, Felipe, *Millennium*, pp. 555, 556.

[244] See Aziz, Ahmad, *An Intellectual History of Islam*, p. 115.

Male Names

Mushir (A) مشير (*musheer*) (شور): counsellor, adviser. See Murshid مرشد; Nasih ناصح.

Mushir-ul-Haqq (A) مشير الحق (*musheer al-Haqq*): counsellor of the Truth (Allah).

Mushtaq (A) مشتاق (*mushtaaq*) (شوق): longing, desiring, eager.

Musir (A) موسر (*moosir*) (يسر): prosperous, affluent, rich.

Musleh (A). See Muslih.

Muslih (A) مصلح (صلح): peacemaker, conciliator, reformer, one who sets things right. والله يعلم المفسد من المصلح "Allah knows well him who works corruption from him who sets aright." (*surat al-Baqarah* 2:220).

Muslih-ud-Din (A) مصلح الدين: reformer of the religion (Islam). Muslih ud-Din Sa'di: see Sa'di.

Muslim (A) مسلم (سلم): (male) follower of the religion of Islam. فان تولوا فقولوا اشهدوا بانا مسلمون "If then they turn back, then say: 'Bear witness that we are Muslims (bowing to Allah's will)." (*surat Aal 'Imraan* 3:64). Abul Husayn Muslim (816-875): author of *Sahih al-Muslim*.

Mustafa (A) مصطفى (*mustafaa*) (صفو): chosen, selected, preferred. An epithet of Muhammad (s). In *surat Saad* Allah says: وانهم عندنا لمن المصطفين الاخيار "In Our sight they [Ibrahim, Ishaaq, Ya'qub] are truly of the elect, the excellent." (*surat Saad* 38:47). Al-Mustafa المصطفى, the chosen: an epithet of Muhammad (s). See Mukhtar مختار; Mufazzal (*mufaddal*) مفضل. Mustafa Kamil: see Kamil.

Male Names

Mustafa Kamal (A) كمال مصطفى (1881-1938): founder of modern Turkey.

Mustafavi (A+P) مصطفوي: *nisba* (relation) through ancestry to the family of Mustafa, i.e. Muhammad (s).

Mustahfiz (A) مستحفظ (حفظ): guardian, protector, custodian.

Mustahfiz-ur-Rahman (A) مستحفظ الرحمن (*mustahfiz al-Rahmaan*). See Rahman.

Mustain (A) مستعين (*musta'een*) (عون): one who asks the help or aid or assistance. Al-Mustain المستعين: Abbasid Khalifa (862-66).

Mustakfi (A) مستكفي (كفى): one who desires another to do something effectually. Al-Mustakfi: Abbasid Khalifa (944-46).

Mustali (A) المستعلي (*musta'alii*) (على): high, elevated, superior. Ruler in Spain (1055-57).

Mustamsik (A) مستمسك (مسك): composed, calm of mind, one who restrains himself. Al-Mustamsik: Khalifa (of the Abbasid house)[245] in Cairo (1497-1508, 1516-17).

Mustanjid (A) مستنجد (نجد): one who implores for help. Al-Mustanjid: Abbasid Khalifa (1160-70).

Mustansir (A) مستنصر (نصر): one who asks aid or help. Al-Mustansir: Abbasid Khalifa (1226-42).

---

[245] See Bosworth, C. E., *The Islamic Dynasties*, p. 8; Hitti; Philip K., *History of the Arabs*, p. 677.

Male Names

Mustapha (A). See Mustafa.

Mustaqim (A) مستقيم (*mustaqeem*) (قوم): straight. اهدنا الصراط المستقيم "Show us the straight path." (*surat al-Faatihah* 1:6).

Mustarshid (A) مسترشد (رشد): one who seeks direction (*rushd* رشد). Al-Mustarshid: Abbasid Khalifa (1118-35).

Mustasim (A) مستعصم (*musta'sim*) (عصم): He who holds fast.

Mustasim Billah مستعصم باالله: Abbasid Khalifa (1242-58).

Mustazhir (A) مستظهر (ظهر): memoriser, one who knows by heart. Al-Mustazhir: Abbasid Khalifa (1094-1118).

Mustazi (A) مستضيء (*mustadi'*) (ضوء): one who seeks light or advice. Al-Mustazi: Abbasid Khalifa (1170-80).

Muta'ali (A) متعالي (*muta'aalii*) (علی): exalted, supreme. Al-Muta'aalii المتعالي, the most High: one of the names of Allah.

Abdul Muta'ali (A) عبد المتعالي (*'abd al-muta'ali*): servant of the most High.

Mutad (A) مُعتد (*mu'tadd*) (عد): prepared, ready.[246] Hisham III al-Mutad: Spanish Umayyad Khalifa (1027-31).

Mutahar (A). See Mutahhar.

Mutahhar (A) مطهَّر (طهر): clean, pure, purified, very beautiful, of

---

[246] See Steingass, F., *A Comprehensive Persian-English Dictionary*, p. 1268.

perfect beauty. انه لقرآن كريم في كتاب مكنون لا يمسه الا المطهرون "This is indeed a noble Qur'an, in a Book well-guarded which nobody touches except the purified." (*surat al-Waaqi'ah* 56:77-79). Ibn Mutahhar al-Hilli: see Allama.

Mutahhari (A) مطهّري: of or relating to Mutahhar. Murtaza Mutahhari (1920-79): Iranian scholar in the field of Islam and philosopher.

Mutamad (A) معتمد (*mu'tamad*) (عمد): trustworthy, reliable, dependable.

Mutamid (A) معتمد (*mu'tamid*) (عمد): one who relies (upon Allah). Al-Mutamid المعتمد: Abbasid Khalifa (870-892).

Mutamin (A) مؤتمن (*mu'tamin*) (امن): one who entrusts his affairs to the management of another. Ruler in Spain (1081-85).

Mutammim (A) متمّم (تم): perfecting, completing.

Mutaqid (A) معتقد (*mu'taqid*) (عقد): confident, believer, faithful friend.

Mutasim (A) معتصم (*mu'tasim*) (عصم): abstaining from sin (by the grace of Allah), preserved, defended.

> **Al-Mutasim Billah** (A) المعتصم بالله: Abbasid Khalifa (833-42).

Mutawakkil (A) متوكّل (وكل): one who puts his trust (in Allah). ان الله يحب المتوكلين "Allah loves those who put their trust (in Him)." (*surat Aal 'Imraan* 3:159).

Male Names

Al-Mutawakkil 'ala Allah الممتوكِّل على الله: Abbasid Khalifa (847-861).

Mutawassit (A) مـتـوسِّـط (وسط): mediator, intercessor, umpire. Abd al-Rahman al-Mutawassit (822-52): Umayyad Khalifa.

Mutazid (A) معتضد (*mu'tadid*) (عضد): one who seeks assistance (from Allah), a petitioner for justice.

Mu'tazid Billah معتضد بالله: Abbasid Khalifa (892-902).

Mutazz (A) معتزّ (*mu'tazz*) (غز): mighty, powerful. Al-Mutazz المعتز: Abbasid Khalifa (866-69).

Mu'ti (A) المعطي (*al-mu'tii*) (عطو): giver, granter, donor. Al-Mu'ti المعطي, the Granter: one of the names of Allah. Comp. Muti' مطيع, obedient.

Abdul Mu'ti (A) عبد المعطي (*'abd al-mu'tii*): servant of the Donor.

Muti' (A) مطيع (*mutee'*) (طوع): obedient, pious, devoted, faithful. A *sahaabi*. Al-Muti': Abbasid Khalifa (946-74). Comp. Mu'ti المعطي, granter. See Taai طائع, obedient.

Muti'-ul-Islam (A) مطيع الإسلام: obedient (follower) of Islam.

Muti'-ur-Rahman (A) مطيع الرحمن (*mutee'al-rahmaan*): obedient (servant) of the most Gracious.

Mutlaq (A) مطلق (طلق): free, unlimited, unrestricted.

142

Male Names

Muttalib (A) مطّلب (طلب): seeker. Abdul Muttalib: grandfather of Muhammad (s).[247]

Muttaqi (A) المتقي (al-muttaqii) (وقى): God-fearing, pious, religious, devout. ربنا هب لنا من ازواجنا وذرياتنا قرة اعين واجعلنا للمتقين اماما "Our Lord! Grant to us wives and offspring who will be the comfort of our eyes, and make us models for devout people." (surat al-Furqaan 25:74). Abbasid Khalifa (940-44). See Taqi تقي.

Muwaffaq (A) موفّق (وفق): successful, prosperous, lucky, fortunate. Ruler in Spain (1054). See Naajih ناجح, successful.

Muzaffar (A) مظفّر (ظفر): victorious, triumphant, victor, conqueror. See Zafir ظافر.

Abul Muzaffar Shihab-ud-Din (A) أبو المظفّر شهاب الدين: Mughal emperor Shah Jahaan (1628-57).

Muzaffar-ud-Din (A) مظفّر الدين: victorious of the religion (Islam). Shah of Iran (1896-1907).

Muzahir (A) مظاهر (muzaahir) (ظهر): protector, defender, supporter.

Muzahir-ud-Din (A) مظاهر الدين: defender of the religion (Islam).

Muzakkir (A) مذكّر (mudhakkir) (ذكر): reminder, warner. An epithet of Muhammad (s). فذكر انما انت مذكر "Remind them! You are only a reminder." (surat al-Ghaashiyah 88:21).

---

[247] See Haykal, Muhammad Husayn, The Life of Muhammad, p. 45. It should be noted that Mutallib is not one of the attributes of Allah.

143

Male Names

Muzzammil (A) مُزَّمِّل (زمل): one wrapped in garments. *Al-Muzzammil* المزمل: title of the 73rd *sura* of the Qur'an. In this *sura*, Allah addresses Muhammad (s): يايها المزمل "O You wrapped in garments." (*surat al-Muzzammil* 73:1).

N

Naabih (A) نابه (نبه): noble, famous, eminent, distinguished, brilliant. See Nabih نبيه, noble.

Naafi (A). See Nafi.

Naaif (A) نائف (naa'if): exalted, lofty, eminent, superior.

Naail (A) نائل (naa'il) (نيل): winner, gift. See Fazl (fadl) فضل.

Naaji (A) ناجي (نجو): saved, liberated. Comp. Naji ‾نجي, intimate friend.

> **Naaji Allah** (A) ناجي الله: saved by Allah. An epithet of Prophet Nuh.[248]

Naajih (A) ناجح (نجح): successful, prosperous. See Muwaffaq موفق. Comp. Najih نجيح, right.

Naashit (A) ناشط (nasheet) (نشط): energetic, dynamic, lively, fresh, vigorous. See Nashit نشيط, energetic.

Naasi (A) ناصع (naasi'): clear, pure.

Naasir (A) ناصر (نصر): helper, protector, friend. Al-Naasir الناصر, the Helper: one of the names of Allah. فما له من قوة ولا ناصر "(On the day of judgment) he will have no strength, nor helper." (surat al-Taariq

---

[248] See Steingass, F., *A Comprehensive Persian-English Dictionary*, p. 1367.

Male Names

86:10). See Nasir نصير; Munasir مناصر, helper.

Abdun Naasir (A) عبد الناصر (*'abd al-naasir*): servant of the Helper. Jamaal Abd al-Naasir (Gamal Abdul Nasser) جمال عبد الناصر (1918-70): president of Egypt.

Naasir-ud-Din ناصر الدين: defender of the faith (Islam). Nasir ud-Din Mahmud Shah: Delhi Sultan (1246-66).[249]

Naazim (A). See Nazim.

Naazir (A) ناضر (*naadir*) (نضر): bright, radiant, blooming. Comp. Nazeer نذير (*nadheer*), warner; Nazir نظير (*nazeer*), equal.

Nabab (P). See Nawab.

Nabi (A) نبي (*nabiyy*) (نبو): Prophet sent by Allah for the guidance of mankind. ان الله وملائكته يصلون على النبي يايها الذين آمنوا صلوا عليه وسلموا تسليما "Allah and His angels bless the *Nabi* [Muhammad]. O you who believe! Ask blessings on him and salute him with a worthy salutation." (*surat al-Ahzaab* 33:56).

Nabi Allah (A) نبي الله: an epithet of Prophet Nuh.

Nabi Bakhsh (A+P) نبي بخش: gift of the Prophet.

Nabih (A) نبيه (*nabeeh*) (نبه): noble, famous, eminent, distinguished, brilliant. See Fatin فطن; Naabih نابه.

---

[249] "[T]hough a Sultan he led the life of a saint. [...] It is related that he earned his livelihood by sewing caps and copying the Holy Qur'an. His wife cooked meals with her own hands." See Hasan, Masudul, *History of Islam*, vol. I, pp. 391-2.

Male Names

Nabil (A) نبيل (*nabeel*) (نبل): noble, highborn, honourable.

Nadim (A) نديم (*nadeem*) (ندم): intimate friend, companion. See Rafiq رفيق.

Nadir (A) نادر (*naadir*) (ندر): extraordinary, rare, exceptional.

    Nadir Shah (A) نادر شاه: Afghan king (1929-33).

Naeb (A). See Naib.

Nafi (A) نافع (*naafi'*) (نفع): beneficial, advantageous, profitable. A reporter of Hadith.[250]

Nafis (A) نفيس (*nafees*) (نفس): precious, invaluable, costly.

Naib (A) نائب (*naa'ib*) (نوب): deputy; sing. of Nuwwaab نواب.

Naim (A) نعيم (*na'eem*) (نعم): happiness, felicity, peaceful, bliss. واجعلني من ورثة جنة النعيم "[My Lord!] Make me one of the inheritors of the *Jannah* [Paradise] of bliss." (*surat al-Shu'araa'* 26:85).

    Ayn-un-Naim (A) عين النعيم: fountain of blessings. An epithet of Muhammad (s).

    Naimullah (A) نعيم الله (*naim allah*): grace of Allah, bliss of Allah.

Najah (A) نجاح (*najaah*) (نجح): prosperity, success.

---

[250] See Imam Malik, *Muwatta*, p. 36.

Male Names

Najat (A) نجاة (*najaah*) (نجو): rescue, salvation, deliverance. ويا قوم ما لي ادعوكم الى النجاة وتدعونني الى النار "And, O my people, how is it that I call you to deliverance while you call me to the fire?" (*surat al-Mu'min* 40:41).

Naji (A) نجِي (*najiyy*) (نجو): intimate friend, bosom friend.[251] Comp. Naaji ناجي, saved.

Najiullah (A) نجي الله (*naji allah*): intimate friend of Allah. An epithet of Muhammad (s).

Najib (A) نجيب (*najeeb*) (نجب): noble, distinguished, aristocratic, of noble descent.

Najibullah (A) نجيب الله (*najib allah*): distinguished (servant) of Allah.

Najib-ud-Din (A) نجيب الدين: distinguished (person) of the religion (Islam).

Najih (A) نجيح (*najeeh*) (نجح): sound, right. Abu Najih: a *sahaabi*.[252] Comp. Naajih ناجح, successful.

Najm (A) نجم: star. *Al-Najm* النجم: title of the 53th *sura* of the Qur'an. وبالنجم هم يهتدون "By the stars, they get directions." (*surat al-Nahl*: 16:16). See Kawkab كوكب (f.); Najma نجمة (f.).

Najm-ud-Dawlah (A) نجم الدولة: star of the state. King of Iran

---

[251] See Madina, Maan Z., *Arabic-English Dictionary of the Modern Literary Language*, p. 654; Cowan, J Milton (ed.) Hans Wehr, *A Dictionary of Modern Written Arabic*, p. 946.

[252] See An-Nawawi, *Forty Hadith*, p. 34.

148

Male Names

(1110-17).

Najm-ud-Din (A) نجم الدين: star of the religion (Islam).

Najwan (A) نجوان (*najwaan*) (نجو): saved, liberated. See Naaji ناجي, saved.

Nameer (A) نمير: pure, clear, healthy, good.

Namir (A) نمر leopard, tiger, panther. Comp. Nameer نمير, pure.

Naqi (A) نقي (*naqiyy*): pure, clean. Ali ibn Muhammad Naqi (827-868): the tenth Imam of the Shi'ites.[253]

Naqib (A) نقيب (*naqeeb*) (نقب): president, head, chief. وبعثنا منهم اثنى عشر نقيبا "We raised among them twelve chieftains." (*surat al-Maa'idah* 5:12). See Ra'is رئيس.

Naseh (A). See Nasih.

Naser (A). See Naasir.

Nashit (A) نشيط (*nasheet*) (نشط): energetic, dynamic, lively, fresh, vigorous. See Naashit ناشط, energetic.

Nashwan[254] (A) نشوان (*nashwaan*) (نشو): elated, exalted, exuberant.

Nasi (A). See Naasi.

---

[253] See Al-Tabatabai, Allamah Sayyid Muhammad Husayn, *Shi'ite Islam*, p. 208.

[254] See Al-Arnaut, Shafiq, *Qamus al-Asma' al-Arabiyya* [Dictionary of Arabic Names] (in Arabic), p. 92; Ahmed, Leila, *Women and Gender in Islam*, p. 114.

149

Male Names

Nasib (A) نسيب (*naseeb*) (نسب): noble, highborn.

Nasif (A) ناصف (*naasif*): just, fair. Malak Hifni Nasif: see Malak.

Nasih (A) ناصح (*naasih*) (نصح): adviser, counsellor. ابلغكم رسالات ربي وانا لكم ناصح امين "I [Hud] convey to you the messages of my Lord and I am a true adviser for you." (*surat al-A'raaf* 7:68). See Murshid مرشد.

> **Nasih-ud-Din** (A) ناصح الدين: counsellor of the religion (Islam).

Nasim (A) نسيم (*naseem*) (grammatically fem.) breeze, gentle wind, fresh air, fragrant air.

> **Nasim-ul-Haqq** (A) نسيم الحق (*naseem al-haqq*): breeze of the Truth (Allah).

Nasir (A) نصير (*naseer*) (نصر): helper, protector, patron. وما لكم من دون الله من ولي ولا نصير "Besides Allah you have no protector nor helper." (*surat al-Tawba* 9:116). See Naasir ناصر; Munasir مناصر, helper.

> **Nasir-ud-Din** (A) نصير الدين: defender of the religion (Islam).

Nasr (A) نصر: victory, triumph. *Al-Nasr* النصر: title of the 110th *sura* of the Qur'an. وما النصر الا من عند الله "Victory comes only by the help of Allah." (*surat al-Anfaal* 8:10). See Zafar ظفر.

Nasrullah (A) نصر الله (*nasr allah*): help of Allah. اذا جاء نصر الله والفتح "When Allah's help and the victory comes." (*surat al-*

Male Names

Nasr 110:1).

Nasr-ud-Din (A) نصر الدين: victory of the religion (Islam).

Nasri[255](A) نصري (*nasriyy*): winner of victory after victory.

Natiq (A) ناطق (*naatiq*) (نطق): endowed with speech, eloquent, rational (being).

Naveed (P) نوید: happy tidings, good news.

Nawab[256] (P) نواب (*nawaab*) (نوب): ruler, administrator. A title assumed by the independent rulers in the Indian sub-continent (see e.g. Siraj ud-Dawla). An honorific title awarded by the British rulers in India (see e.g. Abdul Latif). Nawabzada: son of a Nawab, e.g. Nawabzada Liaqat Ali Khan (see Liaqat).

Nawaz (P) نواز (*nawaaz*): one who caresses, soothes.

Ali Nawaaz (A+P) علي نواز: cherished by Ali.

Shah Nawaaz (P) شاه نواز: friend of king.

Naweed (P). See Naveed.

Nayif (A) نيف (*nayyif*): excess, surplus. See Fayz فيض (*fayd*); Ziyada زيادة.

---

[255] See Abd-el-Jawad, Hassan, 'A Linguistic and Socio-cultural Study of Personal Names in Jordan', *Anthropological Linguistics*, XXVIII, p. 84 (1986).

[256] *Nuwwaab* (A) نواب: pl. of Naa'ib نائب.

Male Names

Nazeer (A) نذير (*nadheer*) (نذر): warner, Prophet sent by Allah to warn mankind. An attribute of Muhammad (s). ان انا الا نذير وبشير لقوم يؤمنون "(Say (O Muhammad!)): I am but a warner, and a bearer of good news for people who believe (in Islam)." (*surat al-A'raaf* 7:188). See Munzir منذر (*mundhir*). Comp. Naazir ناضر (*naadir*), bright; Nazir نظير (*nazeer*), equal.

Nazif (A) نظيف (*nazeef*): pure, clean, innocent.

Nazih (A) نزيه (*nazeeh*) (نزه): pure, virtuous, just, honest. See Adil عادل; Afif عفيف; Sharif شريف.

Nazim (A) ناظم (*naazim*) (نظم): organiser, governor.

Nazim-ud-Din (A) ناظم الدين: organiser of the religion (Islam). Khwaja Nazimuddin: governor-general (1948-51) and prime minister of Pakistan (1951-53).

Nazir (A) نظير (*nazeer*) (نظر): equal, peer, comparable. Comp. Naazir ناضر (*naadir*), bright; Nazeer نذير (*nadheer*), warner.

Nazmi (A) نظمي (*nazmii*): arranger, organiser.

Nazr (A) نذر (*nadhr*): "a vow, promise made to God; a gift.[...]"[257] Nazrul Islam (1899-1976): "One of the most distinguished poets of modern Muslim Bengal...a fiery genius of remarkable vitality and dynamism."[258]

Neku-siyar (P) نيك سير: well-disposed, of good manners and habits.

---

[257] See Steingass, F., *A Comprehensive Persian-English Dictionary*, p. 1394.

[258] See Ahmad, Aziz, *An Intellectual History of Islam*, p. 116.

Mughal emperor (1719).

Niaz (P). See Niyaz.

Nidal[259] (A) نضال (*nidaal*): striving, contest, competition, battle.

Nima (A) نعمة (*ni'mah*) (نعم): blessing, boon, favour, grace, bounty; sing of Ni'mat نعمات. اليوم اكملت لكم دينكم واتممت عليكم نعمتي "This day I perfected your religion and completed my favour to you." (*surat al-Maa'idah* 5:3).

> **Nimatullah** (A) نعمة الله (*ni'mat allah*): blessing of Allah (see *surat al-Baqarah* 2:231). Shah Wali Ni'mat Allah (d.1431): founder of the Ni'matullahi Sufi Order.[260]

Nimat (A) نعمات (*ni'maat*) (نعم): blessings, boons, favours, graces, bounties; pl. of Ni'mah نعمة, blessing. See Ni'mat (f.).

Nimr (A) نمر: leopard, tiger.

Nishtar (P) نشتر: kind of knife.

Niyaz (P) نياز (*niyaaz*): gift.

Niyaazi (P) نيازي: friend, lover.

[259] See Abd-el-Jawad, Hassan, 'A Linguistic and Socio-cultural Study of Personal Names in Jordan', *Anthropological Linguistics*, XXVIII, p. 93 (1986). This name "appeared in Egypt during the Arab-Israeli war." See Schimmel, Annemarie, *Islamic Names*, p. 17.

[260] See Glasse, Cyril, *The Concise Encyclopaedia of Islam*, p. 302.

Male Names

Nizam (A) نظام (*nizaam*) (نظم): order, arrangement, discipline, ruler. Title of the ruler of Hyderabad in pre-independence India.

Nizam-ud-Din (A) نظام الدين: discipline of the religion (Islam). Nizam-ud-Din Awliya (d.1323): Indian saint.[261]

Nizam-ul-Mulk[262] (A) نظام الملك: the organisation of the kingdom. Persian vizier (d.1092) during the Seljuq Sultanate.[263]

Nizami (A) نظامى (*nizaami*): of or relating to Nizam. "Name of a famous poet."[264]

Noman (A). See Numan.

Nomani (A). See Numani.

Noor (A). See Nur.

Nuaym (A) نعيم (*nu'aym*): diminutive of ناعم, gentle, delicate. Abu Nu'aym: a *sahaabi*.

---

[261] "He seems to have exercised a powerful pietistic influence over the Muslim society of his age, which held him in great esteem." See Aziz, Ahmad, *An Intellectual History of Islam*, p. 37.

[262] See Glasse, Cyril, *The Concise Encyclopaedia of Islam*, p. 302.

[263] "The guiding hand throughout the administration of Alp Arslan and Malikshah was that of their illustrious Persian vizier, Nizam-al-Mulk...one of the ornaments of the political history of Islam...the basis of this Persian vizier's glory is his establishment of the first well-organised academics for higher learning in Islam." See Hitti, Philip K., *History of the Arabs*, pp. 477-8.

[264] See Steingass, F., *A Comprehensive Persian-English Dictionary*, p. 1410.

Male Names

Nubugh (A) نبوغ (*nuboogh*): distinction, eminence, excellence, superiority, genius.[265]

Numan (A) نعمان (*nu'maan*) "Blood; name of the kings of Hirah in Arabia, especially of the last, Nu'man bin Munzir; also surname of the celebrated lawyer Abu Hanifa."[266]   Abu Abdullah an-Nu'man bin Bashir: a *sahaabi*.[267]

Numani (A) نعماني (*nu'maaniyy*): Mawlana Shibli Numani (1857-1914): Indian scholar in the field of Islam, and author of *Sirat an-Nabi* (life of the Prophet).[268]   He "took the *nisba* Nu'mani out of respect for Imam Abu Hanifa Nu'man."[269] See Shibli.

Nur (A) نور (*noor*): light, illumination. Al-Noor النور, the Light: one of the names of Allah; also the title of the 24th *sura* of the Qur'an. الله نور السماوات والارض "Allah is the light of the heavens and the earth." (*surat al-Nur* 24:35). قد جاءكم من الله نور وكتاب مبين "A light and a clear Book has now come to you from Allah." (*surat al-Maa'idah* 5:15).

---

[265] See Haim, S., *The Shorter Persian-English Dictionary*, p. 746.

[266] See Steingass, F., *A Comprehensive Persian-English Dictionary*, p. 1412. Also see Haykal, Muhammad Husayn, *The Life of Muhammad*, p. 56; Schimmel, Annemarie, *Islamic Names*, p. 11; Colebrooke, T. E., 'On the Proper Names of the Mohammadans', *Journal of the Royal Asiatic Society of Great Britain and Ireland*, XIII, p. 246 (1881).

[267] An-Nawawi, *Forty Hadith*, p. 42.

[268] "[H]is monumental work is *Shi'r al-'Ajam*, a history of Persian poetry in five volumes, which...was among the sources of E. G. Browne's *Literary History of Persia*." See Aziz, Ahmad, *An Intellectual History of Islam*, p. 108. Also see Hardy, P., *The Muslims of British India*, p. 176.

[269] See Schimmel, Annemarie, *Islamic Names*, p. 11.

Male Names

Abdun Nur (A) عبد النور (*'abd al-nur*): servant of the Light.

Ali Nur (A) علي نور: Ali of light. Ali was the fourth of the 'rightly guided' Khalifas and the first Imam of the Shi'ites.

Nurullah (A) نور الله (*nur allah*): light of Allah (see *surat al-Tawba* 9:32).

Nur Muhammad (A) نور محمد: light of Muhammad (s).

Nur-ud-Din[270] (A) نور الدين: light of the faith (Islam). Nur-ud-Din ibn Zangi: famous general during the Crusades.[271] Nur ud-Din Randeri: Indonesian scholar and author of *Sirat al-Mustakim* and *Bustan al-Salatin* (*The Garden of Kings*).[272]

Nur-ul-Haqq (A) نور الحق (*nur al-haqq*): light of the Truth (Allah).

Nur-ul-Huda (A) نور الهدى: light of the right guidance (of

---

[270] It is a "*[l]aqab*, or sobriquet, e.g.[...] Nur el-Din..." See Sheniti, Mahmud, 'Treatment of Arabic names', *International Conference on Cataloguing Principles Report*, 1961, p. 268; Ashoor, M. S., 'The Formation of Muslim Names' in 9 *Int. Libr. Rev.*, IX, p. 493 (1977).

[271] "In the 12th century the great Muslim leader Nureddin rebuilt the wall [citadel of Aleppo] and the mosques...and constructed his 'Golden Palace'"; "he defeated Raymond of Poitiers, prince of Antioch.[...] This was the finest victory against the West and greatly boosted Nureddin's standing in the Muslim world." See Tate, Georges, *The Crusades and the Holy Land*, pp. 20, 84.

[272] He "is one of the most distinguished thinkers who wrote in Malaya." See Wintedt, R., *Cultural life of Malaya*, pp. 148-9.

Allah).

Nur-un-Nabi (A) نور النبي: light of the Nabi.

Nur-uz-Zaman (A) نور الزمان: light of the era.

Nuri (A) نوري (*nooriyy*): light, luminous. Nuri al-Sa'id.[273]

Nusrat (A) نصر (نصرة): help, aid, assistance, support.

    Nusrat Shah (A+P) نصرة شاه: ruler of Bengal (d.1533).[274]

    Nusrat-ud-Din (A+P) نصرة الدين: help of the religion (Islam).

See Lewis, Bernard, *The Middle East*, p. 350.

[274] He "was a patron of art, architecture and literature. He caused two famous mosques, the *Bara Sona Masjid* (Large Golden Mosque) and *Qadam Rasul* (Foot of the Prophet), to be constructed at Gaur; and a Bengali version of the *Mahabharata* was made under his orders." See Majumdar, R. C., *et al.*, *An Advanced History of India*, p. 341.

Male Names

O

Obaidullah (A). See Ubaidullah.

Osman (A). See Usman (*uthmaan*).

Omar (A). See Umar.

P

Pasha (P) پاشا (*paashaa*): lord, honorific title.

Parvez (P) پرویز (*parwez*): victorious, fortunate, happy. Son of Mughal emperor Jahangir.[275]

Khusrau Parvez (P) خسرو پرویز: Sasanid ruler (d.628).

Pir (P) پیر: saint, spiritual guide, wise.

Pir Ahmad (P+A) پیر احمد: king of Central Anatolia (1464-74).

---

[275] See Majumdar, R. C., *An Advanced History of India*, p. 604.

Male Names

Q

Qaadir (A) قادر (قدر): able, capable, powerful. Al-Qaadir القادر, the Powerful: one of the names of Allah. قل ان الله قادر على ان ينزل آية ولكن اكثرهم لا يعلمون "Say: Allah is able to send down a Sign. But most of them understand not." (*surat al-An'aam* 6:37). See Qadeer قدير; Muqtadir مقتدر. Al-Qaadir bi-llah: Abbasid Khalifa (991-1031).[276]

> **Abdul Qaadir** (A) عبد القادر ('*abd al-qaadir*): servant of the Powerful. Abdul Qaadir al-Jilani (1077-1166): one of the most celebrated saints in Islam. See Muhyi: Muhyi-id-Din.

Qabil (A) قايبل (*qaabeel*): son of Adam.

Qabis (A) قابس (*qaabis*): literate, educated.

Qadir (A) قدير (*qadeer*) (قدر): able, powerful, mighty. Al-Qadeer القدير, the Omnipotent: one of the names of Allah. انك على كل شيء قدير "Verily, over all things You have power." (*sura Aal 'Imraan* 3:26). See Qaadir قادر; Muqtadir مقتدر.

> **Abdul Qadir** (A) عبد القدير ('*abd al-qadeer*): servant of the Powerful.

Qadi (A). See Qazi.

Qahir (A) قاهر (*qaahir*) (قهر): conqueror, subduer. Al-Qaahir القاهر, the Subduer: one of the names of Allah. وهو القاهر فوق عباده "He is the Omnipotent over His servants." (*surat al-An'aam*

---

[276] See Watt, W. Montgomery, *The Majesty that was Islam*, p. 198.

Male Names

6:18). Abbasid Khalifa (932-34).

Abdul Qahir القاهر عبد (*'abd al-qaahir*): servant of the Subduer. Abd al-Qahir al-Baghdadi (d.1037): Shafi scholar.[277]

Qaid (A) قائد (*qaa'id*) (قود): leader, commander. Qaid-i-Azam قائد اعظم, great leader: title of Muhammad Ali Jinnah (1876-1948), founder of Pakistan.

Qaim (A) قائم (*qaa'im*) (قوم): upright, independent, one who performs (a duty) (see *surat Aal 'Imraan* 3:39). Al-Qaim: Abbasid Khalifa (1031-75).

Qais (A) قيس: measure, measurement, example, exemplar.

Qaisar (A) قيصر: Caesar, emperor.

Qamar (A) قمر: moon. *Al-Qamar* القمر: title of the 54th *sura* of the Qur'an. ومن آياته الليل والنهار والشمس والقمر "Among His signs are the night and the day and the sun and the moon." (*surat Haa Mim al-Sajdah* 41:37).

Qamar-ud-Din (A) قمر الدين: moon of religion (Islam).

Qasid (A) قاصد (*qaasid*) (قصد): messenger, courier.

Qasid-ul-Haqq (A) قاصد الحق: (*qaasid al-haqq*): courier of the Truth (Allah).

---

[277] See Keller, *Reliance of the Traveller* (Translation of *'Umdat al-Salik* in Arabic by Ahmad ibn Naqib al-misri), p. 1021.

Male Names

Qasim (A) قاسم (*qaasim*) (قسم): distributor, divider. Al-Qaasim القاسم: son of Muhammad (s). Qasim Amin (1865-1908): Egyptian writer and author of *tahrir al-mar'a* (Emancipation of Women).

> **Abul Qaasim** (A) ابو القاسم: father of Qasim, a *kunya* of Muhammad (s). Abul Qaasim Mansur Firdausi: see Firdausi.

Qayyum (A) قيوم (قوم): eternal, everlasting. Al-Qayyum القيوم, the Eternal: one of the names of Allah. الله لا اله الا هو الحي القيوم "Allah! There is no God except Him, the Living, the Eternal." (*surat al-Baqarah* 2:255).

> **Abdul Qayyum** (A) عبد القيوم (*'abd al-qayyum*): servant of the Eternal.

Qazi (A) القاضي (*al-qaadii*) (قضى): judge, justice. ان ربك يقضي بينهم يوم القيامة فيما كانوا فيه يختلفون "Your Lord will judge between them on the Day of Resurrection concerning that wherein they used to differ." (*surat Yunus* 10:93).

Qidwa (A) قدوة (*qidwah*): model, ideal, example.

Qismat (A) قسمة: distribution, division, part, portion, fate, destiny (see *surat al-Nisaa'* 4:8).

Qiwam (A) قوام (*qiwaam*) (قوم): support, prop.

> **Qiwam-ud-Din** (A) قوام الدين: support of the religion (Islam).

Quddus (A) قدوس (قدس): holy, most holy. Al-Quddus القدوس, the All-holy: one of the names of Allah (see *surat al-Hashr* 59:23).

161

Male Names

Abdul Quddus (A) عبد القدوس (*'abd al-quddus*): servant of the All-holy.

Qudrat (A) قدرة (*qudrah*) (قدر): power, might, strength.

Qudratullah[278] (A) قدرة الله (*qudrat allah*): power of Allah.

Quds (A) قدس: holiness, sanctity. See Qudus.

Qudsi (A). See Qudsiy.

Qudsiy (A): قدسي (*qudsiyy*): holy, sacred.

Qudus (A) قدس: holiness, sanctity.

> **Ruhul Qudus** (A) روح القدس: an epithet of Jibreel. قل نزله روح القدس من ربك بالحق "Say: Jibreel revealed it [the Qur'an] from your Lord with truth." (*surat al-Nahl* 16:102).

Quraishi[279] (A) قريشي (*quraishiyy*): *nisba* (relation) through ancestry to Quraish, the tribe of Muhammad (s). *Quraish* قريش: title of the 106th *sura* of the Qur'an. لايلاف قريش "For the familiarity of the Quraish." (*surat Quraish* 106:1).

---

[278] Care should be taken with names like Qudrat-i-Khuda, lest the person is inadvertently called Mr Khuda!

[279] "Families related to the large unit of the Qurayshites appear now as Qurashi or Qurayshi (Qureshi, Quraeshi etc.) and thus maintain their original Arabic pedigree." See Schimmel, Annemarie, *Islamic Names*, p. 39, also see p. 11. See Colebrooke, T. E., 'On the Proper Names of the Mohammadans', *Journal of the Royal Asiatic Society of Great Britain and Ireland*, XI, p. 222 (1879); Saif-ul-Islam, 'Cataloguing Bengali Muslim Names: problems and possible solutions', *UNESCO J. of Information Science*, II, p. 37 (1980).

Male Names

Qurban (A) قربان (Qurbaan) (قرب): sacrifice (see *surat al-Maa'idah* 5:27); sacrifice on the occasion of *Eid al-Adhaa* عيد الاضحى.

Qurban Ali (A) قربان علي: "[Devotion] to the beloved imam [Khalifa Ali] is expressed by Qurban 'Ali, 'sacrificed to-'".[280]

Qutb[281] (A) قطب: leader, chief, pivot, axis, pole. Sayyid Qutb (1906-66): Egyptian political and religious thinker and author of *fi zilaal al-qur'an* (*In the Shade of the Qur'an*).[282]

Qutb-ud-Din (A) قطب الدين: leader of the religion (Islam). Qutb ud-Din Aybak: Delhi Sultan (1206-10).[283]

---

[280] See Schimmel, Annemarie, *Islamic Names*, p. 35.

[281] It is a title "for the highest members of the saintly hierarchy." Ibid., p. 38. Also see Glasse, Cyril, *The Concise Encyclopaedia of Islam*, p. 327.

[282] "Egypt's most famous Islamic activist of the twentieth century." See *The Oxford Encyclopaedia of the Modern Islamic World*, p. 400.

[283] "[T]he dynasty founded by him in India is known as the 'Slave dynasty.'" See Majumdar, R. C., *et al.*, *An Advanced History of India*, p. 271.

Male Names

R

Raa'i (A) راعي (*raa'iy*): guardian, custodian, patron, protector.

Raaid (A) رائد (*raa'id*) (رود): pioneer, explorer, guide, leader, model.

Raaiq (A) رائق: pure, clear, tranquil, serene.

Raaji (A) الراجي (*al-raajii*): hopeful, hoping, full of hope.

Raazi (A) الراضي (*al-raadii*) (رضى): satisfied, contended, well-pleased. Al-Raazi (*raadi*): Abbasid Khalifa (934-40). Fakhruddin al-Raazi (*raadi*) (1149-1209): famous theologian-philosopher and the author of *mafatih al-ghayb* (The Keys of the Unseen). See Razi (*radiyy*) (رضى), satisfied.

Rabb (A) رب: lord. Al-Rabb الرب, the Lord: one of the names of Allah. الحمد لله رب العالمين "All praise belongs to Allah, the Lord of the universe." (*surat al-Faatihah* 1:2). See Maalik مالك, lord.

Abdur Rabb (A) عبد الرب (*abd al-rabb*): servant of the Lord.

Rabbani (A) رباني (*rabbaaniyy*): divine, from Allah.[284] See Ilahi إلاهي; Rabbiyy ربّي.

---

[284] See *Al-Mawrid: A Modern Arabic-English Dictionary*, p. 576; Cowan, J Milton (ed.) Hans Wehr, *A Dictionary of Modern Written Arabic*, p. 320; Madina, Maan Z., *Arabic-English Dictionary of the Modern Literary Language*, 245, Steingass, F., *A Comprehensive Persian-English Dictionary*, p. 567.

Male Names

Rabbi (A) رَبِّي (*rabbii*): my Lord (Allah).[285] اذ قال ابراهيم ربي الذي يحيي ويميت "When Ibrahim said: My Lord is He who gives life and causes death." (*surat al-Baqarah* 2:258). Comp. Rabbiyy ربِّي, divine.

> **Fazle Rabbi** (A) فضل ربي: bounty of my Lord. هذا من فضل ربي "[Sulayman said:] 'This is of the bounty of my Lord.'" (*surat al-Naml* 27:40).

Rabbiyy (A) رَبِّي: divine.[286] See Rabbani رباني, divine.

Rabi (A) ربيع (*rabee'*) (ربع): spring, springtime.

> **Abu al-Rabi' Sulaymaan** (A) أبو الربيع سليمان: ruler in Morocco (1308-10). Mahmud ibn al-Rabi': a *sahaabi*.[287]

Rabi'a (A) ربيعة (*rabi'ah*): fem. of Rabi. Rabi'ah ibn al-Harith: cousin of Muhammad (s).[288] Comp. Raabi'a رابعة (f.).

Rabih (A) رابح (*raabih*): winner, gainer.

Rabi'yy (A) ربيعي (*rabi'yy*): of the spring.

Rafi' (A) رفيع (*rafee'*) (رفع): high ranking, noble, eminent, exalted.

---

[285] See Steingass, F., *A Comprehensive Persian-English Dictionary*, p. 569

[286] See Madina, Maan Z., *Arabic-English Dictionary of the Modern Literary Language*, p. 245, *Al-Mawrid: A Modern Arabic-English Dictionary*, p. 576.

[287] See Keller, *Reliance of the Traveller* (Translation of *'Umdat al-Salik* in Arabic by Ahmad ibn Naqib al-misri), p. 1068.

[288] See Haykal, Muhammad Husayn, *The Life of Muhammad*, p. 486.

Male Names

Al-Rafi' الرفيع, the Exalter: one of the names of Allah. رفيع الدرجات ذو العرش "Exalted in ranks, the Lord of the Throne." (surat al-Mu'min 40:15). See Sani سني.

Abdur Rafi' (A) عبد الرفيع ('abd al-rafee'): servant of the Exalted.

Rafi-ud-Dawla (A) رفيع الدولة: high-ranking (person) of the state. Mughal emperor (1719).

Rafi-ud-Din (A) رفيع الدين: noble (person) of the religion (Islam). Son of Shah Wali Allah.[289]

Rafid (A) رافد (raafid) (رفد): tributary stream, affluent, helper, supporter, aide.

Rafif (A) رفيف (rafeef): glittering, shining, gleaming.

Rafiq (A) رفيق (rafeeq) (رفق): intimate friend, companion. ومن يطع الله والرسول فاولئك مع الذين انعم الله عليهم من النبيين رفيقا والصديقين والشهداء والصالحين وحسن اولئك "All who obey Allah and the Rasul (Messenger), they are in the company of those on whom Allah has bestowed favour, of the Prophets, and the pious and the martyrs and the righteous. How beautiful is their company." (surat al-Nisaa' 4:69). See Nadim نديم; Sadiq صديق; Wafiq وفيق; Zamil زميل.

Rafiq-ul-Islam (A) رفيق الإسلام (rafeeq al-islam): friend of Islam.

---

[289] An eighteenth-century Urdu version of the Qur'an was prepared by him. See Aziz, Ahmad, *An Intellectual History of Islam*, p. 107.

Male Names

Ragib (A) راغب (*raaghib*) (رغب): desirous, wishful, willing.

Ragid (A) رغيد (*ragheed*): comfort, opulence, affluence.

Rahif (A) رهيف (*raheef*): sharp.

Rahim (A) رحيم (*raheem*) (رحم): merciful, compassionate, kind. Al-Rahim الرحيم, the most Merciful: one of the names of Allah. ان الله غفور رحيم "Allah is All-forgiving and Most Merciful." (*surat al-Baqarah* 2:173). See Ra'uf رؤوف.

> **Abdur Rahim** (A) عبد الرحيم (*'abd al-raheem*): servant of the most Merciful. Abdur Rahim (1867-1948): Indian jurist, judge and author of *The Principles of Muhammadan Jurisprudence*.

Rahimi (A) رحيمي: *nisba* (relation) to Rahim.

Rahman (A) رحمن (*rahmaan*) (رحم): Al-Rahmaan الرحمن, the most Gracious: one of the names of Allah. بسم الله الرحمن الرحيم [290] "In the name of Allah, the most Gracious, the most Merciful." *Al-Rahman* الرحمن: title of the 55th *sura* of the Qur'an.

> **Abdur Rahman**[291] (A) عبد الرحمن. (*'abd al-rahmaan*): servant of the most Gracious. Abd ar-Rahman ibn 'Awf: one of the ten *sahaabis* to whom the Prophet (s) gave the good news of entering

---

[290] See in the beginning of each *sura* except *surat al-Tawba* (9); in *surat al-Naml* (27), in the beginning and also in verse 30.

[291] Recommended by Muhammad (s) as a name favoured by Allah. (*Muslim*: Adab no. 2132).

167

Male Names

into paradise.[292] Abd ar-Rahman I: founder (756-88) of Umayyad dynasty that ruled Spain for three centuries (756-1031). Abd ar-Rahman III (r. 912-961).[293] Tunku Abdul Rahman: the first Malaysian Prime Minister.

Rahmat (A) رحمة (*rahmah*) (رحم): mercy, compassion, kindness. وما ارسلناك الا رحمة للعالمين "We sent you [O Muhammad] not, but as a mercy for all creatures." (*surat al-Anbiyaa'*: 21:107).

Rahmatullah (A) رحمة الله (*rahmat allah*): mercy of Allah. An epithet of Muhammad (s). رحمت الله وبركاته عليكم اهل البيت. "The mercy of Allah and His blessings be upon you, O people of the house!" (*surat Hud* 11:73). Rahmat Allah al-Hindi: Indian scholar and author of *Izhar al-Haqq*.[294]

Raihan (A). See Rayhan.

Rais (A) رئيس (*ra'is*) (رأس): leader, chief, president, superior. See Naqib نقيب; Sayyid سيد.

Rais-ud-Din (A) رئيس الدين: leader of the religion (Islam).

Raja (A) رجاء (*rajaa'*) (رجو): hope, wish. See Amal أمل.

Rajaa' al-Karim (A) رجاء الكريم: hope of the Kind

---

[292] See Lings, Martin, *Muhammad*, p. 329.

[293] "The new palace...begun [by him] in 936, on a vast site a few miles north-west of Cordova, which was easily the biggest and richest city in the western world." See Fernandez-Armesto, Felipe, *Millennium*, p. 26.

[294] "[I]t was translated into Arabic, Turkish, French, English and German." See Ikram, S. M., *History of Muslim Civilization in India and Pakistan*, p. 667.

Male Names

(Allah).

Rajai (A) رجائي (*rajaa'ii*): my hope.

Rajab (A) رجب: the seventh month of the Islamic calendar. Parents may wish to name a child born in this month 'Rajab'.[295]

Raji (A). See Raaji.

Rajih (A) راجح (*raajih*): superior, predominant.

Rakib (A). See Raqib.

Rakin (A) ركين (*rakeen*) (ركن): firm, steady, solid. See Razeen رزين.

Ramadan (A) رمضان (*ramadaan, ramazaan*): "The ninth month of the Arab and Islamic calendar. The word *Ramadan* meant originally 'great heat'..."[296] In this sacred month, on the Night of Power, the Qur'an, the Holy book of the Muslims was revealed to Muhammad (s) through angel Jibreel. شهر رمضان الذي انزل فيه القرآن هدى للناس "The month of Ramadaan in which was revealed the Qur'an, a guidance for mankind." (*surat al-Baqarah* 2:185). In this month, Muslims keep fast from early dawn to sunset. Parents wish to name a child born in this sacred month 'Ramadan/Ramazan'.

Ramazan (A). See Ramadan.

Rami (A) رامي (*raamii*): the constellation Sagittarius.

---

[295] "The Mi'raj is usually dated to the 27th night of the month of Rajab." See Ali, Yusuf, *The Holy Qur'an*, p. 691.

[296] See Glasse, Cyril, *The Concise Encyclopaedia of Islam*, p. 329.

169

Male Names

Ramiz (A) رامز (*raamiz*): one who indicates by signs.

Ramiz-ud-Din (A) رامز الدين: one who indicates by signs to the religion (Islam).

Raqi (A) راقي (*raaqee*): superior, high-ranking, top, educated.

Raqib (A) رقيب (*raqeeb*) (رقب): observer, guard. Al-Raqib الرقيب, the Watcher: one of the names of Allah. وكان الله على كل شيء رقيبا "Allah is watchful over everything." (*surat al-Ahzaab* 33:52).

> **Abdur Raqib** (A) عبد الرقيب (*'abd al-raqeeb*): servant of the Observer.

Rashad (A) رشاد (*rashaad*) (رشد): right guidance, integrity of conduct. See Rushd رشد.

> **Muhammad Rashaad** (A) محمد رشاد: king of Anatolia (1909-18).

Rashed (A) راشد (*raashid*) (رشد): right-minded, rightly-guided. The first four Khalifas after the death of Muhammad (s) are called *al khulafaa' al-Raashidun* الخلفاء الراشدون, 'the rightly guided khalifas'. اولئك هم الراشدون "Such are they who are rightly guided." (*sura Al-Hujuraat* 49:7). See Muhtad مهتد; Hakeem حكيم; Rashid رشيد, wise.

> **Rashed-ud-Din** (A) راشد الدين: rightly-guided (person) of the religion (Islam).

Rashid (A) رشيد (*rasheed*) (رشد): wise, prudent, judicious, rightly guided. Al-Rasheed الرشيد, the Right-minded: one of the names of

170

Male Names

Allah (see *surat Hud* 11:87). See Muhtadi مهتدي; Rashed راشد, rightly-guided. Muhammad Rashid Ridaa (1865-1935): Islamic revivalist, founder of the periodical *al-Mamar* and author of *Tafsir al-Qur'an* (*al-Manar*).

Abdur Rashid (A) عبد الرشيد (*'abd al-rasheed*): servant of the Right-minded.

Izz-ud-Dawlah Abdur Rashid (A): عز الدولة عبد الرشيد: Ghaznavid ruler (1050-53).

Rashid ud-Din (A) رشيد الدين: wise (person) of the faith (Islam). Arab historian (1247-1318), author of *jami' al-tawaariikh* (Assembly of Histories).[297]

Rashiq (A) رشيق (*rasheeq*) (رشق): graceful, elegant.

Rasikh (A) راسخ (*raasikh*): well-established, well-founded, stable, steady.

Rasim (A) راسم (*raasim*): planner, designer.

Rasin (A) رصين (*raseen*): calm, composed.

Rasmi (A) رسمي (*rasmiyy*): ceremonial, ceremonious, formal.

Rasul[298] (A) رسول (*rasool*): Messenger of Allah. محمد رسول الله

---

[297] It is "[t]he first genuine universal history in Islam--probably in the world..." See Lewis, Bernard, *Islam in History*, p. 119.

[298] A Muslim is a servant only to Allah. So, names like Abdur Rasul, Ghulam Rasul are improper.

Male Names

"Muhammad is the Messenger of Allah." (*surat al-Fath* 48:29). See Nabi نبي, Prophet.

Rauf (A) رؤوف (*ra'oof*) (رأف): merciful, kind, compassionate. Al-Ra'uf الرؤوف, the most Kind: one of the names of Allah. ربنا انك رؤوف رحيم "Our Lord! You are full of kindness, Most Merciful." (see *surat al-Hashr* 59:10). See Rahim رحيم.

Abdur Rauf (A) عبد الرؤوف (*'abd al-ra'oof*): servant of the most Kind. Abd al-Rauf: Indonesian scholar and author.

Rayhan (A) ريحان (*raihaan*) (روح): ease, fragrant herb, sweet basil. والحب ذو العصف والريحان فبأي آلاء ربكما تكذبان "Husked grain and scented herb. Then which of the favours of your Lord will you deny?" (*surat al-Rahmaan* 55:12-13).

Raza (A). See Reza.

Razi (A) رضي (*radiyy*) (رضى): satisfied, contended, pleased. يرثني ويرث من آل يعقوب واجعله رب رضيا "[Zakariya said to Allah] 'Who shall inherit of me and inherit (also) of the house of Yaqub. And make him, my lord, one with whom You are well-pleased!'" (*surat Maryam* 19:6). See Raazi (*raadi*) راضي, satisfied.

Razin (A) رزين (*razeen*): calm, composed, self-possessed.

Razzaq (A) رزاق (*razzaaq*) (رزق): provider. Al-Razzaaq الرزاق, the All-provider: one of the names of Allah. ان الله هو الرزاق ذو القوة المتين "For Allah is He Who gives all sustenance--Lord of unbreakable might." (*surat al-Dhaariyaat* 51:58).

Abdur Razzaq (A) عبد الرزاق (*'abd al-razzaaq*): servant of the

172

Male Names

All-provider. Abd al-Razzaq al-Sanhuri (1895-1971): "Egyptian jurist, legal scholar, and architect of civil codes in several Arab countries."[299]

Reza (A) رضاء (*ridaa'*) (رضي): contentment, satisfaction, pleasure, consent. See Rizwaan (*ridwaan*) رضوان, contentment. Muhammad Reza Pahlavi: Shahanshah of Iran (1941-79).

    Reza-ul-Karim (A) رضاء الكريم (*ridaa' al-karim*): satisfaction of the most Generous (Allah).

Rezwan (A). See Rizwaan.

Riaz (A). See Riyaz.

Rida (A): See Reza. Ridaa' Ali ibn Musa (765-817): the eighth Imam of the Shi'ites.[300] Rashid Ridaa: see Rashid.

Ridawi (A). See Rizvi.

Ridwan (A). See Rizwaan.

Rif'at (A) رفعة (*rif'ah*) (رفع): high rank, high standing. Former title of the Egyptian Prime Minister. والى السماء كيف رفعت "And the heaven, how it is raised?" (*surat al-Ghaashiyah* 88:18). See Sanaa سناء. Muhammad Saadiq Rifat Pasha (1807-56): prominent writer.

Rifaa'at (A) رفاعة (*rifaa'ah*): "name of twenty three companions of

---

[299] See *The Oxford Encyclopaedia of the Modern Islamic World*, vol. I, p. 7.

[300] See Al-Tabatabai, Allamah Sayyid Muhammad Husayn, *Shi'ite Islam*, p. 205.

Muhammad."[301]

Rifqi (A) رفقي (*rifqii*): kind.

Riyaz (A) رياض (*riyaad*): pl. of Rawza روضة (*rawdah*), garden.

Riyaz-ul-Islam (A) رياض الإسلام: gardens of Islam.

Riza (A). See Reza. Ahmad Riza Khan (1856-1921): Indian Sufi scholar and author of the 12-volume *Fatwa-i-Rizvia*.[302]

Rizk (A) رزق (*rizq*): livelihood, subsistence, blessing of Allah. كلوا من رزق ربكم واشكروا له "Eat of the sustenance (provided) by your Lord and render thanks to Him." (*surat Sabaa* 34:15).

Rizk Allah (A) رزق الله: livelihood from Allah.

Rizvi (A) رضوي (*ridawiyy*): *nisba* (relation) through ancestry to the eighth Imam Reza (*ridaa'*) of the Shi'ites.

Rizwaan (A) رضوان (*ridwaan*) (رضي): satisfaction, contentment. تراهم ركعا سجدا يبتغون فضلا من الله ورضوانا "You [O Muhammad!] see them bowing, prostrating,seeking bounty from Allah and [His] satisfaction." (*surat al-Fath* 48:29). See Reza رضاء (*ridaa'*), satisfaction.

---

[301] See Steingass, F., *A Comprehensive Persian-English Dictionary*, p. 581. Rifaa'a ibn Rafi: Name of a sahaabi. See Keller, *Reliance of the Traveller* (Translation of *'Umdat al-Salik* in Arabic by Ahmad ibn Naqib al-misri), p. 911.

[302] "Th[e] mystic 'path' (*tariqa*) appeared towards the end of the nineteenth century, under the influence of Ahmad Riza Khan." See Kepel, Gilles, *Allah in the West*, p. 91. "He was a prolific issuer of *fatwas*...Few dared to cross swords with him, indeed few dared to even stand in his way. He...came to exercise a mesmeric hold over vast numbers." See Shourie, Arun, *The World of Fatwas*, p. 5.

Male Names

Rohi (A). See Ruhi.

Ruh (A) روح: spirit, soul.

>**Ruhullah** (A) روح الله (*ruh allah*): spirit of Allah. An epithet of Prophet 'Isa.[303] Ayatullah Ruhullah Khomeini: see Ayatullah.

>**Ruh-ul-Amin** (A) روح الأمين: the faithful spirit, an epithet of Jibreel.[304] نزل به الروح الامين "The Faithful Spirit came down with it (the Qur'an)." (*surat al-Shu'araa'* 26:193). See Amin.

>**Ruh-ul-Haqq** (A) روح الحق (*ruh al-haqq*): spirit of the truth. An epithet of Muhammad (s).

>**Ruhul Qudus** (A) روح القدس: the holy spirit. Epithet of Jibreel.[305] وآتينا عيسى ابن مريم البينات وايدناه بروح القدس "We gave 'Isa, son of Maryam, clear signs and We strengthened him with the Holy Spirit." (*surat al-Baqarah* 2:87).

Ruhi (A) روحي (*ruhiyy*): spiritual.

Ruhollah (A). See Ruh.

---

[303] See Steingass, F., *A Comprehensive Persian-English Dictionary*, p. 592; Colebrooke, T. E., 'On the Proper Names of the Mohammadans', *Journal of the Royal Asiatic Society of Great Britain and Ireland*, XI, p. 212 (1879).

[304] See Ali, Yusuf, *The Holy Qur'an*, p. 1081, n. 3224.

[305] See Pickthall, Marmaduke, *The Glorious Qur'an*, p. 2, n. 1.

Male Names

Rukn (A) ركن: pillar, prop, support. See *surat Hud* 11:80.

Rukn-ud-Din (A) ركن الدين: pillar of the religion (Islam). Rukn-ud-Din Barbak Shah: Bengal Sultan (1460-74).

Rukn-ud-Dawlah[306](A) ركن الدولة: prop of the state. Rukn ud-Dawlah Hasan: Buwayhid *ameer* (947-77).

Rushd (A) رشد: right guidance. ولقد آتينا ابراهيم رشده من قبل "We gave Ibrahim aforetime his right judgment." (*surat al-Anbiyaa'* 21:51). See Rashad رشاد.

Ibn Rushd: Abul Walid Muhammad ibn Ahmad ibn Rushd (1126-98): "The greatest Moslem philosopher, judged by his influence especially over the West,"[307] author of *tahaafut al-tahaafut* (The Incoherence of the Incoherence).[308] In the West, he is known as Averroes.

Rushdi[309] (A). See Rushdiy.

---

[306] See Colebrooke, T. E., 'On the Proper Names of the Mohammadans', *Journal of the Royal Asiatic Society of Great Britain and Ireland*, XI, p. 207 (1879).

[307] See Hitti, Philip K., *History of the Arabs*, p. 582.

[308] He was known as "Averroes in Europe, and translated into Latin, he became the great authority on Aristotle's philosophy, and was so celebrated that he could be referred to simply as 'the Commenter'." See Glasse, Cyril, *The Concise Encyclopaedia of Islam*, p. 174. "[T]he intellectual movement initiated by ibn-Rushd continued to be a living factor in European thought until the birth of modern experimental science." See Hitti, Philip K., *History of the Arabs*, p. 582.

[309] See Abd-el-Jawad, Hassan, 'A Linguistic and Socio-cultural Study of Personal Names in Jordan', *Anthropological Linguistics*, XXVIII, p. 84 (1986).

Male Names

Rushdiy (A): رشدي (*rushdiyy*): rightly guided, on the right way, following the right path.

Rustam (P) رستم: "the most renowned hero among the Persians."[310] King of Iran (867-95).

Ruwwad (A) رواد: (*ruwwaad*) pioneers, explorers, guides, leaders, models; pl. of Raaid رائد.

---

[310] See Steingass, F., *A Comprehensive Persian-English Dictionary*, p. 575.

Male Names

S

Saabih (A) صابح: coming or arrival in the morning. Comp. Sabih صبيح pretty (f.).

Saabir (A) صابر (صبر): patient, tolerant. يايها الذين آمنوا استعينوا بالصبر والصلوة ان الله مع الصابرين "O you who believe! seek help with *sabr* (patience) and *salaat* (prayer). Allah is with those who are patient." (*surat al-Baqarah* 2:153). See Halim حليم; Sabur صبور.

Saadaat (A) سادات: "Princes, lords (especially the descendants of Muhammad (s)";[311] pl. of Sayyid سيد. "[S]aiyidu's-saadaat, Lord of lords, an honorific title of the descendants of Muhammad; also of Muhammad himself."[312]

>   **Anwar as-Saadaat** (A) أنور السادات: more brilliant of the Sayyids.

>   **Ashraf as-Saadaat** (A) اشرف السادات: most noble of the Sayyids.

>   **Iftikhar as-Saadaat** (A) افتخار السادات: pride of the Sayyids.

Saadiq (A) صادق (صدق): true, truthful, honest, sincere, devoted. واذكر في الكتاب اسماعيل انه كان صادق الوعد "And make mention in the

---

[311] See Steingass, F., *A Comprehensive Persian-English Dictionary*, p. 639.

[312] *Ibid.*, p. 715.

Male Names

book of Ismail. He was true to what he promised." (*surat Maryam* 19:54). See Mukhlis مخلص.

Saafi (A) صافي (صفو): pure, clear, crystal. See Safi صفي.

Saaid (A) صاعد (*saa'id*): rising, ascending.

Saaim (A) صائم (*saa'im*) (صوم): fasting. See Saaima (f.).

Saalim[313] (A) سالم (سلم): safe, secure, perfect, complete. Saalim ibn 'Umayr: a *sahaabi*.[314] See Salim سليم.

Saami (A) سامي (سمو): eminent, exalted, high-minded, sublime. Al-Saami السامي: a celebrated poet.[315] See Jalil جليل; Nabil نبيل; Rafi' رفيع. Comp. Sami' سميع, hearing.

Saamir (A) ثامر (*thaamir*): fruit-bearing, fruitful, productive. Comp. Saamir سامر, entertainer.

Saamir (A) سامر: entertainer. See Samir سمير. Comp. ثامر, fruit-bearing.

Sabah[316] (A) صباح (*sabaah*): morning.

---

[313] See Abd-el-Jawad, Hassan, 'A Linguistic and Socio-cultural Study of Personal Names in Jordan', *Anthropological Linguistics*, XXVIII, p. 84 (1986).

[314] See Haykal, Muhammad Husayn, *The Life of Muhammad*, p. 243.

[315] See Colebrooke, T. E., 'On the Proper Names of the Mohammadans', *Journal of the Royal Asiatic Society of Great Britain and Ireland*, XI, p. 229 (1879).

[316] A popular name in Kuwait. In the cabinet of ministers of 1991 as many as six ministers bore this name besides the Emir of Kuwait al-Sabah. See *Encyclopedia of the Third World*, vol. II, p. 1050.

179

Male Names

Sabat (A) ثبات (*thabaat*): firmness, stability, certainty, endurance, boldness, truth.

Sabeer (A) صبير (صبر): patient, tolerant. See Sabur صبور.

Saber (A). See Saabir صابر; Sabeer صبير.

Sabet (A). See Sabit ثابت (*thaabit*). '

Sabiq (A) سابق (*saabiq*): first, winner.

Sabir (A). See Saabir; Sabeer.

Sabit (A) ثابت (*thaabit*): strong, well-established, certain, sure. Thabit ibn Arqam: a *sahaabi*.[317] See Sabat ثبات (*thabaat*).

Abu Saabit Aamir (A) أبو ثابت آمر: ruler in Morocco (1307-8).

Sabuh (A) صبوح: shining, brilliant. See Jamil جميل.

Sabri (A). See Sabriy.

Sabriy[318] (A) صبري (*sabriyy*): patient.

Sabur (A) صبور (صبر) (*saboor*): patient, tolerant. Al-Sabur الصبور, the Patient: one of the names of Allah. See Saabir صابر; Sabir صبير. Sabur ibn-Ardashir: Persian vizier of Buwayhid Sultan Baha al-Dawlah.

---

[317] See Haykal, Muhammad Husayn, *The Life of Muhammad*, p. 391.

[318] See Abd-el-Jawad, Hassan, 'A Linguistic and Socio-cultural Study of Personal Names in Jordan', *Anthropological Linguistics*, XXVIII, p. 84 (1986); Paxton, Evelyn, 'Arabic Names', *Asian Affairs*, LIX, p. 199 (1972).

Male Names

Abdus Sabur (A) عبد الصبور (*'abd al-saboor*): servant of the Patient.

Sa'd (A) سعد: good luck, good fortune, success, happiness, prosperity, lucky; sing. of Su'ud سعود. Sa'd ibn Abu Waqqaas: a well-known *sahaabi*;[319] Sa'd al-Musta'een: ruler of Granada (Spain) (1445).

Sa'd-ud-Din (A) سعد الدين: success of the religion (Islam).

Sa'dullah (A) سعد الله (*sa'd allah*): joy of Allah. An epithet of Muhammad (s). Muhammad Saadullah (1886-1950): Indian political leader.

Sadat (A). See Saadaat.

Sadek (A). See Saadiq صادق.

Sa'di (A) سعدي (*Sa'dii*): happy, Lucky, blissful fortunate. Muslih-ud-Din Sa'di (1184-1292): celebrated Persian poet, author of *Gulistan* and *Bustan*.[320]

Sadid (A) سديد (*sadeed*) (سد): correct, right, sound, appropriate, unerring, hitting the target. يايها الذين آمنوا اتقوا الله وقولوا قولا سديدا "O you who believe! Fear Allah, and speak words straight to the point." (*surat al-Ahzaab* 33:70).

---

[319] See Haykal, Muhammad Husayn, *The Life of Muhammad*, p. 83.

[320] See Steingass, F., *A Comprehensive Persian-English Dictionary*, p. 683; Glasse, Cyril, *The Concise Encyclopaedia of Islam*, p. 341.

Male Names

Sadiq[321] (A) صديق (*sadeeq*) (صدق): friend, companion (see *surat al-Shu'araa'* 26:101). See Rafiq رفيق.

Sadr[322] (A) صدر: chest, breast, forefront, start, dawn, prime. قال رب اشرح لي صدري "(Musa said:) 'O my Lord! Relieve my mind.'" (*surat Taa Haa* 20:25). See Awwal أول.

    Sadr-ud-Din (A) صدر الدين: (person at) forefront of the faith (Islam).

Saduh (A) صدوح: singer, singing.

Saduq (A) صدوق: honest, truthful, sincere, trustworthy.

Saeed (A) سعيد (*sa'eed*) (سعد): happy, lucky, blissful, fortunate. يوم يات لا تكلم نفس الا باذنه فمنهم شقي وسعيد "On the day when it comes no soul will speak except by His permission, some among them will be wretched and some will be blessed." (*surat Hud* 11:105). See Mas'ud مسعود. Abu Sa'eed Khudri: a *sahaabi*.[323]

    Abu Saeed Usman (*uthmaan*) (A) أبو سعيد عثمان: ruler in Morocco (1310-31).

    Saeed-uz-Zaman (A) سعيد الزمان: luckiest of the age.

---

[321] Names such as, Sadiq al-Rahman, meaning 'friend of the Most Gracious (Allah)', are not proper as the relationship of man with Allah is that of a servant عبد and not a friend.

[322] "Originally an Arabic honorific, *sadr* has been used informally since at least the tenth century to denote a prominent member of the '*ulama*'." See *The Oxford Encyclopaedia of the Modern Islamic World*, vol. III, p. 449.

[323] See *Riyadh-us-Saleheen*, vol. I, p. 416.

Male Names

Safdar (P) صفدر: brave.

Saffaah (A) سفاح (سفح): giver of liberty, liberal.

Abu Abbas as-Saffah ابو عباس السفاح: the first Khalifa
(749-754) of the Abbasid dynasty.

Safi (A) صفي (*safiyy*) (صفو): pure, sincere and honest friend. See
Saafi صافي, pure.

Safiullah (A) صفي الله (*safiyy allah*): the pure (one) of Allah. An
epithet of Adam.[324]

Safiy-ud-Din (A) صفي الدين: the pure (one) of the faith (Islam).
Shaykh Safi al-Din: forefather of the Safawid dynasty (1502-1736)
in Persia from whom the dynasty derived its name.

Safir (A) سفير (*safeer*) (سفر): ambassador, mediator, intercessor.

Safwaan (A) صفوان: pure, clear, smooth stone. Safwaan ibn Baydaa al-
Fahri: a *sahaabi*.

Saghir (A) صغير (*sagheer*) (صغر): small, young. قل رب ارحمهما كما
ربياني صغيرا "Say: My Lord! Have mercy on them (parents) both as
they raised me up during my childhood." (*surat Bani Israa'il* 17:24).

Saghir Ali صغير علي: little Ali.

Sagir (A). See Saghir.

---

[324] See Colebrooke, T. E., 'On the Proper Names of the Mohammadans', *Journal of the Royal Asiatic Society of Great Britain and Ireland*, XI, p. 198 (1879).

Male Names

Sahab (A) سحاب (*sahaab*): clouds.

Sahl (A) سهل (sahl): smooth, simple, facile, easy, even. Abul Abbas Sahl ibn S'ad: a *sahaabi*.[325] Abu Muhammad Sahl (d.896): "[A] Sunni theologian and mystic".[326]

Said (A). See Saeed.

Saif (A). See Sayf.

Saim (A). See Saaim.

Sajed (A). See Sajid.

Sajid (A) ساجد (*saajid*) (سجد): prostrate in worship, bowing in adoration to Allah. أمن هو قانت آناء الليل ساجدا وقائما يحذر الآخرة ويرجوا رحمة ربه "Is one who worships devoutly during the hours of the night prostrating himself or standing [in adoration], fearing the Hereafter and hoping for the mercy of his Lord [like one who does not]?" (*surat al-Zumar* 39:9).

> **Sajid-ur-Rahman** (A) ساجد الرحمن: (*saajid al-rahmaan*): one who prostrates to the Merciful (Allah).

Sajjad[327] (A) سجاد (*sajjaad*) (سجد): worshipper of Allah, worshipper engaged in *sujud* (prostration) before Allah. Name of Zainul Abidin, the

---

[325] See An-Nawawi, *Forty Hadith*, p. 104.

[326] See *Shorter Encyclopaedia of Islam*, p. 488.

[327] As the meaning of Sajjad is worshipper, names such as Sajjad Ali or Sajjad Husayn are improper.

fourth Imam of the Shi'ites.

Sakhaa (A) سخاء (*sakhaa'*) (سخو): generosity, liberality.

Sakhawat (A) سخاوة (*sakhaawah*) (سخو): generosity, liberality.

Sakib (A). See Saqib.

Salabat (A) صلابة (*salaabat*) (صلب): strong, majesty, dignity, awe.

Saladin (A). See Salah.

Salah (A) صلاح (*salaah*) (صلح): piety, righteousness, honesty, goodness.

> **Salah-ud-Din**[328] (A) صلاح الدين: rectitude of the faith (Islam). Salah ud-Din Yusuf Ayyubi (1138-93): Sultan of Egypt known to the Western world as Saladin who came out victorious in the battle against Richard the Lion-heart, king of England during the Crusades.[329]

Salam (A) سلام (*salaam*) (سلم): peace, safety, security. *As-salaamu alaikum* عليكم السلام, 'peace be upon you': greeting amongst Muslims. *Al-Salaam* السلام, the All-peaceable: one of the names of Allah. (*surat al-Hashr* 59:23). ونادوا اصحاب الجنة ان سلام عليكم" And they call

---

[328] "Saladin (Salah al-Din)...is probably the best known bearer of this type of name, and is responsible for its continued popularity..." See Paxton, Evelyn, 'Arabic Names', *Asian Affairs*, LIX, p. 199 (1972).

[329] "Saladin was the strongest personality of his time." Tate, Georges, *The Crusades and the Holy Land*, Chapter V, 'Saladin's Victory', p. 97 . "Christians in the West were uneasily aware that this Muslim ruler had behaved in a far more 'Christian' manner than had their own Crusaders when they conquered Jerusalem." See Armstrong, Karen, *Jerusalem: One City Three faiths*, p. 294.

Male Names

to the inhabitants of Paradise: Peace be upon you." (*surat al-A'raaf* 7:46).

Abdus Salam (A) عبد السلام (*'abd al-salaam*): servant of the All-peaceable.

Salama (A) سلمة (*salamah*): peace; fem. of Salam سلم. Salamah ibn 'Amr ibn al-Akwa': a *sahaabi*.[330]

Salamat (A) سلامة (*salaamah*) (سلم): safety, security, soundness, integrity.

> **Salamatullah** (A) سلامة الله (*salaamat allah*): security of Allah.

Saleh (A). See Salih.

Salek (A) سالك (*saalik*): traveller, wayfarer. "A member of a Sufi order whose intention is actively to seek the realisation of God."[331]

Salem (A). See Saalim سالم.

Salih (A) صالح (*saalih*) (صلح): pious, righteous, upright, just, virtuous, devoted. رب هب لي حكما والحقني بالصالحين "O my Lord! bestow wisdom on me and unite me to the righteous." (*surat al-Shu'araa'* 26:83). A Prophet. اتعلمون ان صالحا مرسل من ربه "Do you know that Saalih is a *rasul* from his Lord?" (*surat al-A'raaf* 7:75).

---

[330] See Haykal, Muhammad Husayn, *The Life of Muhammad*, p. 327; Keller, *Reliance of the Traveller* (Translation of *'Umdat al-Salik* in Arabic by Ahmad ibn Naqib al-misri), p. 1092.

[331] See Glasse, Cyril, *The Concise Encyclopaedia of Islam*, p. 350.

Male Names

As-Saalih 'Imaad-ud-Din Ismail (A) الصالح عماد الدين اسماعيل: Sultan of Egypt (1342-45).

Salil (A) سليل (*saleel*): drawn (sword), scion, son.

Salim (A) سليم (*saleem*) (سلم): sound, perfect, complete, safe, secure. يوم لا ينفع مال ولا بنون الا من اتى الله بقلب سليم "The day when wealth and sons avail not [any man] except him who brings to Allah a sound heart." (*surat al-Shu'araa'* 26:88-89). See Saalim سالم. Salim bin Thabet: a *sahaabi*. Mughal emperor Jahangir (d.1627) was known as Prince Salim before his accession to the throne of Delhi.[332] Salim I (d.1520): Ottoman Sultan.

> **Salimullah** (A) سليم الله (*salim allah*) (1884-1915): soundest (servant) of Allah. Nawab of Dhaka (Bangladesh).[333]

> **Salim-uz-Zaman** (A) سليم الزمان: soundest (person) of the age.

Salit (A) سليط (*saleet*): strong, solid, firm, sharp.

Salman (A) سلمان (*salmaan*): safe.

---

[332] Mughal emperor Akbar gave this name to his son out of respect for the blessings he asked from the famous saint Shaykh Salim Chishti. See Schimmel, Annemarie, *Islamic Names*, p. 37; Majumdar, R. C., *et al.*, *An Advanced History of India*, p. 604.

[333] He was the founder of the political party, Muslim League in 1906 which played a major role in the independence movement of the Indian sub-continent, resulting in partition in 1947 into India and Pakistan. See Majumdar, R. C., *et al.*, *An Advanced History of India*, p. 977. Also see Hardy, P., *The Muslims of British India*, p. 164.

Male Names

Salmaan al-Farsi (A) سلمان الفارسي:[334] a very close *sahaabi* whom Muhammad (s) "gave good tidings of Paradise".[335]

Samad (A) صمد: eternal. Al-Samad الصمد, the Everlasting: one of the names of Allah. قل هو الله احد الله الصمد "Say: He is Allah, the One! Allah, the Everlasting," (*surat al-Ikhlaas* 112:1-2).

Abdus Samad (A) عبد الصمد (*'abd al-samad*): servant of the Eternal. Khwaja Abdus Samad: sixteenth-century Persian calligrapher and painter at the Mughal court.

Samah (A) سماح (*samaah*) (سمح): generosity, bounty, good-heartedness.

Sami' (A) سميع (*samee'*) (سمع): hearing, listening. Al-Sami' السميع, the All-Hearing: one of the names of Allah. انك سميع الدعاء "You are the hearer of *du'aa'* (prayer)." (*surat Aal 'Imraan* 3:38). Comp. Saami سامي, eminent.

Abdus Sami (A) عبد السميع (*'abd al-samee'*): servant of the All-hearing.

Samih (A) سميح (*sameeh*): magnanimous, generous, kind, forgiving, good-hearted.

---

[334] "Allah's blessings be upon them, and there was Bilal from Ethiopia, and there was Souhaid the Roman, and there was Salman the Persian..." See Grand Sheikh of Al-Azhar University, 'Message from His Eminence' in Weeramantry, C.G., *Islamic Jurisprudence*, p. xviii; see Keller, *Reliance of the Traveller* (Translation of *'Umdat al-Salik* in Arabic by Ahmad ibn Naqib al-misri), p. 1093.

[335] See Lings, Martin, *Muhammad*, p. 329.

Male Names

Samim (A) صميم (*sameem*) (صم): sincere, genuine, pure, true, essence, heart.

Samin (A) ثمين (*thameen*) (ثمن): valuable, precious, priceless.

Samir (A) سمير (*sameer*) (سمر): companion (in nightly conversation), entertainer (with stories, music etc.). See Saamir سامر, entertainer. Comp. Saamir ثامر, fruit-bearing.

Samud (A) صمود (*samood*): steadfastness, firmness, endurance.

Sanaa' (A) سناء (*sanaa'*) (سنو): brilliance, radiance, splendour. Comp. Sanaa ثناء (*thanaa'*), praise.

Sanaa (A) ثناء (*thanaa'*) (ثنو): praise, commendation, eulogy. Comp. Sanaa' سناء, brilliance.

    Sanaaullah (A) ثناء الله (*thanaa' allah*): praise of Allah.

Sanad (A) سند: support, prop.

    Sanad-ud-Dawlah[336] (A) سند الدولة: prop of the state.

Sani (A) سنيّ (*saniyy*) (سنو): brilliant, majestic, exalted, eminent, splendid. See Rafi' رفيع.

Saqib (A) ثاقب (*thaaqib*) (ثقب): penetrating, piercing, sharp-witted, sagacious, astute, acute. النجم الثاقب "The piercing star!" (*surat al-Taariq* 86:3).

---

[336] See Colebrooke, T. E., 'On the Proper Names of the Mohammadans', *Journal of the Royal Asiatic Society of Great Britain and Ireland*, XI, p. 207 (1879).

Male Names

Saqif (A) ثقيف (*thaqeef*): proficient, skilful. A *sahaabi*.

Sardar (P) سردار (*sardaar*): chief, noble man, officer of rank. An honorific title.

Sarkar (P) سركار (*sarkaar*): chief, overseer. A title of respect.

Sarwar[337] (P) سرور: leader, chief, master. *Sarwari Ambiya*: Chief of the Prophets, an epithet of Muhammad (s).[338]

Sattar (A) ستار (*sattaar*) (ستر) veiler (of sin). Al-Sattar الستار, the Veiler of sin: one of the names of Allah.

> **Abdus Sattar** (A) عبد الستار (*'abd al-sattar*): servant of the Veiler of sin. President of Bangladesh (1981-82).

Sayed (A). See Sayyid.

Sayem (A). See Saaim.

Sayf (A) سيف: sword.

> **Sayfullah** (A) سيف الله (*sayf allah*): sword of Allah. Title of honour awarded to Khalid ibn Walid by Muhammad (s) for his bravery in battle.

> **Sayf-ud-Din Hamza Shaah** (A+P) سيف الدين حمزة شاه: Bengal Sultan (1410-12).

---

[337] A name such as Ghulam Sarwar, meaning servant of the leader, i. e. Muhammad (s) is improper because man's relationship with Allah is as that of a servant to his Lord.

[338] See Steingass, F., *A Comprehensive Persian-English Dictionary*, p. 679.

Male Names

Sayf-ud-Dawlah (A) سيف الدولة: sword of the state. Ruler (944-67) of the Hamdani dynasty who "held his court in Aleppo and became noted as a patron of literature".[339]

Sayf-ul-Islam (A) سيف الإسلام: sword of Islam.

Sayyed (A). See Sayyid.

Sayyid (A) سيّد: lord, master, chief. An epithet of Muhammad (s). سيدا "lordly" (see *surat Aal 'Imraan* 3:39). It is "[a] title of respect used for the descendants of the Prophet through his daughter Fatimah and 'Ali ibn Abu Talib."[340] See Mawla مولى; Ra'is رئيس.

Sayyid Ahmad Khan (1817-1898): Indian reformer who uplifted the political situation and education of Muslims in India. He is the author of *Mahomedan Commentary on the Holy Bible* (1862) and *A Series of Essays on the Life of Mohammad* (1870).

Sayyid Ahmad Brelvi (Barelwi) (d.1831): Indian religious reformer and the founder of *Mujahidin* (holy warriors) movement to eradicate syncretistic elements from Hinduism which crept into Islam in the Indian Sub-continent. He is the author of *Sirat-i-Mustaqim*.

Sekandar (A). See Sikandar.

---

[339] See Watt, W. Montgomery, *The Majesty that was Islam*, p. 165.

[340] See Glasse, Cyril, *The Concise Encyclopaedia of Islam*, p. 353. See Steingass, F., *A Comprehensive Persian-English Dictionary*, p. 715; Saif-ul-Islam, 'Cataloguing Bengali Muslim Names: problems and possible solutions', *UNESCO J. of Information Science*, II, p. 38 (1980).

Male Names

Selim (A). See Salim.

Shaafi (A) شافي (*shafii*): healing, one who cures, salutary, satisfactory. Comp. Shaafi' شافع; Shafi' شفيع, mediator.

Shaafi' (A) شافع : intercessor, mediator. See Shafi' شفيع, mediator. Comp. Shaafi شافي, one who cures. Muhammad ibn Idris ash-Shaafi'i (767-820): founder of the Shafi School of Law.[341]

Shaahid (A) شاهد (شهد): witness. يايها النبي انا ارسلناك شاهدا ومبشرا ونذيرا "O Nabi, We have sent you as a witness, and a bringer of good news and a warner." (*surat al-Ahzaab* 33:45).

> **Al-Shaahid** (A) الشاهد: the witness, an epithet of Muhammad (s).

Shaahin (P). See Shahin.

Shaban (A) شعبان (*sha'baan*): "[E]ighth lunar month. Mas. pr. name."[342] It is a month of religious significance for Muslims. *Nisf min Sha'baan* (Middle of Sha'baan), or *Shab-e-Barat* (Night of the Destiny) is a blessed, sacred night observed by Muslims by offering special prayers. Parents may wish to name a child born in this sacred month 'Shaban'. Al-Ashraf Sha'ban (1363-76): Mamluk Sultan.

Shabbar (P) شبر: son of Prophet Harun, by which name Muhammad (s)

---

[341] He was known as the "father of Muslim Jurisprudence." See Coulson, N J., *Conflicts and Tensions in Islamic Jurisprudence*, p. 5. "His *al-Risala* was the first work in the history of mankind to investigate the theoretical and practical bases of jurisprudence." See Keller, *Reliance of the Traveller*, p. 1095.

[342] See Haim, S., *The Shorter Persian-English Dictionary*, p. 437.

Male Names

is said to have called his grandson Hasan.[343]

Shabbir (P) شبير: son of Prophet Harun, by which name Muhammad (s) is said to have called his grandson Husayn.[344] Allama Shabbir Ahmad Usmani (*uthmaani*) (1887-1949): "an *'alim* from Deoband...In November 1945 at Calcutta, such *'ulama* founded the *Jam'iyyat al-'ulama-i-Islam* to campaign in support of the All-India Muslim League."[345]

Shad (A) شاد (*shaad*): happy.

Shadi (A) شادي (*shaadi*) (شدو): singer.[346]

Shafa'at (A) شفاعة (*shafaa'at*) (شفع): intercession, mediation. قل لله الشفاعة جميعا "To Allah belongs all intercession." (*surat al-Zumar* 39:44). Shafa'at Ahmad Khan (1893-1947): Indian political leader.[347]

Shafaqat (A) شفقة (*shafaqah*) (شفق): compassion, pity, kindness, tenderness. See Ishfaq اشفاق, compassion.

Shafi' (A) شفيع (*shafee'*) (شفع): intercessor, mediator. ما من شفيع الا من بعد اذنه "No intercessor [can plead with Him] except after His permission [has been obtained] (*surat Yunus* 10:3). See Shaafi' شافع, intercessor. Comp. Shaafi شافي, one who cures. Mian Mohammad Shafi

---

[343] See Steingass, F., *A Comprehensive Persian-English Dictionary*, p. 731.

[344] *Ibid.*, p. 732.

[345] See Hardy, P., *The Muslims of British India*, p. 242.

[346] See Steingass, F., *A Comprehensive Persian-English Dictionary*, p. 722.

[347] See Hardy, P., *The Muslims of British India*, p. 196.

Male Names

(1869-1932): Indian political leader.

Shafiq (A) شفيق (*shafeeq*) (شفق): compassionate, kind-hearted, affectionate, warm-hearted. See Mushfiq مشفق; Shafuq شفوق.

Shafuq (A) شفوق (شفق): compassionate, sympathetic, affectionate. See Shafeeq شفيق; Mushfiq مشفق.

Shah (P) شاه (*shaah*) (abbreviation: Shah شه[348]): king, emperor. "[A] title assumed by fakirs."[349] Originally, the royal title of the kings of the Pahlavi dynasty (1925-1979).[350] Shah Abbas: see Abbas. Shah Waliullah: see Wali.

> **Shah Alam** (P+A) شاه عالم (*shaah 'aalam*): king of the world. Shah Alam Bahadur Shah شاه عالم بهادر شاه: Mughal emperor (1707-1712).

> **Shahbaz** (P) شاهباز (*shaahbaaz*): royal falcon, royal, generous, noble.

> **Shah Jahan** (P) شاه جهان (*shaah jahaan*): king of the world. Mughal emperor (d.1666) who built the Taj Mahal, one of the architectural wonders of the world. See Jahan.

> **Shah Jalal** (P+A) شاه جلال (*shaah jalaal*) (d. 1340): saint

---

[348] See Haim, S., *The Shorter Persian-English Dictionary*, p. 448; Steingass, F., *A Comprehensive Persian-English Dictionary*, p. 768.

[349] See Steingass, F., *A Comprehensive Persian-English Dictionary*, p. 726.

[350] See Glasse, Cyril, *The Concise Encyclopaedia of Islam*, p. 307.

Male Names

buried at Sylhet (Bangladesh).[351]

Shah Nawaaz (P) شاه نواز (*shaah nawaaz*): friend of king.

Shahzada (P) شاه زاده (*shaah zaadah*): prince. Sultan Shahzada: Bengal Sultan (1487).

Shahabuddin (A). See Shihab: Shihabuddin.

Shahadat (A) شهادة (*shahaadah*) (شهد): testimony, evidence, fundamental belief in Islam. *Kalima Shahaadat*: اشهد ان لا اله الا الله وحده لا شريك له واشهد ان سيدنا محمدا عبده ورسوله "I testify that there is no God except Allah, He is one, He has no partner. I testify that our leader Muhammad is his servant and Rasul." ولا نكتم شهادة الله انا اذا لمن الآثمين "We will not conceal the testimony of Allah, for then we will commit sin." (*surat al-Maa'idah* 5:106).

Shahan (P) شاهان (*shaahaan*): kings; pl. of Shah شاه, king.[352]

Shahan Shah (P) شاهان شاه: king of kings.[353] Title[354] of royalty in Iran before the revolution in 1979 when Iran became an Islamic republic.

---

[351] The conquest of Sylhet in expansion of Muslim rule in Bengal "is attributed...to the moral and material support which the Muslim troops received from Hadrat Shah Jalal..." See Ikram, S. M., *History of Muslim Civilization in India and Pakistan*, p. 133.

[352] See Steingass, F., *A Comprehensive Persian-English Dictionary*, p. 727

[353] *Ibid.*, p. 728.

[354] "'Azud was the first ruler in Islam to bear the title shaahanshah." See Hitti, Philip K., *History of the Arabs*, p. 472.

Male Names

Shahed (A). See Shaahid.

Shaheen (P). See Shahin.

Shahid (A) شهيد (*shaheed*) (شهد): witness, martyr in the cause of Islam and as such held in very high esteem and honour.[355] والذين آمنوا باللّه ورسله اولئك هم الصديقون والشهداء عند ربهم "And those who believe in Allah and His Messengers, they are the pious and the martyrs in the eye of their Lord." (*surat al-Hadeed* 57:19). *Sayyid al-Shuhada*: 'the lord among martyrs' an epithet of Imam Husayn, grandson of Muhammad (s) who attained martyrdom in the battle of Karbala.[356] See Shaahid شاهد. Husain Shaheed Suhrawardy (1893-1963): Prime Minister of Bengal and Pakistan.

Shahin[357] (P) شاهين (*shaaheen*): royal white falcon; the beam of scales.

Shahiq (A) شاهق (*shaahiq*): high, towering, lofty, tall.

Shahir (P) شهير (*shaheer*) (شهر): famous, eminent, renowned.

Shahryar (P) شهر يار: friend of the city, i.e. king. The king of *The*

---

[355] "[T]hose who are slain in the path of God, in religious war, or die because of other specified causes (for instance during pilgrimage) are honoured by the laqab *shahid* 'martyr'." See Schimmel, Annemarie, *Islamic Names*, p. 59. "Such are assured a place in paradise and are buried in the clothes they were in battle." See Glasse, Cyril, *The Concise Encyclopaedia of Islam*, p. 360.

[356] See Al-Tabatabai, Allamah Sayyid Muhammad Husayn, *Shi'ite Islam*, p. 196.

[357] See Steingass, F., *A Comprehensive Persian-English Dictionary*, p. 728; Bland, N., 'On the Muhammadan Science of Interpretation of Dreams', *J. of the Royal Asiatic Society*, XVI, p. 156.

Male Names

Thousand and One Nights narrated by his bride Shahrazaad.[358] Son of Mughal emperor Jahangir.

Shahzad, Shahzada (P). See Shah.

Shaikh (A). See Shaykh.

Shaikh-ul-lslam (A) شيخ الإسلام: leader of Islam. Title of the highest religious office in Ottoman Turkey.

Shajaat (A) شجاعة (*shajaa'ah*) (شجع): courage, bravery, valour.

Shaji (A) شجيع (*shajee'*) (شجع): courageous, bold, brave. See Shuja شجاع, courageous.

Shaker (A). See Shakir.

Shakil[359] (P) شكيل (*shakeel*): well formed, handsome.

Shakir (A) شاكر (*shaakir*) (شكر): thankful, grateful. Al-Shaakir الشاكر, the All-thankful: one of the names of Allah. فان الله شاكر عليم "Allah is All-thankful, All-knowing." (*surat al-Baqarah* 2:158). Muslims wish to acknowledge as often as possible their gratefulness to Allah for all the bounties He has provided for them in this world. See Shakur شكور.

Shakur (A) شكور (*shakoor*) (شكر): thankful, grateful. Al-Shakur الشكور, the All-thankful: one of the names of Allah. والله شكور حليم

---

[358] See Hitti, Philip K., *History of the Arabs*, p. 292.

[359] The word is derived from Arabic. See Haim, S., *The Shorter Persian-English Dictionary*, p. 441.

Male Names

"Allah is All-thankful, All-clement." (*surat al-Taghaabun* 64:17). See Shaakir شاكر.

Abdus Shakur (A) عبد الشكور (*'abd al-shakoor*): servant of the All-thankful.

Shams (A) شمس: sun. Al-Shams الشمس, 'the Sun': title of the 91st *sura* of the Qur'an. اقم الصلوة لدلوك الشمس الى غسق الليل وقرآن الفجر ان قرآن الفجر كان مشهودا "Establish prayers at the sun's decline till the darkness of the night, and the recital of the Qur'an at dawn. For the recital of the Qur'an is witnessed." (*surat Bani Israa'il* 17:78). See Aftab افتاب; Khurshid خورشيد; Mihr مهر.

Shams-ud-Din (A) شمس الدين: sun of the religion (Islam). Famous poet (d.1391) of Iran. Shams-ud-Din Ilyas Shah: Bengal Sultan (1345-58).

Shams-ud-Dawlah (A) شمس الدولة: sun of the kingdom. Buwayhid Sultan (982-86).

Shamsher (P) شمشير: sword. See Sayf سيف; Muhannad مهند.

Sharaf (A) شرف: nobility, high rank, eminence, distinction, honour, glory, dignity. See Karamat كرامة; Sharafat شرافة.

Sharaf-ud-Dawlah (A) شرف الدولة: honour of the state. Buwayhid Sultan (983-9).

Sharaf-ud-Din (A) شرف الدين: honour of the religion (Islam).

Sharafat (A) شرافة (*sharaafah*) (شرف): honour, nobleness. See Sharaf شرف.

198

Male Names

Shariat (A) شريعة (*shari'ah*) (شرع): drinking place, divine law, Islamic law. ثم جعلناك على شريعة من الامر فاتبعها ولا تتبع اهواء الذين لا يعلمون "And now We have set you [O Muhammad] on a clear road of [our] commandment; so follow it, and follow not the whims of those who know not." (*surat al-Jaathiyah* 45:18).

Shariatullah (A) شريعة الله (*shari'at allah*): divine law of Allah. Nineteenth-century Bengali political and religious reformer (1764-1840).[360]

Shariati (A) شريعتي: of or relating to Shariat. Ali Shari'ati (1933-77): "one of the most important social thinkers of twentieth-century Iran."[361]

Sharif (A) شريف (*shareef*) (شرف): noble, honourable, highborn. Originally Sharif referred to "[t]he descendants of the Prophet through his daughter Faatimah and 'Ali ibn Abi Taalib".[362] See Nabeel نبيل; Hasib حسيب.

Sharif-ud-Din (A) شريف الدين: noble (person) of the religion (Islam).

Shaukat (A). See Shawkat.

Shawkat (A) شوكة: power, might, bravery, valour. Shawkat Ali (1873-1938): Indian political leader who fought for the cause of Muslims in pre-independent India. He is elder brother of Muhammad Ali (see

---

[360] See Ahmad, Aziz, *An Intellectual History of Islam in India*, p. 10.

[361] See *The Oxford Encyclopaedia of the Modern Islamic World*, vol. IV, p. 46.

[362] See Glasse, Cyril, *The Concise Encyclopaedia of Islam*, p. 363. Also see Steingass, F., *A Comprehensive Persian-English Dictionary*, p. 743.

Male Names

Muhammad).

Shaykh (A) شيخ: title of a political or spiritual leader of a Muslim community; chief, head, old man (see *surat al-Qasas* 28:23).

Sheikh (A). See Shaykh.

Sher (P) شير: lion. An epithet of Khalifa Ali. Sher Ali: Afghan king (d.1879).

> **Sher-e-Khuda** (P) شير خدا: lion of Khuda (Allah). Epithet of Hamza, an uncle of Muhammad (s).

> **Sher Shah** (P) شير شاه: king of the lions. Sher Shah Sur: Delhi Sultan (1540-45).

Sherif (A). See Sharif.

Shibl (A) شبل: lion cub. Shibl bin Khaled: a *sahaabi*. See Shibli.

Shibli (A) شبلي: *nisbah* (relation) to Shibl. Shibli Numani: See Numani.

Shihab (A) شهاب (*shihaab*) (شهب): flame, meteor, shooting star, star (see *surat al-Saaffaat* 37:10). See Kaukab كوكب (f.).

> **Shihab-ud-Din** (A) شهاب الدين: meteor of the religion (Islam). Twelfth-century philosopher.[363]   Shihab-ud-Din Shah Jahan: Mughal emperor (d.1666).

Shikdar (P). See Shiqdar.

---

[363] See Al-Tabatabai, Allamah Sayyid Muhammad Husayn, *Shi'ite Islam*, p. 108.

Male Names

Shiqdar (P) شقدار (*shiqdaar*): land tax collector during the Muslim rule in India,[364] now a family title. Comp. Sikdar سكدر.

Shoeb (A). See Shuayb.

Shuayb (A) شعيب (*shu'ayb*): a Prophet (see *surat al-A'raaf* 7:88). 'Amr ibn Shu'ayb: a hadith narrator.[365]

Shubul[366] (A) شبول (*shubool*): lion cubs; pl. of Shibl شبل.

Shuhrah (A) شهرة: fame, renown.

Shuja (A) شجاع (*shujaa'*) (شجع): courageous, bold, brave. A *sahaabi*.[367] See Humaam همام, brave.

> **Shah Shuja** (P+A) شاه شجاع (*shaah shujaa'*): son of Mughal emperor Shah Jahan.[368]

> **Shuja-ud-Din** (A) شجاع الدين: brave (person) of the religion (Islam).

Shuja't (A) شجاعة (*shujaa'at*) (شجع): courage, boldness, bravery.

Shukr (A) شكر (*shukr*): thanks, gratitude, gratefulness. See Shukri.

---

[364] See Steingass, F., *A Comprehensive Persian-English Dictionary*, p. 750.

[365] See Keller, *Reliance of the Traveller*, p. 1039.

[366] See Wortabet, *Arabic English Dictionary*, p. 297.

[367] See Haykal, Muhammad Husayn, *The Life of Muhammad*, p. 364.

[368] See Majumdar, R. C., *et al.*, *An Advanced History of India*, p. 604.

Male Names

Shukri[369] (A) شكري (*shukriyy*): thanking and acknowledging gratefulness to Allah.

Siddiq (A) صديق (*siddeeq*) (صدق): righteous, very truthful, honest. In the Qur'an, Prophet Yusuf (see *surat Yusuf* 12:46), Prophet Ibrahim (see *surat Maryam* 19:41) and Prophet Idris (see *surat Maryam* 19:56) are mentioned as Siddiq.

Al-Siddiq (A) الصديق: the truthful. Title of Khalifa Abu Bakr, the first of the 'rightly guided' Khalifas.[370]

Siddiqullah (A) صديق الله (*siddiq allah*): the truthful (one) to Allah. An epithet of Prophet Yusuf. يوسف ايها الصديق "O Yusuf! [he said] O you truthful one!" (*surat Yusuf* 12:46).

Siddiqi (A) صديقي (*siddiqiyy*): *nisba* (relation) through ancestry to the first Khalifa Abu Bakr al-Siddiq (d.634). Abdur Rahman Siddiqui (d.1953): Bengali political leader and editor of *Morning News*.

Siham (P) سهام (*sihaam*): arrows; pl. of Sahm سهم.

Sikandar (P) سكندر: Alexander. Sikandar Hayat Khan (1892-1942): Indian political leader.

Sikandar Shah (P) سكندر شاه: Bengal Sultan (1358-90).

---

[369] See Abd-el-Jawad, Hassan, 'A Linguistic and Socio-cultural Study of Personal Names in Jordan', *Anthropological Linguistics*, XXVIII, p. 84 (1986); Paxton, Evelyn, 'Arabic Names', *Asian Affairs*, LIX, p. 199 (1972).

[370] See Haykal, Muhammad Husayn, *The Life of Muhammad*, p. 620.

202

Male Names

Sikdar[371] (P) سكدر: peace keepers. Comp. شقدار.

Silm (A) سلم: peace. See Silma (f.).

Sina (A). See Ibn Sina.

Sinan[372] (A) سنان (*sinaan*): spear. Umm Sinan: a *sahaabia*.

> **Sinan-ud-Din** (A) سنان الدين (*sinaan al-din*): spear of the religion (Islam).

Siraj (A) سراج (*siraaj*) (سرج): lamp, light. In the following verse of the Qur'an, Muhammad (s) is described as *siraj munir*, a shining lamp: يايها النبي انا ارسلناك شاهدا ومبشرا ونذيرا وداعيا الى الله باذنه وسراجا منيرا "O Nabi (prophet), We have sent you as a witness and a bringer of good news and a warner, and as a summoner to Allah by His permission and as a shining lamp." (*surat al-Ahzaab* 33:45-46). See Chirag (P) چراغ; Misbah مصباح; Nibras نبراس (f.).

> **Siraj-ud-Dawlah** (A) سراج الدولة: lamp of the state. The last independent Nawab of Bengal who fought against Robert Clive at the historic Battle of Plassey (1757).

> **Siraj-ud-Din** (A) سراج الدين: lamp of the religion (Islam). Siraj-ud-Din Bahaadur Shaah II: the last Mughal emperor of India

---

[371] See Saif-ul-Islam, 'Cataloguing Bengali Muslim Names: problems and possible solutions', Librarianship & Archives Administration, *UNESCO J. of Information Science*, II, p. 38 (1980).

[372] "'Spear's point, a name of high antiquity". See Colebrooke, T. E., 'On the Proper Names of the Mohammadans', *Journal of the Royal Asiatic Society of Great Britain and Ireland*, XIII, p. 246 (1881).

Male Names

(1837-58).

Soad (A). See Saad.

Sobhan (A). See Subhan.

Sohel (P). See Suhayl.

Sohrab (P). See Suhrab.

Solaiman (A). See Sulayman.

Subah[373] (A) صباح (*subaah*): beautiful, graceful.

> **Subah-ud-Din** (A) صباح الدين (*subaah al-din*): beautiful (person) of the religion (Islam).

Subhan (A) سبحان (*subhaan*) (سبح): praise, glory. Al-Subhaan السبحان, the Glory: one of the names of Allah. *Subhaanalllah* سبحان الله, Glory to Allah. *Subhaana Rabbil 'Azeem* سبحان رب العظيم Glory to my Lord, the Greatest! *Subhaanallahi 'ammaa yasifun* سبحان الله عما يصفون "Glorified be Allah above all that they attribute to Him" (*surat al-Mu'minun* 23:91).

> **Abdus Subhan** (A) عبد السبحان (*'abd al-subhaan*): servant of the Glory.

Subhi (A): of or relating to Subh. See Subh (f.).

---

[373] "There are Kuwaiti personal names for the Sheikhs or ruling class in Kuwait, as... Subaah." See Yassin, M. Aziz F., 'Personal Names Address in Kuwaiti Arabic', *Anthropological Linguistics*, XX, p. 54.

Male Names

Sufi[374] (A) ‌صوفي (*sufiyy*): a mystic, someone believing in Sufi mysticism. Muhammad al-Sufi.[375]

Sufiyan (A) سفيان (*sufiyaan*): ship builder. A *sahaabi*.[376]

Suhail (A). See Suhayl.

Suhayl[377] (A) سهيل: Canopus, the second brightest star in the sky.[378] Suhail bin 'Amr:[379] a *sahaabi*.

Suhrab (P) سهراب (*suhraab*): son of the Iranian epic hero Rustam.

Suhrawardy. See Shahid.

Sulaiman (A). See Sulayman.

Sulayman (A) سليمان (*sulaymaan*): a Prophet, the biblical Solomon, son of Prophet Dawud. He is renowned for his wisdom granted by Allah (*surat al-Naml* 27:15). The Qur'an mentions that he had command over *jinn* and birds. وحشر لسليمان جنوده من الجن والانس والطير فهم يوزعون "And before Sulayman were marshalled his armies, of *jinns* and

---

[374] Originally it was an honorific title; now "a person is simply called Sufi or Sufiyya". See Schimmel, Annemarie, *Islamic Names*, p. 39.

[375] See Choueiri, Youssef, *Islamic Fundamentalism*, p. 87.

[376] See Keller, *Reliance of the Traveller* (Translated from the Arabic), p. 1032.

[377] See Colebrooke, T. E., 'On the Proper Names of the Mohammadans', *Journal of the Royal Asiatic Society of Great Britain and Ireland*, XIII, p. 247 (1881).

[378] See *Al-Mawrid: A Modern Arabic-English Dictionary*, p. 649.

[379] See Haykal, Muhammad Husayn, *The Life of Muhammad*, p. 172.

Male Names

men and birds, and they were all kept in order and ranks." (*surat al-Naml* 27:17). Sulayman invited Bilqis (Queen of Sheba) to accept Islam. See Bilqis (f.). Sulayman the Magnificent: Ottoman Khalifa (1494-1566).[380]

Suleyman (A). Sulayman.

Sultan (A) سلطان (*sultaan*): ruler, authority, power.[381] Title of a Muslim king, e.g. Sultan Salah ud-Din. واجعل لي من لدنك سلطانا نصيرا " "And grant me from your presence a sustaining power." (*surat Bani Israai'l* 17:80). See Haakim حاكم.

Suud (A) سعود (*su'uud*) (سعد): pl. of Sa'd سعد, good fortune.

---

[380] "Sulayman was known to his people by the honorific title of *al-Qanuni* (the lawgiver) because of the high esteem in which later generations held the codes which bore his name.[...] To Europeans, however, Sulayman was known as the Magnificent, and magnificent he was. His court was certainly one of the most resplendent in Eurasia." See Hitti, Philip K., *History of the Arabs*, pp. 713-14.

[381] See *The Oxford Encyclopaedia of the Modern Islamic World*, vol. IV, p. 135.

T

Taai (A) طائع (*taa'i'*) (طوع): obedient, willing (see *surat Fussilat* 41:11). Al-Taai: Abbasid Khalifa (974-91).

Tabari (A): Abu Ja'far Muhammad ibn Jarir Al-Tabari (838-923): famous historian[382] and commentator on the Qur'an, *Jami al-Bayan fi Tafsir al-Qur'an* which "became a standard work upon which later Koranic commentators drew."[383] The *nisba* al-Tabari connects him to his birth place Tabaristan in Persia.

Tabassum (A) تبسّم (بسم): smile. *Tabassama* فتبسم "[Sulayman] smiled" (*surat al-Naml* 27:19).

Tabataba'i. See Allama.

Tafazzul (A) تفضّل (*tafaddul*) (فضل): courteousness, favour, kindness, beneficence.

Tafazzul Husayn (A) تفضّل حسين (*tafaddul husayn*): favour of Husayn.

Ta Ha (A) طه (Taa Haa): mystic letters at the beginning of *surat Ta Ha* (20:1), from which the *sura* derives its title. An epithet of Muhammad (s).

---

[382] "His monumental work on universal history [*Annals of the Apostles and Kings*], the first complete one in the Arabic tongue...begins with the creation of the world and goes down to A.H. 302 (915)." See Hitti, Philip K., *History of the Arabs*, p. 390.

[383] *Ibid.*

Male Names

Tahir (A) طاهر (*taahir*) (طهر): virtuous, pure.

Al-Tahir (A) الطاهر: nickname of Abdullah, son[384] of Muhammad (s), who died in infancy.

Tahmid (A) تحميد (*tahmeed*) (حمد): praising Allah, saying *al-hamdu li-llaah* الحمد لله.

Tahsin (A) تحسين (*tahseen*) (حسن): adornment, ornament, decoration, embellishment, betterment. Ata Khan Tahsin: eminent eighteenth-century Indian writer in Urdu.[385]

Taib (A) تائب (*taa'ib*) (توب): repentant, penitent. التائبون "Those who turn repentant (to Allah)..." (*surat al-Tawba* 9:112).

Taif (A) طيف: vision, spectre.

Taif-ur-Rahman (A) طيف الرحمن (*taif al-rahmaan*): vision of the Merciful (Allah).

Taisir (A) تيسير (*taiseer*) (يسر): making easy, facilitating, simplification.

Taj (A) تاج (taaj): crown.

Taj Khan (A+P) تاج خان: lord of Chunar in Bengal (1531).

Taj-ud-Din (A) تاج الدين: crown of the religion (Islam). Taj-ud-Din Ibrahim: king of Central Anatolia (1424).

---

[384] See Haykal, Muhammad Husayn, *The Life of Muhammad*, p. 68.

[385] See Aziz, Ahmad, *An Intellectual History of Islam in India*, p. 106.

Male Names

Taj-ul-Islam (A) تاج الإسلام: crown of Islam.

Tajammul (A) تجمّل (جمل): dignity, magnificence, splendour, adornment.

Tajammul Husayn (A) تجمّل حسين: adornment of Husayn.

Talal[386] (A) طلال (*talaal*): "طلالة, being pleasant, agreeable, joy, a beautiful...form or appearance."[387] Talal I: king of Jordan (1951-2).

Taleb (A). See Talib.

Taleem (A). See Talim.

Talib (A) طالب (*taalib*) (طلب): student, seeker, pursuer.

Abu Talib (A) أبو طالب: Abu Talib ibn Abd al-Muttalib: See Abu.

Talim (A) تعليم (*ta'leem*) (علم): education, instruction.

Talukdar[388] (A+P) تعلق دار: small landlord. Originally a title, now used as a family name.

Tamim (A) تميم (*tameem*) (تمّ): well-formed, solid. Ruler in North

---

[386] It should be noted that Talal طلال means 'ruins', while Tilal طلال (*tilaal*) is pl. of Tall طلّ, drizzle, dew (see *surat al-Baqarah* 2: 265).

[387] See Steingass, F., *A Comprehensive Persian-English Dictionary*, p. 817.

[388] See Steingass, F., *A Comprehensive Persian-English Dictionary*, p. 309; Saif-ul-Islam, 'Cataloguing Bengali Muslim Names: problems and possible solutions', *UNESCO J. of Information Science*, II, p. 38 (1980).

Male Names

Africa (1062-1108). Abu Ruqayya Tamim: a *sahaabi*.[389]

Tamir (A) تامر (*taamir*): rich or abounding in dates.

Tamiz (A) تمييز (*tamyeez*) (ميز): distinction, distinguishing, judgment.

Tamiz-ud-Din (A) تمييز الدين: distinction of the religion (Islam).

Tamjid (A) تمجيد (*tamjeed*) (مجد): praise, glorification, extolment.

Tanvir (A) تنوير (*tanweer*) (نور): illumination, blossoming.

Tanzil (A) تنزيل (*tanzeel*) (نزل): revelation, sending down. تنزيل العزيز الرحيم "A revelation of the All-mighty, the Merciful." (*surat Ya Sin* 36:5).

Tanzil-ur-Rahman (A) تنزيل الرحمن (*tanzil al-rahmaan*) revelation of the Merciful (Allah).

Taqi (A) تقي (*taqiyy*) (وقي): Godfearing, devout, pious. تلك الجنة التي نورث من عبادنا من كان تقيا "This is the *Jannah* [Paradise] which We grant the Godfearing among Our servants to inherit." (*surat Maryam* 19:63). See Muttaqi متقي. Muhammad al-Jawaad Taqi (809-835): the ninth Imam of the Shi'ites.[390]

Taqi-ud-Din (A) تقي الدين: Godfearing (person) of the religion (Islam). Taqi ud-Din Ahmad ibn Taymiyah: see Ibn

---

[389] See An-Nawawi, *Forty Hadith*, p. 44.

[390] See Al-Tabatabai, Allamah Sayyid Muhammad Husayn, *Shi'ite Islam*, p. 207.

210

Male Names

Taymiyah. Takiyeddin: chief astronomer of the Ottoman Court.[391]

Tarib (A) طرب: lively, gleeful, merry.

Tariq (A) طارق (*taariq*): morning star, night star (see *surat al-Taariq* 86:1-2). *Al-Tarriq* الطارق: title of the 86th *sura* of the Qur'an.

> **Tariq Ibn Ziyad** (A) طارق بن زياد: celebrated general who invaded Spain bringing it under Muslim rule for eight centuries (d.720). Gibraltar (in Arabic, *jabal tariq*, mountain of Tariq), where he landed before conquering Spain, bears his name.

Tarub (A) طروب (طرب): lively, gleeful, merry.

Tasadduq (A) تصدّق (صدق): beneficence, benevolence.

> **Tasadduq Husayn** (A) تصدّق حسين: benevolence of Husayn.

Taslim (A) تسليم (*tasleem*) (سلم): greeting, salutation. يايها الذين آمنوا صلوا عليه وسلموا تسليما "O you who believe! Ask blessings on him (Muhammad) and salute him with a worthy salutation." (*surat al-Ahzaab* 33:56).

Taufik (A). See Tawfiq.

Taufiq (A). See Tawfiq.

Tauhid (A). See Tawhid.

---

[391] See Lewis, Bernard, *The Middle East*, p. 210.

Male Names

Tauqir (A). See Tawqir.

Tawfiq (A) توفيق (*tawfeeq*) (وفق): prosperity, good luck, good-fortune, success (granted by Allah). و ما توفيقي الا باش "[Shu'ayb said:] My success is granted only by Allah." (*surat Hud* 11:88). Ruler of Egypt (1879-92).

Tawhid (A) توحيد (*tawheed*) (وحد): belief in the unity of Allah.

Tawqir (A) توقير (*tawqeer*) (وقر): honour, great respect, high regard.

Tawwab (A) تواب (*tawwaab*) (توب): merciful, forgiving. Al-Tawwaab التواب, the All-compassionate: one of the names of Allah. وانا التواب الرحيم "I am the most Forgiving, the most Merciful." (*surat al-Baqarah* 2:160). See Ghafur غفور.

Abdut Tawwab (A) عبد التواب ('*abd al-tawwab*): servant of the most Forgiving.

Taysir (A). See Taisir.

Tayyib (A) طيّب (*tayyib*) (طيب): good, good-natured, generous, good-tempered. ولا تتبدلوا الخبيث بالطيب "Do not exchange the bad for the good. " (*surat al-Nisaa'* 4:2).

Al-Tayyib (A) الطيّب: nickname of Abdullah,[392] son of Muhammad (s) who died in infancy.

Tazim (A) تعظيم (*ta'zeem*): glorification, exaltation, honour.

---

[392] See Haykal, Muhammad Husayn, *The Life of Muhammad*, p. 68.

Male Names

Tazim-ud-Din (A) تعظيم الدين: glorification of the religion (Islam).

Thaabit (A): See Sabit ثابت.

Thanvi. See Ashraf.

Tirmidhi (A). See Tirmizi.

Tirmizi (A) الترمذي (*al-tirmidhiyy*): Abu Isa Muhammad al-Tirmidhi (824-92): author of one of the *sahih hadith*. "The *nisba* al-Tirmidhi connects him with Tirmidh, a place...where he is said to have died."[393]

Torab (A). See Turab.

Tufayl (A) طفيل: diminutive of Tifl طفل, baby. Al-Tufayl ibn 'Amr: a *sahaabi*.[394]

Turab (A) تراب (*turaab*): soil, dust. والله خلقكم من تراب ثم من نطفة ثم جعلكم ازواجا "Allah created you from dust; then from a sperm-drop; then He made you in pairs." (*surat Faatir* 35:11).

> **Abu Turab** (A) أبو تراب: a *kunya* of Khalifa Ali, the fourth of the 'rightly guided' khalifas, conferred upon him by Muhammad (s).

---

[393] See Gibb, H A R & Kramers, J H., *Shorter Encyclopaedia of Islam*, p. 595.

[394] See Haykal, Muhammad Husayn, *The Life of Muhammad*, p. 119. "And from Yemen came Abu Huraira and Tufail..." (Grand Sheikh of Al-Azhar University, 'Message from His Eminence' in Weeramantry, *Islamic Jurisprudence*, p. xviii).

Male Names

U

Ubaid (A). See Ubayd عُبَيْد.

Ubayd (A) عُبَيْد (عَبْد): diminutive of Abd عَبْد, servant, servant of lower rank.

Ubaydullah (A) عُبَيْد الله ('*ubayd allah*): lowly servant of Allah. Cousin of Muhammad (s).[395] Ubayd Allah al-Mahdi (909-34): the first Fatimid Khalifa.

Ula (A) عُلى ('*ulaa*): high rank, prestige, glory. See Rif'at رِفْعة.

Umar (A) عُمَر ('*umar*): the meaning of 'Umar'[396] is linked with 'Aamir',[397] 'prosperous, full of life, large, substantial'. The root word *umr* عُمْر, means 'life' (*surat Faatir* 35:11).

Umar bin al-Khattab (A) عُمَر بن الخطّاب (d.644): the second of the 'rightly guided' Khalifas (634-44) who earned the title *al-Faruq* (see Faruq). He was one of the ten *sahaabis* to whom Muhammad (s) gave the good news of

---

[395] See Haykal, Muhammad Husayn, *The Life of Muhammad*, p. 637.

[396] It may be noted that 'Umar' is plural of 'Umrah' عُمْرة , meaning 'minor pilgrimage to Makkah'. See Madina, Maan Z., *Arabic-English Dictionary of the Modern Literary Language*, p. 456; Steingass, F., *A Comprehensive Persian-English Dictionary*, p. 866. See *surat al-Baqarah* 2:196.

[397] See Al-Arnaut, Shafiq, *Qamus al-Asma' al-Arabiyya* [Dictionary of Arabic Names] (in Arabic), p. 68; Colebrooke, T. E., 'On the Proper Names of the Mohammadans', *Journal of the Royal Asiatic Society of Great Britain and Ireland*, XIII, pp. 241-2 (1881).

Male Names

entering into paradise.[398]

Umar Khayyam (A) عمر خيّام: celebrated Persian poet, author of *Rubaiyyat* (c.1048-c.1129).[399] See Khayyam.

Umdat (A) عمدة: support. See Imad عماد.

Umdat-ud-Dawlah[400] (A) عمدة الدولة: support of the state.

Usama (A) اسامة (*usaamah*): lion. Usama ibn Zayd (d.673): a *sahaabi*.[401]

Usman (*'uthmaan*) **ibn 'Affaan** (A) عثمان بن عفان: the third of the 'rightly guided' Khalifas (644-56). He married two daughters of Muhammad (s), Ruqayya and after her death, Umm Kulthum. He was one of the ten *sahaabis* to whom Muhammad (s) gave the good news of entering into paradise.[402] Under his guidance the Qur'an was compiled in its final form. Usman I: founder (1299-1326) of the Ottoman dynasty

---

[398] See Lings, Martin, *Muhammad*, p. 329.

[399] "[T]he algebrist 'Umar (or Omar) Khayyam, famous in the east for his mathematical writings, and in the West for his quatrains..." See Lewis, Bernard, *The Middle East*, p. 266.

[400] See Colebrooke, T. E., 'On the Proper Names of the Mohammadans', *Journal of the Royal Asiatic Society of Great Britain and Ireland*, XI, p. 207 (1879).

[401] See *Riyadh-us-Saleheen*, vol I, p. 236; Haykal, Muhammad Husayn, *The Life of Muhammad*, p. 497.

[402] See Lings, Martin, *Muhammad*, p. 329.

Male Names

(1299-1924).[403]

Uzayr (A) عزير: a Prophet (*surat al-Tawbah* 9:30), the biblical Ezra.

---

[403] "This was the greatest Moslem state of modern times; not only that, but one of the most enduring Moslem states of all time. No less than thirty-six sultans, all in the direct male line of 'Uthman, reigned from 1300 to 1922." See Hitti, Philip K., *History of the Arabs*, p. 713.

W

Waahid (A) واحد (وحد): one, unique, matchless. Al-Waahid الواحد, the One: one of the names of Allah. هو الله الواحد القهار "He is Allah, the One, the Absolute."(*surat al-Zumar* 39:4). See Farid فريد; Wahid وحيد.

> **Abdul Waahid** (A) عبد الواحد (*'abd al-waahid*): servant of the One. Ruler of North Africa and Spain (1224).

Waasiq (A) واثق (*waathiq*) (وثق): confident, sure, certain. See Wasiq (*wathiq*) وثيق, strong. Al-Waasiq (*al-waathiq*): Abbasid Khalifa (842-47).

Wadud (A) ودود (*wadood*) (ودّ): lover, warm-hearted, affectionate. Al-Wadud الودود, the All-loving: one of the names of Allah. وهو الغفور الودود "And He is the Forgiving, the All-loving." (*surat al-Buruj* 85:14).

> **Abdul Wadud** (A) عبد الودود (*'abd al-wadood*): servant of the All-loving.

Wafai (A) وفائي (*wafaa'iyy*) (وفى): associated with faithfulness, fidelity, loyalty, faith.

Wafi (A) وفي (*wafiyy*) (وفى): true, trustworthy, reliable, perfect, complete. Comp. adj.: Awfaa أوفى, more reliable (see *surat al-Tawba* 9:111). See Salih صالح; Barr بر.

Wafiq (A) وفيق (*wafeeq*) (وفق): companion, friend. See Rafiq رفيق.

217

Male Names

Wahhab (A) وهَّاب (*wahhaab*) (وهب): donor, grantor. Al-Wahhab الوهاب, the All-giver: one of the names of Allah. قال رب اغفر لي وهب لي ملكا لا ينبغي لاحد من بعدي انك انت الوهاب "He [Sulayman] said: forgive me and bestow on me sovereignty such as shall not belong to any after me: For You are the Grantor of bounties [without measure]". (*surat Saad* 38:35).

> **Abdul Wahhab** (A) عبد الوهاب (*'abd al-wahhab*): servant of the All-giver. Muhammad ibn Abd al-Wahhab (1703-87): founder of the Wahhabi movement.[404]

Wahid (A) وحيد (*waheed*) (وحد): unique, matchless, singular. See Farid فريد; Waahid واحد.

> **Wahid-ud-Din** (A) وحيد الدين: unique (manifestation) of the religion (Islam). Muhammad Wahid-ud-Din: king of Anatolia (1918-22).

> **Wahid-uz-Zaman** (A) وحيد الزمان: unique (person) of the age.

Waiz (A)[405] واعظ (*waa'iz*): admonisher, preacher.

Wajed (A). See Wajid.

Wajid (A) واجد (*waajid*) (وجد): finder, lover. Al-Waajid الواجد, the

---

[404] "The most impressive reform of modern times was the violent and austere call to primitive purity launched by Muhammad bin 'Abd al-Wahhab (d. 1792), which arose from the emptiness of the Arabian desert and got lost in the superfluities of oil-wealth." See Fernandez-Armesto, Felipe, *Millennium*, p. 563.

[405] See Bland, N., *Journal of the Royal Asiatic Society*, XVI, p. 155.

Male Names

Finder: one of the names of Allah.

Wajih (A) وجيه (*wajeeh*) (وجه): noble, honoured, well-esteemed, illustrious. اسمه المسيح عيسى ابن مريم وجيها في الدنيا والآخرة "His name is Masih, Isa, son of Maryam, high honoured in this world and the Hereafter." (*surat Aal 'Imraan* 3:45).

Wakil (A) وكيل (*wakeel*) (وكل): advocate, representative. Al-Wakeel الوكيل, the Trustee: one of the names of Allah. والله على كل شيء وكيل "And Allah is in charge of all things." (*surat Hud* 11:12). See Naib نائب.

Wali (A) ولي (*waliyy*): guardian, protector, friend, saint. Al-Waliyy الولي, the Protector: one of the names of Allah. وهو الولي الحميد "He is the Protecting Friend, the Praiseworthy." (*surat al-Shuraa* 42:28).

Waliullah (A) ولي الله (*wali allah*): friend of Allah. An epithet of Muhammad (s). الا ان اولياء الله لا خوف عليهم ولا هم يحزنون "Behold! verily the friends of Allah are [those] on whom fear [comes] not, nor shall they grieve." (*surat Yunus* 10:62). Bahmanid Sultan in Northern Deccan (India) (1522-25).

Shah Waliullah (P+A) شاه ولي الله (1703-1762): "the foremost *'alim* of eighteenth-century India"[406] and translator of the Qur'an in Persian.

Walid (A) وليد (*waleed*) (ولد): newborn, newborn child, nascent, new,

---

[406] See *The Oxford Encyclopaedia of the Modern Islamic World*, vol. I, p. 2.

Male Names

boy, son. Al-Walid الوليد: Umayyad khalifa (705-715).[407]

Waqar (A) وقار (*waqaar*) (وقر): majesty, dignity, veneration. ما لكم
لا ترجون لله وقارا "What is the matter with you that you are not
conscious of Allah's majesty...?" (*surat Nuh* 71:13). Waqar al-Mulk: a
title of honour.

Waris (A) وارث (*waarith*) (ورث): heir, inheritor, successor. Al-Waaris
الوارث, the Inheritor: one of the names of Allah. وزكريا اذ نادى
ربه رب لا تذرني فردا وانت خير الوارثين "And [remember]
Zakariya, when he cried to his Lord: My Lord! Leave me not childless,
though You are the best of inheritors." (*surat al-Anbiyaa'* 21:89).

Wasi (A) واسع (*waasi'*) (وسع): broad-minded, liberal, learned, scholarly.
Al-Waasi' الواسع, the All-embracing: one of the names of Allah. ان
الله واسع عليم "Allah is All-embracing, All-knowing." (*surat al-Baqarah*
2:115).

Abdul Wasi (A) عبد الواسع (*abd al-waasi'*): servant of the
All-embracing.

Wasim (A) وسيم (*waseem*) (وسم): handsome.

Wasim-ud-Din (A) وسيم الدين: handsome (person) of the
religion (Islam).

---

[407] "During the reigns of al-Walid and Hisham the Islamic empire reached its greatest
expansion, stretching from the shores of the Atlantic Ocean and the Pyrenes to the Indus
and the confines of China--an extent hardly rivalled in ancient times and surpassed in
modern times only by the British and Russian empires." See Hitti, Philip K., *History of
the Arabs*, p. 206.

Male Names

Wasiq (A) وثـيق (*watheeq*) (وثق): solid, strong, secure. See Waasiq واثق (*waathiq*), confident.

Wazir (A) وزير (*wazeer*) (وزر): minister, vizier (see *surat al-Furqaan* 25:35).

Wilayat (A) ولاية (*wilaayah*): custody, guardianship.

Male Names

Y

Yahya (A) يحيى (*yahyaa*): a Prophet, the biblical John, son of Prophet Zakariya. وزكريا ويحيى وعيسى والياس كل من الصالحين "And Zakariya and Yahya and 'Isa and Ilyaas. Each one [of them] was of the righteous." (*surat al-An'aam* 6:85).

Yamin (A) يمين (*yameen*) (يمن) (f.): right, right side, right hand. لأصحاب اليمين "...for the companions of the right-hand." (see *surat al-Waaqi'ah* 56:38).

Yaqub (A) يعقوب (*ya'qoob*): a Prophet, the biblical Jacob, son of Prophet Ishaq. وهبنا له اسحاق ويعقوب وكلا جعلنا نبيا "We bestowed on him (Ibrahim) Ishaq (as a son) and Yaqub [as a grandson] and each one of them We made a Prophet." (*surat Maryam* 19:49).

Yaqut (A) ياقوت (*yaaqoot*): ruby, sapphire, topaz (see *surat al-Rahmaan* 55:58).

Yaqzan (A) يقظان (*yaqzaan*) (يقظ): vigilant, awake, on the alert. Ruler in Western Algeria (907-9).

Yar (P) يار (*yaar*): friend.

Shahr yar (P) شهر يار. See Shahryar.

Yar Muhammad (P+A) يار محمد: friend of Muhammad (s).

Male Names

Yasar[408] (A) يسار (*yasaar*) (يسر): prosperity, wealth, affluence, ease. See Maisara ميسرة (f.).

Yasin (A) يس (*ya seen*): the opening letters of the first verse of *surat Ya Sin* (36:1). An epithet of Muhammad (s).

Yasir (A) ياسر (*yaasir*): easy. 'Ammar bin Yasir: a *sahaabi*.

Youssef (A). See Yusuf.

Yumn (A) يمن: happiness.

    Abul Yumn (A) أبو اليمن: father of happiness.

Yunus (A) يونس: a Prophet, the biblical Jonah. Yunus يونس: title of the 10th *sura* of the Qur'an. He is known as Zu-n Noon (*dhu al-Noon*), 'Lord of the fish'. The Qur'an narrates that he was swallowed by a big fish and later rescued by the grace of Allah. (See *surat al-Anbiyaa'* 21:87-88). وان يونس لمن المرسلين "And Yunus was one among those sent [by Us]." (*surat al-Saffat* 37:139).

Yusri (A) يسري (*yusriy*): easy. See Yasir.

Yusuf (A) يوسف: a Prophet, the biblical Joseph, son of Prophet Yaqub (see *surat al-An'aam* 6:84). Yusuf يوسف: title of the 12th *sura* of the Qur'an. This *sura* relates that Prophet Yusuf while an infant told his father, Prophet Yaqub that he had dreamt that eleven stars, the sun and the moon had prostrated before him (12:4). This *sura* also tells how the

---

[408] This name is not recommended by the Prophet (s). Narrated by Muslim: "Do not name your boy Yasaar, nor Rabaah, nor Nujayh, nor Aflah..." See Sabiq, Sayyid, *Fiqh us-Sunnah*, vol. IV, p. 311.

wife of Aziz (Zulaykha) was smitten by his beauty. See Jamal (m.); Malak (m.); Zulaykha (f.).

Abu Yusuf (A) أبو يوسف (735-795): one of the chief pupils of Imam Abu Hanifa who became chief judge during the Abbasid regime.

Male Names

Z

Zaahir (A) ظاهر (ظهر): distinct, manifest, plain, clear. Al-Zaahir الظاهر, the Evident: one of the names of Allah. (see *surat al-Hadeed* 57:3). Comp. Zahir ظهير, helper.

Abduz Zaahir (A) عبد الظاهر (*'abd al-zaahir*): servant of the Evident.

Muhammad Zaahir Shaah (A+P) محمد ظاهر شاه: Afghan king (1933).

Zaaid (A) زائد (*zaa'id*): increasing, exceeding, excessive, growing, surplus.

Zaaki (A) زاكي (*zaakiy*). See Zaki زكيّ.

Zafar (A) ظفر: victory. See Nasr نصر.

Zafarullah (A) ظفر الله (*zafar allah*): victory of Allah.

Zafir (A) ظافر (*zaafir*) (ظفر): victorious, triumphant, winner, conqueror. See Ghalib غالب; Muzaffar مظفر; Muntasir منتصر. Al-Zafir: Fatimid Khalifa (1149-54).

Zaghlul (A) زغلول (*zaglool*): young pigeon. Sa'd Zaghlul (d.1927): Egyptian nationalist leader.

Zahed (A). See Zahid.

Male Names

Zahi (A) زاهي (*zaahii*) (زهو): beautiful, brilliant, glowing.

Zahid (A) زاهد (*zaahid*) (زهد): devout, ascetic.

Zahir (A) ظهير (*zaheer*) (ظهر): helper, supporter, protector, patron. والملائكة بعد ذلك ظهير "And furthermore the angels are his [Muhammad's] helpers." (*surat al-Tahreem* 66:4). Comp. Zaahir ظاهر, distinct. Zahir Shah: king of Afghanistan (1933-73).

> **Zahir-ud-Din** (A) ظهير الدين: helper of the religion (Islam). Zahir-ud-Din Babur (d.1530): founder of the Mughal empire.

> **Zahir-ud-Dawlah**[409] (A) ظهير الدولة: helper of the state.

Zahin (A) ذهين (*dhaheen*) (ذهن): sagacious, ingenious.

Zahur (A) ظهور (ظهر): prominent, high.

Zaid (A). See Zayd.

Zaim (A) زعيم (*za'eem*): leader, Chief.

> **Zaim-ud-Din** (A) زعيم الدين: leader of the religion (Islam).

Zain (A). See Zayn.

Zakaai (A) ذكائي (*dhakaa'iyy*): intelligent, bright, brilliant.

Zakaria (A) زكريا (*zakariyaa*): a Prophet, the biblical Zachariah and

---

[409] See Colebrooke, T. E., 'On the Proper Names of the Mohammadans', *Journal of the Royal Asiatic Society of Great Britain and Ireland*, XI, p. 207 (1879).

Male Names

father of Prophet Yahya (see *surat Maryam* 19:7).

Zaker (A). See Zakir.

Zaki (A) ˚زكي (*zakiyy*): pure, chaste, sinless. قال انما انا رسول ربك
لأهب لك غلاما زكيا "He said: I am only a Messenger of your Lord, to
give you [Maryam] a son most pure." (*surat Maryam* 19:19). See Zaaki
زاكي. Comp. Zaki (*dhakiyy*) ˚ذكي, intelligent, bright, brilliant.

> **Zakiy-ud-Din** (A) ˚زكي الدين: pure (person) of the religion
> (Islam).

Zakir (A) ذاكر (*dhaakir*) (ذكر): one who glorifies or eulogises Allah.
والذاكرين الله كثيرا والذاكرات اعد الله لهم مغفرة واجرا عظيما
"...men who remember Allah much and women who remember, Allah has
prepared for them *maghfira* (forgiveness) and a vast reward." (*surat al-
Ahzaab* 33:35). Zakir Husain[410] (1897-1969): Vice-President of India
(1962-67).

Zaman (A) زمان (*zamaan*): time, age, era.

> **Nur-uz-Zaman** (A) نور الزمان: light of the age.

> **Shams-uz-Zaman** (A) شمس الزمان: sun of the age.

> **Zaman Shah** (A+P) زمان شاه: king of the age.   King of
> Afghanistan (1793-1800).

Zamil (A) زميل (*zameel*): companion, friend. See Rafeeq رفيق.

---

[410] Such names are improper on the ground that a Muslim glorifies only Allah.

Male Names

Zamir (A) ضمير (*dameer*) (ضمر): heart, mind, conscience.

Zamir-ud-Din (A) ضمير الدين (*damir al-din*): heart of the religion (Islam).

Zarif (A) ظريف (*zareef*) (ظرف): elegant, witty, graceful.

Zayan (A) زيان (*zayaan*) (زين): beautiful, graceful.

Zayd[411] (A) زيد: growth, increase, increment, addition. Zayd ibn Harisa (*haarithah*): adopted son of Muhammad (s) (see *surat al-Ahzaab* 33:37). Comp. Zaaid زائد: increasing.

Zaydan (A) زيدان (*zaydaan*): growth and increase.

Zayn (A) زين: beautiful, pretty, beauty, grace.

Zayn-ud-Din (A) زين الدين: grace of the religion (Islam). Sultan of Egypt (1295-97); a Bengali poet.[412]

Zayn-ul-Abidin (A) زين العابدين: ornament of the worshippers (of Allah). Title of Imam Sajjad, son of Imam Husayn and the fourth Imam of the Shi'ites.[413]

---

[411] When Zayd al-Khayl came to pay allegiance to Muhammad (s), "[t]he Prophet then changed the name of his guest from Zayd al-Khayl (meaning literally, 'increase of horses') to Zayd al-Khayr ('increase of goodness'). See Haykal, Muhammad Husayn, *The Life of Muhammad*, p. 431.

[412] He was the court poet of Yusuf Shah (1474-81) and the author of *Rasul Vijay* (Victory of the Prophet). See Aziz, Ahmad, *An Intellectual History of Islam*, p. 113.

[413] See Al-Tabatabai, Allamah Sayyid Muhammad Husayn, *Shi'ite Islam*, p. 201.

Male Names

Zhobin (P) ژوبین (*zhobeen*): kind of spear.[414]

Zia (A) ضياء (*diyaa'*) (ضوء): light, glow, illumination. جعل الذي هو
ضياء الشمس "He [Allah] it is who has made the sun a [source of]
radiant light." (*surat Yunus* 10:5). See Nur نور.

> **Zia-ud-Din** (A) ضياء الدين (*diaa' al-din*): light of the religion
> (Islam). Ziauddin Barni (1282-1356): famous historian, who wrote
> on Muslim rule in India, author of *Tarikh-i-Firuz Shahi*.[415]

> **Zia-ul-Haqq** (A) ضياء الحق (*diaa' al-haqq*): light of the
> Truth (Allah). Muhammad Zia ul-Haq (d.1988): President of
> Pakistan (1978-88) who "moved towards establishing a 'truly
> Islamic order' in Pakistan."[416]

> **Zia-ur-Rahman** (A) ضياء الرحمن (*diaa' al-rahmaan*): light
> of the most Gracious (Allah). Ziaur Rahman (d.1981):
> President of Bangladesh who "made Islam the first basic
> principle of the Constitution."[417]

Ziad (A). See Ziyad.

Zihni (A) ذهني (*dhihniyy*): intellectual, cerebral.

Zill (A) ظل: shadow, shade.

---

[414] See Steingass, F., *A Comprehensive Persian-English Dictionary*, p. 637.

[415] See Majumdar, R. C., *et al.*, *An Advanced History of India*, p. 271.

[416] See *Encyclopedia of the Third World*, vol. II, p. 1472.

[417] See *Encyclopedia of the Third World*, vol. I, p. 115.

Male Names

Zill Allah[418] (A) الله ظل‎: shadow of Allah.

Zill-ur-Rahman (A) الرحمن ظل‎ (*zill al-rahmaan*): shadow of the Merciful (Allah), i.e. Khalifa (vicegerent) of Allah.

Ziyad (A) زياد‎ (*ziyaad*) (زيد‎): increase, addition, surplus. Ziyad bin Naim: a *sahaabi*.

Ziyada (A) زيادة‎ (*ziyaadah*) (زيد‎): increase, addition, surplus, superabundance. See Faiz فيض‎ (*faid*); Ziyada زيادة‎.

Ziyadatullah (A) الله زيادة‎ (*ziyaadat allah*): surplus bestowed by Allah.

Ziyan (A) زيان‎ (*ziyaan*) (زين‎): ornament, decoration. See Zinat زينة‎ (f.).

Zoha (A). See Zuha (*duhaa*).

Zubair (A). See Zubayr.

Zubayr (A) زبير‎: diminutive of Zubrah زبرة‎, small piece of iron.

Al-Zubayr ibn al-'Awwaam (A) العوام بن الزبير‎ (d.656): cousin of Muhammad (s) who was the fifth convert to Islam.[419]

---

[418] See Colebrooke, T. E., 'On the Proper Names of the Mohammadans', *Journal of the Royal Asiatic Society of Great Britain and Ireland*, XI, p. 215 (1879).

[419] See Haykal, Muhammad Husayn, *The Life of Muhammad*, p. 83; Keller, *Reliance of the Traveller*, p. 643. "[H]e is one of the ten to whom Paradise was promised by Muhammad (s)". See *Shorter Encyclopaedia of Islam*, p. 660.

Male Names

Zuha (A) ضحى (*duhaa*): forenoon. *Al-Dhuaa* الضحى: title of the 93rd *sura* of the Qur'an. كانهم يوم يرونها لم يلبثوا الا عشية او ضحاها "On the day when they behold it, it will be as if they had tarried but for an evening or the morning thereof." (*surat al-Naazi'aat* 79:46).

Shams-uz-Zuha (A) شمس الضحى (*shams al-duhaa*): sun of the forenoon.

Zuhair (A) زهير: small flower.

Zuhur (A) ظهور (ظهر): fame, splendour, emergence. See Zuhur (f.). Comp. Zuhur زهور, flowers.

Zuhur-ul-Islam (A) ظهور الإسلام: fame of Islam.

Zulfiqar[420] (A). See Zulfaqar. Zulfikar Ali Bhutto (1928-79): President (1971-73) and Prime Minister (1973-78) of Pakistan. See Zulfaqar.

Zulfaqar (A) ذو الفقار (*dhu al-faqaar*): the cleaver of vertebrae.[421] *Faqaar* is pl. of *faqaarah*, spine.[422] Name of the sword of Muhammad

---

[420] "[Ali's] mysterious two-edged sword *Dhu'l-fiqar* is not only used as a proper name." See Schimmel, Annemarie, *Islamic Names*, p. 34. See Colebrooke, T. E., 'On the Proper Names of the Mohammadans', *Journal of the Royal Asiatic Society of Great Britain and Ireland*, XI, p. 210 (1879).

[421] See Hitti, Philip K., *History of the Arabs*, p. 183.

[422] See Steingass, F., *A Comprehensive Persian-English Dictionary*, p. 934; Cowan, J Milton (ed.) Hans Wehr, *A Dictionary of Modern Written Arabic*, p. 723.

Male Names

(s) which was inherited by Khalifa Ali.[423]   See Zulfiqar.

Zul Qarnayn[424] (A) ذو القرنين (*dhu al-qarnayn*) "owner of the two horns" i.e. world conqueror. A king of ancient times (see *surat al-Kahf* 18:83). King of Anatolia (1152-62).

Zu-n Noon (A) ذو النون (*dhu al-noon*): 'Lord of the fish', an epithet of Prophet Yunus who was swallowed by a big fish and later rescued by the grace of Allah   (see *surat al-Anbiyaa'* 21:87-88).   Well-known Egyptian Sufi (796-859); king of Anatolia (1142).

---

[423] See Hitti, Philip K., *History of the Arabs*, p. 183; Colebrooke, T. E., 'On the Proper Names of the Mohammadans', *Journal of the Royal Asiatic Society of Great Britain and Ireland*, XI, p. 210 (1879).

[424] "Popular opinion identifies Zul Qarnain with Alexander the Great." See Ali, Yusuf, *The Holy Qur'an*, p. 845, n. 2428. "In the case of Dhu'l Karnein, possessor of the two horns, which appears in the Koran, is supposed to apply to Alexander the Great, but it was also borne by other princes." See Colebrooke, T. E., 'On the Proper Names of the Mohammadans', *Journal of the Royal Asiatic Society of Great Britain and Ireland*, XI, p. 212 (1879).

FEMALE NAMES

A

Aalaa (A) آلاء (*aalaa'*): pl. of إلى,[1] benefit, favour, blessing. فاذكروا آلآء الله لعلكم تفلحون "Remember (all) the bounties of your Lord, that you may be successful" (*surat al-A'raaf* 7:69).

Aalam (A) عالم (*'aalam*) (علم): world; sing. of *'Aalameen* عالمين. الحمد لله رب العالمين "Praise be to Allah, Lord of the worlds." (*surat al-Faatihah* 1:2). See Dunya دنيا. Comp. Alam علم, flag. See Aalam (m.).

> **Aalam Ara** (A+P) عالم آرا (*'aalam aaraa*): adorning the world.

Aalia (A). See Aaliya.

Aaliya (A). عالية (*'aaliyah*): high, tall, towering, lofty, exalted, high-ranking, sublime, superior, excellent; fem. of Aali.

Aamina (A) آمنة (*aaminah*): mother of Muhammad (s). Comp. Amina أمينة, trustworthy.

Aamira (A) عامرة (*'aamirah*) (عمر): prosperous, full of life, large, substantial; fem. of 'Aamir.

Aaqiba (A). See Aqiba عاقبة.

Aaqila (A) عاقلة (*'aaqilah*): wise, judicious, intelligent, prudent; fem.

---

[1] See Madina, Maan Z., *Arabic-English Dictionary of the Modern Literary Language*, p. 21.

of Aaqil. Comp. Aqila عقيلة, the best.

Aarifa (A) عارفة (*'aarifah*): learned, expert, authority; fem. of Aarif. See Areefa عريفة, learned.

Abeda (A). See Abida.

Abida (A) عابدة (*'aabidah*): worshipper, adorer, devout; fem. of Abid. See Abid (m.).

Abir (A) عبير (*'abeer*) (عبر): fragrance, aroma, scent, perfume composed of musk, sandal-wood, and rose-water. See Ambarin عنبرين.

Abla (A) عبلة (*'ablah*): well-rounded, perfectly formed, a woman possessing a beautiful figure.

Adala (A) عدالة (*'adaalah*): justice.

Adiba (A) أديبة (*'adeebah*): polite, well-mannered, well-bred, courteous, polished, writer; fem. of Adib.

Adila (A) عادلة (*'aadilah*): honest, upright, righteous; fem. of Adil.

Afaf (A) عفاف (*'afaaf*) (عف): chastity, purity, honesty, righteousness, modesty, decency.

Afia (A) عافية (*'aafiyah*) (عفو): good health, vigour, vitality.

Afifa (A) عفيفة (*'afeefah*): chaste, virtuous, honest, righteous, upright, decent; fem. of Afif.

Afkar (A) أفكار (*afkaar*): pl. of Fikr فكر, intellect, thought.

234

Female Names

Afnan (A) أفنان (*afnaan*): pl. of Fann فن, variety and Fanan فنن, branch, twig. ذواتا أفنان "Of spreading branches." (*surat al-Rahmaan* 55:48)

Afra (A) عفرا (*afraa*): whitish red.[2]

Afrah (A) أفراح (*afraah*): pl. of Farah فرح, joy, happiness.

Afrin (P) افرين (*afreen*): praise, lucky.

Afroz (P) افروز: illuminated.

Afroza (P) افروزا (*afrozaa*): burning, polishing.

Afsana (P) افسانه (*afsaana*): fable, fiction, romance.

Afsar (P) افسر: crown.

    Afsar Ara (P) افسر آرا: adorning the crown.

Afza (P) افزا (*afzaa*): increase, augmentation.[3]

Agharid (A) أغاريد (*aghaareed*) (غرد): pl. of Ugrudah أغرودة, twittering, song.

Aghsan (A) أغصان (*aghsaan*) (غصن): pl. of Ghusn غصن, branch, twig.

Ahdaf (A) أهداف (*ahdaaf*) (هدف): pl. of Hadaf هدف, aim, goal, target.

---

[2] See Steingass, F., *A Comprehensive Persian-English Dictionary*, p. 856.

[3] *Ibid.*, p. 82.

Female Names

Ahlam (A) أحلام (*ahlaam*) (حلم): pl. of Hulm حلم, dream.

Aida (A). See Ayda.

Ain (A). See Ayn.

Aisha (A) عائشة (*'aa'ishah*) (عيش): living, well-off, well-to-do, prosperous. Aisha (d.678): wife of Muhammad (s) and daughter of Khalifa Abu Bakr, known as *Umm al-Mumineen* أم المؤمنين (Mother of the Faithful) and a transmitter of many *hadith*.

Akhtar (P) اختر: star, good luck.

Akifa (A) عاكفة (*'aakifa*) (عكف): devoted to, dedicated to; fem. of Akif. See Akif (m.).

Alhan (A) ألحان (*alhaan*): melody.

Alia (A). See Aliya.

Alifa (A) أليفة (*aleefah*): friendly, sociable, amicable; fem. of Alif.

Aliya (A) عليَّة (*'aliyyah*): high, lofty, sublime; fem. of Ali. See Ali (m.). Comp. Alyaa علياء, sky. Al-'Aliyya b. Ayfa': a *sahaabia*.

Aliyya (A). See Aliya.

Almas (A) ألماسة (*almaasah*): diamond.

Altaaf (A) ألطاف (*altaaf*): pl. of Lutf لطف, kindness.

Alyaa' (A) علياء (*'alyaa'*) (علي): heaven(s), sky, sublimity, lofty.

236

Female Names

Comp. Alia علِيّة, high.

Amaal (A) آمال (*aamaal*) (امل): pl. of Amal أمل, hope, expectation.

Amal (A) أمل (امل): hope, expectation; sing. of Amaal آمال. See Raja رجاء, hope.

Aman (A) أمان (*amaan*) (امن): trust, safety, protection, tranquillity, peace of mind, calmness. See Aman (m).

Amanat (A) أمانات (*amaanaat*) (امن): pl. of Amanah أمانة, trust, deposit. ان الله يامركم ان تؤدوا الامانات الى اهلها "Allah commands you that you restore trusts to their owners." (*surat al-Nisaa'* 4:58).

Amani[4](A) أماني (*amaanii*): pl. of Umniyah أمنية, wish, aspiration, hope. See Amani (P).

Amani (P) أماني (*amaanii*): security, trust.[5] See Amani (A).

Ama (A) أمة (*amah*): female slave, servant. ولامة مؤمنة خير من مشركة "A believing slave girl is better than an idolatress." (*surat al-Baqarah* 2:221). See Kaniz كنيز, female slave.

Amat-ul-Islam (A) أمة الإسلام: (female) servant of Islam.

Amat-ul-Karim (A) أمة الكريم (*amat al-karim*): (female) servant of the most Generous.

---

[4] See Abd-el-Jawad, Hassan, 'A Linguistic and Socio-cultural Study of Personal Names in Jordan', *Anthropological Linguistics*, XXVIII, p. 94 (1986).

[5] See Steingass, F., *A Comprehensive Persian-English Dictionary*, p. 98.

Female Names

Amatullah (A) أمة الله (*amat allah*): (female) servant of Allah.

Ambara (A) عنبرة (*anbarah*): perfume, ambergris; fem. of Ambar.

Ambarin (A) عنبرين (*anbareen*): perfumed.

Ameera (A) أميرة (*ameerah*) (أمر): princess; fem. of Ameer. See Ameer (m.).

Amina (A) أمينة (*ameenah*) (امن): trustworthy, honest; fem. of Amin أمين. See Amin (m.). Comp. Aamina آمنة.

Amira (A). See Ameera أميرة; Aamira عامرة.

Amjaad (A) أمجاد (مجد): pl. of Majd مجد, glory, honour. Comp. Amjad أمجد, more glorious. See Amjad (m.).

Amna (A) أمنة (امن) (*amnah*): safety.

Amra (A) عمرة (*'amrah*): "any covering for the head, as a crown, tiara..."[6] 'Amra bint Abdur Rahman: a *sahaabia*.

Anadil (A) عنادل (*'anaadil*): pl.[7] of Andalib عندليب, nightingale.

Andalib (A) عندليب (*'andaleeb*) nightingale; sing. of Anadil عنادل.[8] See Bulbul بلبل.

---

[6] See Steingass, F., *A Comprehensive Persian-English Dictionary*, p. 867.

[7] *Ibid.*, p. 868.

[8] *Ibid.*, p. 870.

Female Names

Anisa (A) أنيسة (*aneesah*): friendly, sociable, intimate friend; fem. of Anis.

Anjum (A) انزم: pl. of Najm نزم, star.

Anjuman (P) انجمن: assembly.

    Anjuman Ara (P) انجمن آرا: adorning the assembly.

Ansam (A) أنسام (*ansaam*): pl. of Nasam نسم, breath, breath of life.

Anwaar (A) أنوار (نور): rays of light; pl. of Nur نور. Comp. Anwar أنور, brighter. See Anwar (m.).

Aqiba (A) عاقبة (*'aaqibah*): result, consequence. وله عاقبة الامور "To Allah rests the end of all affairs." (*surat al-Hajj* 22:41).

Aqila (A) عقيلة (*'aqeelah*): the best, the very best.[9]

Ara (P) آرا (*aaraa*): adorning.

    Husn-e-Ara (A+P) حسن آرا: adorning the beauty.

    Jahan Ara (P) جهان آرا: adorning the world. Jahanara Begam: daughter of Mughal emperor Shah Jahan, well known for her piety.[10]

Areefa (A) عريفة (*'areefah*) (عرف): learned, expert, authority; fem. of

---

[9] See Madina, Maan Z., *Arabic-English Dictionary of the Modern Literary Language*, p. 445.

[10] See Majumdar, R. C. *et al.*, *An Advanced History of India*, p. 477.

Female Names

Areef. See Aarifa عارفة, learned.

Arifa (A). See Aarifa عارفة; Areefa عريفة.

Arij (A) أريج (*areej*): fragrance, aroma, sweet smell, scent, perfume.

Arjumand (P) ارجمند: excellent, beloved, noble.

Arjumand Banu (P) ارجمند بانو: noble princess.

Arzu (P) آرزو (*aarzu*): wish, hope, love. See Arzu (m.). See Munya منية; Murad مراد (m.).

Asar (A) آثار (*aathaar*): pl. of Asar اثر (*athar*) sign, mark, trace. فانظر الى آثار رحمت الله كيف يحي الارض بعد موتها "Look, then, at the prints of Allah's mercy, how He revives the earth after its death." (*surat al-Rum* 30:50).

Ashraf (A) أشرف (شرف) nobler, more honourable; comp. adj. of Sharif شريف.

Ashraf Jahan (A+P) أشرف جهان: the noblest of the world.

Ashwaq (A) أشواق (*ashwaaq*): pl. of Shawq شوق, longing, desire, wish.

Asia (A). See Asiya.

Asila (A) أثيلة (*atheelah*) (أثل): highborn, of noble origin. See Asila أصيلة, highborn.

Asila (A) أصيلة (*aseelah*): of noble origin, highborn, pure, pristine; fem. of Asil أصيل. See Asila أثيلة (*atheelah*), highborn.

Female Names

Asima (A) عاصمة (*'aasimah*): protector, guardian; fem. of Asim. See Asim (m.).

Asira (A) أثيرة (*atheerah*): honoured, chosen, preferred; fem. of Asir (*atheer*).

Asiya (A) آسية (*aasiyah*): firm, powerful. Wife of Fir'awn.[11] The Qur'an mentions that she took care of Prophet Musa in his infancy but does not refer to her by name. She was very virtuous and prayed to Allah: رب ابن لي عندك بيتا في الجنة "My Lord! build for me a home near you in Paradise." (*surat al-Tahrim* 66:11).

Asma (A) أسمى (*asmaa*) (سمو): higher, more exalted, more sublime, more eminent; comp. adj. of Saami سامي. See Saami (m.). Comp. Asmaa' أسماء names; 'Asmaa عصماء, chaste. See Ulya عليا, higher.

Asmaa'[12] (A) أسماء (*asmaa'*): pl. of Ism اسم, name. له الأسماء الحسنى "All beautiful names belong to Him [Allah]." (*surat al-Hashr* 59:24). Daughter of Khalifa Abu Bakr.[13] Comp. Asma أسمى, higher; 'Asmaa عصماء, chaste.

'Asmaa (A) عصماء (*'asmaa'*) (عصم): chaste, virtuous, precious, valuable,

---

[11] See Steingass, F., *A Comprehensive Persian-English Dictionary*, p. 62; Siddiq, Muhammad Sayed, *The Blessed Women of Islam*, p. 6; Colebrooke, T. E., 'On the Proper Names of the Mohammadans', *Journal of the Royal Asiatic Society of Great Britain and Ireland*, XIII, p. 268 (1881).

    It should be noted that the Prophet (s) changed the name of a *sahaabia* from 'Asiyya to Muti'a. "Her name was 'Asiyya (rebel) and the Messenger of Allah renamed her Muti'a (obedient)." See Sa'd, Muhammad Ibn, *The Women of Madina*, p. 239.

[12] See Abd-el-Jawad, Hassan, 'A Linguistic and Socio-cultural Study of Personal Names in Jordan', *Anthropological Linguistics*, XXVIII, p. 94 (1986).

[13] See Haykal, M. H., *The Life of Muhammad*, p. 164.

Female Names

excellent;[14] fem. of أعصم. Comp. Asma أسمى, higher; Asmaa'أسماء names.

Asman (P) آسمان (*asmaan*): heaven, sky.

Asmani (P) آسماني (*asmaanii*): heavenly, divine.

Asra (A) أسرى (سري): to travel by night, to make someone travel by night. *Asra* refers to the night journey of Muhammad (s) to the seven heavens. See Israa' إسراء (m.).

Atia (A). See Atiya.

Atifa (A) عاطفة (*'aatifah*): compassion, affection, kindness; fem. of Atif.

Atika (A) عاتكة (*'aatikah*): clear, pure.[15] Daughter of Abd al-Muttalib, grandfather of Muhammad (s). Comp. Atiqa عتيقة, noble. "'Atika bint Zaid (d.672), a woman famous for her beauty, intelligence, and poetic ability."[16]

Atiqa (A) عتيقة (*'ateeqah*): ancient, noble; fem. of Atiq. See Atiq (m.). Comp. Atika عاتكة, clear.

Atira (A) عاطرة (*'aatirah*): fragrant, aromatic, perfumed.

---

[14] See Cowan, J Milton (ed.) Hans Wehr, *A Dictionary of Modern Written Arabic*, p. 617.

[15] *Ibid.*, p. 589.

[16] See Ahmed, Leila, *Women and Gender in Islam*, p. 76.

Female Names

Atiya (A): عطيَّة (*'atiyyah*) (عطو): gift, present. Umm 'Atiyyah: a *sahaabia.*[17] See Inam إنعام; Nawal نوال, gift.

Atiyya (A). See Atiya.

Attar (A) عطّار (*attar*): perfumer.

Atuf (A) عطوف (*atoof*): affectionate, kind hearted, compassionate, loving.

Awatif (A) عواطف (*awaatif*) (عطف): pl. of Aatifa عاطفة, affection, compassion, kindness, feeling.

Ayda (A) عائدة (*'aa'idah*) (عود): returning, visitor.

Ayman (A). See Umm: Umm Ayman.

Ayn (A) عين (*'ayn*): source, spring (*surat Aal 'Imraan* 3:13).

    Ayn-un-Nahr (A) عين النهر: source of the spring.

Azhaar (A) أزهار (زهر): pl. of Zahrah زهرة, flower, blossom. Comp. Azhar (m.).

Azima (A) عظيمة (*'azeemah*) (عظم): magnificent, glorious; fem. of Azim. See Azim (m.).

Aziza (A) عزيزة (*'azeezah*): noble, honourable, illustrious, highly esteemed, dearly loved, beloved; fem. of Aziz. See Aziz (m.)

---

[17] See *Riyadh-us-Saleheen*, vol. I, p. 402; Siddiqi, Muhammad Saeed, *The Blessed Women of Islam*, p. 134.

Female Names

Azra (A) عذراء (*'adhraa'*): virgin, maiden. "[H]eroine of the love romance of Wamiq and 'Adhra."[18]

Azwa (A) أضواء (*adwaa'*): pl. of Zau (*dau*) ضوء, light, splendour, limelight.

Azza (A) عزّة (*'azzah*): young female deer, female fawn.

---

[18] See Schimmel, Annemarie, *Islamic Names*, p. 43.

244

Female Names

B

Baaria (A) بارعة (*baari'ah*) (برع): originator; fem. of Baari'. See Baari (m.).

Badai' (A) بدائع (*badaa'i'*): pl. of Badia' بديعة, wonder, marvel.

Badi'a (A) بديعة (*badee'ah*) (بدع): wonder, marvel; sing. of Badaa'i' بدائع.

Badr (A) بدر: full moon.

> **Badr-ud-Din** (A) بدر الدين: full moon of the religion (Islam). Badr al-Din Lu'lu': see Lulu.

> **Badr-un-Nisa** (A) بدر النساء: full moon of the women.

Badriyyah[19] (A) بدرية: full moon-like.

Baha (A) بهاء (*bahaa'*) (بهو): beauty, glory, splendour, magnificence.

Bahar (P) بهار (*bahaar*): spring, blossom.

> **Bahar Banu** (P) بهار بانو: blooming princess.

Bahia (A). See Bahiya.

---

[19] See Yassin, M. Aziz F., 'Personal Names Address in Kuwaiti Arabic', *Anthropological Linguistics*, XX, p. 55.

Female Names

Bahija (A) بهيجة (*baheejah*): glad, happy, joyful, delighted, delightful, cheerful; fem. of Bahij.

Bahira (A) باهرة (*baahirah*): brilliant, superb, magnificent, gorgeous, spectacular; fem. of Bahir.

Bahiya (A) بهيّة (*bahiyyah*): beautiful, brilliant, elegant, radiant, pretty, charming; fem. of Bahi بهي.

Bahiyya (A). See Bahiya.

Bahja (A) بهجة (*bahjah*): splendour, magnificence, pomp, joy, happiness.

Baiza (A) بيضاء (*baidaa'*) (بيض): white, bright, brilliant, innocent, pure; fem. of Abyad ابيض. الخيط الابيض "white thread" (*surat al-Baqarah* 2:187).

Bajila (A) بجيلة (*bajeelah*) (بجل): honoured, dignified, highly regarded.

Bakhita (P) بخيتة (*bakheetah*): lucky, fortunate; fem. of Bakhit.

Balqis[20] (A). See Bilqis.

Banafsaj (A) بنفسج: violet, flower.

Banu (P) بانو (*baanu*): princess, lady, Mrs.

---

[20] "Balqis, the queen of Sheba." See Mernissi, F., *The Forgotten Queens of Islam*, p. 43. "Balkis", see Colebrooke, T. E., 'On the Proper Names of the Mohammadans', *Journal of the Royal Asiatic Society of Great Britain and Ireland*, XIII, p. 268 (1881).

Female Names

Baraim (A) براعم (*baraa'im*): pl. of Bur'um برعم, blossom, bud.

Baraka (A) بركة (*barakah*) (برك): blessing; sing. of Barakat بركات. See Barakat (m.). Name of Umm Ayman (see Umm). Baraka bint Yasar: a *sahaabia*.

Barat (A) براءة (*baraa'ah*) (برئ): innocence, guiltlessness.

Bari'a (A) بريئة (*baree'ah*): innocent, blameless, guiltless, sound; fem. of Bari'.

Baria (A). See Baaria بارعة.

Barraqa (A) براقة (*barraqah*): bright, brilliant, shining, sparkling, glittering; fem. of Barraq.

Basham (A) بشام (*bashaam*): a fragrant shrub.[21]

Bashira (A) بشيرة (*basheerah*) (بشر): bringer of good news; fem. of Bashir. See Bashir (m.).

Basima (A) باسمة (*baasimah*): smiler, smiling; fem. of Basim.

Basira (A) بصيرة (*baseerah*) (بصر): sagacious, endowed with insight; fem. of Basir. See Basir (m.).

Basma (A) بسمة (*basmah*): smile.

Bassama (A) بسّامة (*bassaamah*): smiling; fem. of Bassam.

---

[21] See Steingass, F., *A Comprehensive Persian-English Dictionary*, p. 188.

247

Female Names

Batul (A) بتول (*batool*): virgin, maiden. An epithet of Maryam, mother of Prophet 'Isa (Jesus), and of Fatima, daughter of Muhammad (s).

Begam, Begum[22] (P) بیگم: honorific title, queen, lady of rank.

Benazir (P+A) بینظیر (*benazeer*): matchless, unique.

Bibi (P) بیبی (*beebee*): lady of rank, an horrific title used at the end of a woman's name in the Indian sub-continent, no more in common use. See Pari.

Bilqis (A) بلقیس (*bilqees*): Queen of Sheba known as Bilqis in the Arabian tradition.[23] While the Qur'an does not mention her by name, it relates that Prophet Sulayman sent a letter to her by means of a bird, the Hudhud, inviting her to submit to Allah.[24] Upon receiving the letter, she says: انه من سلیمان وانه بسم الله الرحمن الرحیم "It is from Sulayman, and is: [as follows]: In the name of Allah, Most Gracious, Most Merciful." (*surat al-Naml* 27:30). Accepting the true religion (Islam), she said: رب انی ظلمت نفسی واسلمت مع سلیمان لله رب العالمین "My Lord! I have indeed wronged myself, and I submit [in Islam], with Sulayman to Allah, the Lord of the worlds." (*surat al-Naml* 27:44). See Sulayman (m.).

Budur (A) بدور (*budoor*): pl. of Badr بدر, full moon.

---

[22] "The Turkish ladies are usually called Begums." See Colebrooke, T. E., 'On the Proper Names of the Mohammadans', *Journal of the Royal Asiatic Society of Great Britain and Ireland*, XIII, p. 276. (1881).

[23] See Ali, Yusuf Ali, *The Holy Qur'an*, n. 3264.

[24] "The Bible tells us that the Queen of Sheba (in modern Yemen) came to visit Solomon, attracted by his representation for wisdom." See Armstrong, Karen, *Jerusalem: One City Three faiths*, p. 47.

Female Names

Bulbul (P) بلبل : nightingale. See Andalib (A) عندليب.

Burum (A) برعم: bud, blossom; sing. of Baraim براعم.

Busaina (A) بثينة (*buthaina*): diminutive of Basna (*bathnah*) بثنة, beautiful woman.

Bushra (A) بشرى (*bushraa*) (بشر): good news, glad tidings. الذين آمنوا وكانوا يتقون لهم البشرى في الحياة الدنيا وفي الآخرة "Those who believe and keep their duty [to Allah], for them are good news in the life of this world and in the Hereafter." (*surat Yunus* 10:63-64). Bushra bint Mulayl: a *sahaabia*. See Bishara بشارة (m.).

Bustan (A) بستان: garden.

Female Names

D

Dahlia (A) دهلية (*dahliyah*): dahlia (flower). See Dalia داليا.

Daiba (A) دائبة (*daa'ibah*): diligent, industrious.

Dalal (A) دلا ل (*dalaal*): coquetry, pampering.[25]

Dalia (A) داليا (*daaliyaa*). See Dahlia.

Dalila (A) دليلة (*daleelah*): guide, model, leader; fem. of Dalil. See Dalil (m.).

Danesh (P) دانش (*daanesh*): wisdom, learning.

> **Danesh Ara** (P) دانش آرا: endowed with wisdom, learning.

Dara (A) دارة (*daarah*) (دور): halo. Comp. Dara (P) (m.).

Daria (A) دارية (*daariyah*) (دري): learned, knowing.

Daulat (A) دولة (*dawlah*) (دول): wealth, empire, state, power.

> **Daulat Khatun** (A+P) دولت خاتون "The fourteenth sovereign of the Bani Khurshid dynasty... acceded to the throne in 1316."[26]

---

[25] See Madina, Maan Z., *Arabic-English Dictionary of the Modern Literary Language*, p. 223.

[26] See Mernissi, Fatima, *The Forgotten Queens of Islam*, p. 105.

Female Names

Dawha (A) دوحة (*dawhah*): lofty tree.

Dil (P) دل: heart, mind.

> **Dilara** (P) دل آرا: "Beloved; a sweetheart; name of the wife of Dara, and mother of Roshang (Roxana)."[27]

> **Dildar** (P) دلدار (*dildaar*): holder of the heart. Wife of Mughal emperor Babur.[28]

> **Dilruba** (A) دلربا (*dilrubaa*): heart-ravishing, a beloved object.

> **Dilshad** (P) دلشاد (*dilshaad*): of happy heart, happy, glad. Dilshad Khatun: wife of Sultan of Iraq.[29]

Dima (A) ديمة (*deema*) (دوم): "An incessant gentle rain unaccompanied by wind, thunder, or lightning."[30]

Duha (A) ضحى (*duhaa*): forenoon. *Al-Duhaa* الضحى: title of the 93rd *sura* of the Qur'an.

---

[27] See Steingass, F., *A Comprehensive Persian-English Dictionary*, p. 531.

[28] See Colebrooke, T. E., 'On the Proper Names of the Mohammadans', *Journal of the Royal Asiatic Society of Great Britain and Ireland*, XIII, p. 277 (1881).

[29] "Mention is made in Sir G. Ousely's work of a beautiful and learned lady, the wife of the Sultan of the Arabian Irak, in the eighth century of the Hejra, who studied the art of poetry with her husband under Selman of Sava." *Ibid.*, XI, p. 237 (1879).

[30] See Steingass, F., *A Comprehensive Persian-English Dictionary*, p. 553; "continuous rain", see Cowan, J Milton (ed.) Hans Wehr, *A Dictionary of Modern Written Arabic*, p. 303.

Female Names

Dunia (A). See Dunya.

Dunya (A) دنيا (*dunyaa*): world, earth. ربنا آتنا في الدنيا حسنة وفي الآخرة حسنة وقنا عذاب النار "Our Lord! Give to us in the world that which is good and in the Hereafter that which is good, and guard us from the doom of fire." (*surat al-Baqarah* 2:201). See Aalam عالم, world.

Durr (A) در (*durr*): pearls. Shajarat al-Durr: the tree of pearls. See Shajarat al-Durr

Durra (A) درة (*durrah*): pearl. A *sahaabia*.

Durriya (A) درية (*durriyyah*): glittering, sparkling, twinkling, brilliant (see *surat al-Nur* 24:35).

Durriyya (A). See Durriya.

252

F

Faaiza (A) فائزة (*faa'izah*): victorious, triumphant, successful; fem. of Faaiz. See Faaiz (m.).

Faariha (A) فارحة (*faarihah*): happy, glad, delighted, cheerful, joyful; fem. of Faarih. See Fariha فرحة, happy.

Faatin (A) فاتن (فتن): beautiful, pretty, attractive, glamorous, captivating, ravishing.

Faatina (A) فاتنة (*faatinah*) (فتن): fem. of Faatin. See Faatin (f.)

Fadia (A) فادية (*faadiyah*): redeemer, ransomer; fem. of Fadi.

Fadila (A). See Fazila.

Faheema (A) فهيمة (*faheemah*) (فهم): intelligent, judicious, learned, erudite; fem. of Faheem.

Fahhama (A) فهامة (*fahaamah*) (فهم): very intelligent, very understanding. See Fahima فهمة; Faheema فهيمة.

Fahima (A) فهمة (*fahimah*) (فهم): quick-witted, sharp-witted; fem. of Fahim. See Faheema فهيمة.

Fahm (A) فهم: intellect, intelligence, insight.

Fahm Ara (A+P) فهم آرا: adorned with intellect, intelligent.

Female Names

Fahmida (P) فهميده (*fahmeeda*): intelligent, judicious.

Faida (A) فائدة (*faa'idah*) (فيد): benefit, advantage, gain, worth, welfare; fem. of Faid.

Faiqa (A) فائقة (*faa'iqah*) (فوق): excellent, outstanding, distinguished, superior, ascendant; fem. of Faiq.

Fajr (A) فجر: dawn, rise, beginning, start. See Fajr (m.); Sabiha; Subh.

Fakhar (A) فخار (*fakhaar*): honour, pride, glory.

Fakhr (A) فخر: glory, pride, honour.

Fakhr-un-Nisa[31] (A) فخر النساء: glory of the women.

Fakhriya (A) فخريّة (*fakhriyyah*): proud (for noble cause); fem. of Fakhri.

Falak (A) فلك: orbit, sky, celestial sphere. وهو الذي خلق الليل والنهار والشمس والقمر كل في فلك يسبحون "It is He who created the night and the day, and the sun and the moon. They float each in an orbit." (*surat al-Anbiyaa'* 21:33). See Sama سماء, sky.

Faliha (A) فالحة (*faalihah*): fortunate, lucky, successful, prosperous; fem. of Falih.

Faqiha (A) فقيهة (*faqeehah*): jurist, scholar in *fiqh* (Islamic jurisprudence); fem. of Faqih.

---

[31] See Colebrooke, T. E., 'On the Proper Names of the Mohammadans', *Journal of the Royal Asiatic Society of Great Britain and Ireland*, XIII, p. 274 (1881).

Female Names

Farah (A) فرح: joy, happiness, delight. See Farha فرحة; Bishr بشر (m.).

Farha (A) فرحة (*farhah*): gladness, happiness, delight. See Farah فرح.

Farhana (A) فرحانة (*farhaanah*): glad, happy, cheerful, delighted; fem. of Farhan.

Farhi[32] (A) فرحي (*farhii*): glad, happy.

Faria (A) فارعة (*faari'ah*): tall, towering, lofty, high; fem. of Fari. Al-Fari'a: a *sahaabia*.

Farida (A) فريدة (*fareedah*) (فرد): unique, matchless; fem. of Farid.

Fariha (A) فرحة (*farihah*): happy, glad, joyful.

Farzana (P) فرزانه (*farzaanah*): wise, learned.

Fasiha (A) فصيحة (*faseehah*) (فصح): eloquent, fluent, well-spoken; fem. of Fasih. See Fasih (m.).

Fathiya (A) فتحيّة (*fathiyyah*): one who wins victory after victory; fem. of Fathi.

Fatiha (A) فاتحة (*faatihah*) (فتح): opening, introduction, dawn, first. *Al-Faatihah* الفاتحة: title of the first *sura* of the Qur'an.

Fatima (A) فاطمة (*faatimah*): daughter of Muhammad (s) and wife of

---

[32] See Abd-el-Jawad, Hassan, 'A Linguistic and Socio-cultural Study of Personal Names in Jordan', *Anthropological Linguistics*, XXVIII, p. 83 (1986).

Female Names

Khalifa Ali known as *Sayyadat al-Nisaa'* (the Chief of Women).[33] The Fatimid dynasty ruled North Africa, and then Egypt and Syria from 909-1171, claiming to be descendants of Muhammad (s) through his daughter Fatimah.

Fattana (A) فتّانة (*fattaanah*): extremely beautiful, charming, captivator.

Fauziya (A). See Fawziya.

Fawz (A) فوز: victory, triumph, success, winning, achievement. See Fawz (m.).

Fawziya (A) فوزيّة (*fawziyyah*) (فوز): triumphant, victorious; fem. of Fawzi.

Fawziyya (A). See Fawziya.

Fayza (A). See Faaiza.

Fazila (A) فاضلة (*faadilah*) (فضل): virtuous, honest, excellent, superior, kind, outstanding, eminent, learned; fem. of Fazil (*fadil*). A *sahaabia*.

Fazila (A) فضيلة (*fadeelah*) (فضل): high degree of excellence, virtue, merit. See Hasana حسنة; Fazila فاضلة (*faadila*).

Fazilat-un-Nisa (A) فضيلة النساء: excellence of the women.

---

[33] Muhammad (s) said to his daughter: "Thou art the highest of the women of the people of Paradise, excepting only the Virgin Mary, daughter of 'Imran." See Lings, Martin, *Muhammad*, p. 329.

Female Names

Fidda (A) فضَّة (*fiddah*): silver. زين للناس حب الشهوات من النساء والبنين والقناطير المقنطرة من الذهب والفضة والخيل المسومة والانعام والحرث "Beautified for mankind is love of the joys [that come] from women and offspring, heaped-up hoards of gold and silver; horses branded [with their mark] and cattle and land." (see *surat Aal 'Imraan* 3:14).

Firasa (A) فراسة (*firaasah*): insight, vision, acumen.

Firdaus (A) فردوس: paradise, heaven. ان الذين آمنوا وعملوا الصالحات كانت لهم جنات الفردوس نزلا "Those who believe and do good works, the gardens of paradise are waiting for their welcome." (*surat al-Kahf* 18:107). See Jannat.

Firdausi (A) فردوسيّ (*firdausiyy*): heavenly. See Firdausi (m.)

Firuza (P) فيروزه: turquoise, a bright greenish-blue colour.

Firuzi (P) فيروزي: victorious, glorious, of the colour of the turquoise.

Fuada (A) فؤادة (*fu'adah*): heart; fem. of Fuad. See Fuad (m.)

Funun (A) فنون (*funoon*) (فن): variety, art.

Furozan (P) فروزان: luminous, radiant.

257

Female Names

G

Ghaania (A) غانية (*ghaaniyah*): beauty, beautiful girl, pretty girl.

Ghada (A) غادة (*ghaadah*) (غيد): delicate young girl, beautiful young woman, youthful and beautiful woman.

Ghadir (A) غدير (*ghadeer*): brook, rivulet, small stream.

Ghaida (A) غيداء (*ghaidaa'*) (غيد): delicate, soft. See Naima ناعمة.

Ghalia (A) غالية (*ghaaliyah*): precious, priceless, valuable, dear, beloved.

Ghaliba (A) غالبة (*ghaalibah*): conqueror, victor, winner; fem. of Ghalib. See Ghalib (m.).

Ghania (A). See Ghaniya.

Ghaniya (A) غنيّة (*ghaniyyah*): rich, wealthy, prosperous; fem. of Ghani. See Ghani (m.). Comp. Ghaania غانية, beauty.

Ghazal (A) غزال: gazelle, deer.

Ghazala[34] (A) غزالة: gazelle, deer. "[A] number of khariji women won renown for their prowess in battle, among them Ghazala, who

---

[34] See Abd-el-Jawad, *Anthropological Linguistics*, XXVIII, p. 86 (1986).

Female Names

defeated al-Hajjaj in a duel."[35]

Ghina (A) غِنى (*ghinan*): affluence, opulence, prosperity, satisfaction, contentment. Comp., Ghinaa' غِناء, singing.

Ghinaa' (A) غِناء: singing, song. Comp. Ghina غِنى, affluence.

Ghufran (A) غفران (*ghufraan*) (غفر): pardon, forgiveness. See Ghufran (m.).

Ghusn (A) غصن: branch, twig; sing. of Ghusun غصون.

Ghusun (A) غصون (*ghusoon*): pl. of Ghusn غصن, branch, twig.

Gul (P) گل: flower, rose.

> **Gul Badan** (P+A) گلبدن: beautiful body resembling rose. Daughter (d.1603) of Babur, founder of the Mughal empire.[36]

> **Gul Bahar** (P) گل بهار: rose spring.

> **Gul Barg** (P) گلبرگ: rose petal.

> **Gulistan** (P) گلستان: rose garden.

> **Gul-izar** (P+A) گل عذار: rosy-cheeked.

> **Gul Rana** (P) گلرعنا: beautiful delicate scented rose.

---

[35] See Ahmed, Leila, *Women and Gender in Islam*, p. 71.

[36] See Majumdar, R C., *et al.*, *An Advanced History of India*, p. 572.

Female Names

Gul Rang (P) گل رنگ: rose-coloured.

Gul-ru (P) گل رو: rosy-faced.

Gul Rukh (P) گل رخ: rose-face.

Gulshan (P) گلشن: rose garden.

Gulzaar (P) گلزار: rose garden.

Gulab (P) گلاب (gulaab): rosewater.

H

Haafiza (A) حافظة (*haafizah*): honorific title of a woman who has memorised the whole of the Qur'an, guardian, protector; fem. of Haafiz. فالصالحات قانتات حافظات للغيب بما حفظ الله "So the righteous women are obedient, guarding in secret that which Allah has guarded." (*surat al-Nisaa'* 4:34).

Haalima (A) حالمة (*haalimah*): dreamer, visionary. Comp. Halima حليمة, patient.

Haameda (A). See Haamida.

Haamida (A) حامدة (*haamidah*): praiser (of Allah); fem. of Haamid. See Haamid (m.).

Haarisa (A) حارثة (*haarithah*): cultivator; fem. of Haaris (*haarith*).

Habiba (A) حبيبة (*habeebah*): beloved, darling, sweetheart; fem. of Habib. See Mahbuba محبوبة. Umm Habibah: wife of Muhammad (s). See Umm.

Hadaya (A) هدايا (*hadaayaa*): pl. of Hadiyya هديّة, gift, present.

Hadia (A) هادية (*haadiyah*): leader, guide; fem. of Hadi. See Murshida مرشدة; Hadi (m.).

Hadil (A) هديل (*hadeel*): cooing of a pigeon.

Hadiya (A) هديّة (*hadiyyah*): gift, present; sing. of Hadaya هدايا.

Female Names

Hafeza (A). See Haafiza.

Haffafa (A) هفّافة (*haffafah*): glittering, shining, thin, peaceful, gentle wind.[37]

Hafiza (A) حفيظة (*hafeezah*): guardian, protector; fem. of Hafiz. See Hafiz (m.).

Hafsa (A) حفصة (*hafsah*): wife of Muhammad (s);[38] daughter of Khalifa 'Umar.

Haifa (A). See Hayfa هيفاء.

Hajar[39] (A) هاجر (*haajar*): wife of Prophet Ibrahim and mother of Prophet Ismail.

Hakeema (A) حكيمة (*hakeemah*): wise, sage, judicious, prudent; fem. of Hakeem. A *sahaabia*. See Hakeem (m.).

Hala (A) هالة (*haalah*): halo, ring, glory. Wife of Abdul Muttalib, grandfather of Muhammad (s).[40] See Dara (A).

Halima (A) حليمة (*haleemah*): patient, tolerant; fem. of Halim. See Halim (m.); Saabira صابرة. Comp. Haalima حالمة, dreamer.

---

[37] See Steingass, F., *A Comprehensive Persian-English Dictionary*, p. 1501-2.

[38] See Haykal, M H., *The Life of Muhammad*, p. 251.

[39] *Ibid.* p. 24.

[40] "On the same day that 'Abdullah married Aminah, his father 'Abd al Muttalib married a cousin of hers named Halah." *Ibid.*, p. 46.

Female Names

Halima al-Sa'diyyah: foster mother of Muhammad (s).[41]

Hamama (A) حمامة (*hamaamah*): dove, pigeon. Daughter of Khalifa Abu Bakr.

Hamda (A) حمدة (*hamdah*): praise, laudation of Allah; fem. of Hamd. See Hamd (m.).

Hamdan[42] (A) حمدان (*hamdaan*): much praise. A tribe in Arabia.[43] The Hamdaani dynasty ruled al-Jazira and Syria from 905 to 1004.

Hameda (A). See Haamida.

Hamida (A) حميدة (*hameedah*): praised, commended, praiseworthy, commendable; fem. of Hamid. See Hamid (m.); Mahmuda محمودة. Hamida Banu Begum: mother of Mughal emperor Akbar.[44]

Hana (A) هناء (*hanaa'*): happiness, bliss.

Hanaan (A) حنان (حن ً): compassion, affection, love, tenderness, warm heartedness. يا يحيى خذ الكتاب بقوة وآتيناه الحكم صبيا وحنانا من لدنا وزكاة وكان تقيا "[And it was said to his son]: O Yahya! Hold fast the Book. And We gave him wisdom when a child, and compassion from our presence, and purity; and he was devout."

---

[41] See Haykal, M H., *The Life of Muhammad*, p. 49.

[42] See Colebrooke, T E., *Journal of the Royal Asiatic Society of Great Britain and Ireland*, XIII, p. 238.

[43] See Haykal, M H., *The Life of Muhammad*, p. 473.

[44] See Colebrooke, T E., *Journal of the Royal Asiatic Society of Great Britain and Ireland*, XIII, p. 277.

(*surat Maryam* 19:12-13). Comp. Hannan حنّان, compassionate (m.).

Hania (A). See Haniya.

Hanifa (A) حنيفة (*haneefah*): true, one of true faith, upright; fem. of Hanif. See Hanif (m.).

Hanin (A) حنين (*haneen*): desire, longing.

Haniya (A) هنيّة (*haniyyah*): pleasant. *Hanii'an* "comfortably" (*surat al-Mursalaat* 77:43).

Hanna (A) حنّة (*hannah*) (حن): compassion, sympathy, pity. Mother of Maryam.[45]

Hanun (A) حنون (*hanoon*): compassionate, merciful, affectionate, tender-hearted, soft hearted.

Hanuna (A) حنونة (*hanoonah*): compassionate; fem. of Hanun. See Hanun (f.).

Hasana (A) حسنة (*hasanah*) (حسن): good deed, kind act, favour; sing. of Hasanaat حسنات. Umm Sharabil Hasana: a *sahaabia*. See Hasanat (m.); Fazila فضيلة (*fadeelah*).

Hasiba (A) حسيبة (*haseebah*): highborn, respected, noble; fem. of Hasib. See Hasib (m.); Nabila نبيلة.

---

[45] See Siddiq, Muhammad Sayed, *The Blessed Women of Islam*, p. 7. "Anne (f.) English, French, and German form...of the Hebrew female name *Hanna* 'He (God) has favoured me (i.e. with a child)'. This is the name borne in the Bible by the mother of Samuel, and according to non-biblical tradition also by the mother of the Virgin Mary." See Hanks & Hodges, *A Dictionary of First Names*, p. 21.

Female Names

Hasifa (A) حصيفة (*haseefah*): judicious, wise, prudent, sagacious; fem. of Hasif. See Hakeema حكيمة.

Hasina (A) حصينة (*haseenah*): well-fortified, guarded, chaste, virtuous.

Hasna (A) حسناء (*hasnaa'*) (حسن): beauty, beautiful woman, See Hussana حسّانة. Comp. Hasna حصناء, chaste.

Hasna (A) حصناء (*hasnaa'*): chaste, virtuous, modest. Comp. Hasna حسناء, beauty.

Hassana (A) حسّانة (*hassanah*): beautiful woman, sweetheart.

Hawa (A) حوّاء (*hawwaa'*): Eve, wife of Adam, mother of mankind. Hawwa' bint Zayd: a *sahaabia*.

Haya' (A) حياء (*hayaa'*): shyness, bashfulness, coyness, modesty.

Haya (A) حياة (*hayaah*) (حي): life. See Hayat (m.). Comp. Haya حياء, shyness.

 Ayn-ul-Hayat (A) عين الحياة: fountain of life.

Hayfa (A) هيفاء (*haifaa'*) (هيف): slender, slim.

Hazar (P) هزار: kind of nightingale.

Hazima (A) حازمة (*haazimah*): firm, energetic, judicious, discreet, prudent; fem. of Hazim.

Hena (A). See Hinna.

265

Female Names

Hiba (A) هبة (*hibah*): gift.

Hikma (A) حكمة (*hikmah*): wisdom. See Hikmat (m.).

Hilal (A) هلال (*hilaal*): crescent, new moon. See Hilal (m.).

Hinna (A) حنّاء (*hinna'*): henna, camphor.[46]

Hishma (A) حشمة (*hishmah*): modesty, bashfulness, decency, decorum.
See Ihtisham احتشام (m.).

Hiyam (A) هيام (*hiyaam*) (هيم): love, passion.

Huda (A) هدى: right guidance, right path. See Huda (m.). Huda al-
Sha'rawi (1879-1947): president (1919) of the women's branch of the
Wafd party in Egypt. "[I]n 1947, the Egyptian state awarded Sha'rawi its
highest decoration"[47] in recognition for her services for establishing
women's rights.

Humaira (A). See Humayra.

Humayda (A) حميدة: praised; fem. of Humayd.

Humayra (A) حميراء (*humayraa'*): of red colour.[48] Name of Aisha,

---

[46] See Madina, M Z., *Arabic-English Dictionary of the Modern Literary Language*, p.
174.

[47] See *The Oxford Encyclopaedia of the Modern Islamic World*, vol. IV, p. 45. Also
see Ahmed, Leila, *Women and Gender in Islam*, p. 174.

[48] See *Al-Mawrid: A Modern Arabic-English Dictionary*, p. 491.

266

Female Names

wife of Muhammad (s).[49]

Hurriya (A) حرية (*hurriyyah*): freedom, liberty.

Husayna (A) حسينة (*husaynah*): diminutive of Husn حسن, beauty. See Husn.

Hushayma (A) حشيمة (*hushaymah*): diminutive of Hishma حشمة, modesty. See Hishma.

Husn (A) حسن: beauty, gracefulness, prettiness. حسنهن "Their beauty" (*surat al-Ahzaab* 33:52). See Malaha ملاحة, beauty.

    Husn-e-Ara (A+P) حسن آرا: adorned with beauty.

Husna (A) حسنى (*husnaa*) (حسن): more beautiful, kindness, good outcome; fem. of Ahsan أحسن.[50] وله الاسماء الحسنى فادعوه بها "The most beautiful names belong to Allah. So call on him by them." (*surat al-A'raaf* 7:180). See Ahsan (m.).

Husni (A) حسني (*husnii*): possessing beauty.

Husniya (A) حسنية (*husniyyah*): possessing beauty.

Hussana (A) حسّانة (*hussanah*) (حسن): beauty, beautiful woman. See Hasna حسناء.

Huzuz (A) حظوظ (*huzooz*): pl. of Hazz حظ, fortune, good luck.

---

[49] See Siddiq, Muhammad Sayed, *The Blessed Women of Islam*, p. 26.

[50] See Madina, Maan Z., *Arabic-English Dictionary of the Modern Literary Language*, p. 156.

267

I

Iba (A) إباء (*ibaa'*): sense of honour, self-esteem, magnanimity, generosity.

Ibrisami (A+P) ابريسمي (*ibreesimi*): silken.

Ibtihaj (A) ابتهاج (*ibtihaaj*) (بهج): joy, delight.

Ibtihal (A) ابتهال (*ibtihaal*) (بهل): prayer, supplication, *du'aa'*.

Ibtisam (A) ابتسام (*ibtisaam*) (بسم): smiling, smile. See Tabassum تبسُّم.

Ibtisama (A) ابتسامة (*ibtisaamah*) (بسم): smile. See Basma بسمة.

Idrak (A) إدراك (*idraak*): intellect, perception, achievement, attainment.

Iftikhar (A) افتخار (*iftikhaar*) (فخر): pride.

Iftitan (A) افتتان (*iftitaan*) (فتن): enchantment, captivation.

Ihtisham (A) احتشام (*ihtishaam*) (حشم): chastity, modesty, decency, decorum.

Ijlal (A) إجلال (*ijlaal*) (جل): glorification, exaltation, honour, distinction, respect.

Ikhlas (A) إخلاص (*ikhlaas*) (خلص): sincerity, honesty, integrity, fidelity, faithfulness. *Al-Ikhlaas* الإخلاص: title of the 112th *sura* of the Qur'an.

Female Names

See Wafaa' وفاء.

Iklil (A) إكليل (*ikleel*): crown.

Ikram (A) إكرام (*ikraam*) (كرم): honour, glory, respect. See Ikram (m.).

Ilham (A) إلهام (*ilhaam*) (لهم): inspiration, revelation.

Iltimas (A) التماس (*iltimaas*) (لمس): request, appeal, entreaty.

Iman (A) إيمان (*imaan*) (أمن): belief, faith in Allah. See Iman (m.).

Imtinan (A) امتنان (*imtinaan*) (من ّ): gratitude, gratefulness, thankfulness.

Imtisal (A) امتثال (*imtithaal*) (مثل): obedience, conforming to, in compliance with.

Imtiyaz (A) امتياز (*imtiyaaz*) (ميز): distinction, mark of honour.

Inam (A) إنعام (*in'aam*) (نعم): gift, present. See Atiya عطية.

Inas (A) إيناس (*inaas*) (أنس): friendliness, cordiality, sociability.

Inshirah (A) إنشراح (*inshiraah*) (شرح): joy, delight, happiness, cheerfulness.

Intisar (A) انتصار (*intisaar*) (نصر): victory, triumph; sing. of Intisaaraat انتصارات. See Nasr نصر; Zafar ظفر (m.).

Intisarat (A) انتصارات (*intisaaraat*) (نصر): pl. of Intisar انتصار,

269

Female Names

victory, triumph.

Iradat (A) إرادة (*iraadah*) (رود): wish, desire.

Irtiza (A) ارتضاء (*irtidaa'*): contentment, approval.

Is'ad (A) إسعاد (*is'aad*) (سعد): making happy or prosperous, blessing, favouring.

Ishraq (A) إشراق (*ishraaq*) (شرق): brilliance, radiance, shining.

Ishrat (A) عشرة (*'ishrah*): pleasure, enjoyment, delight.

Islah (A) إصلاح (*islaah*) (صلح): making right, making good, improvement, betterment.

Ismat (A) عصمة (*'ismah*) (عصم): purity, chastity, modesty.

Ismati[51] (A) عصمتي (*'ismatiyy*): expressive of modesty.

Istabraq (A) إستبرق: brocade. عاليهم ثياب سندس خضر وإستبرق "Their raiment will be green silk and brocade." (*surat al-Dahr* 76:21).

Itidal (A) اعتدال (*i'tidaal*) (عدل): rectitude, moderateness, moderation, mildness.

Itimad (A) اعتماد (*i'timaad*) (عمد): reliance, dependence, confidence. Wife of Abbasid Khalifa Mu'tamid (1068-91).[52]

---

[51] See Colebrooke, T. E., On the Proper Names of the Mohammadans, *Journal of the Royal Asiatic Society of Great Britain and Ireland*, XI, p. 237 (1879).

[52] See Hitti, Philip K., *History of the Arabs*, p. 539.

Female Names

Izaz (A) إعزاز (*i'zaaz*) (عزّ): honour, esteem, regard, affection. Comp. I'jaz إعجاز, inimitability (m.).

Izdihar (A) ازدهار (*izdihaar*) (زهر): prosperity, flourishing, bloom.

Izza (A) عزة (*'izzah*): honour, fame, power. 'Izza bint al-Harith: a *sahaabia*. See Izzat (m.).

271

Female Names

J

Jaan (P) جان (*jaan*): life; sing. of Jaanaan جانان.

Jaanaan (P) جانان (*jaanaan*): pretty, sweetheart; pl. of Jaan جان, life.[53] Comp. Janan جنان (A), heart.

Jadida (A) جديدة (*jadidah*): new, pristine.

Jahan (P) جهان (*jahaan*): world, dunya دنيا.

    Ashraf Jahan (A+P) أشرف جهان: noblest of the world.

    Jahan Ara (P) جهان آرا: adorning the world. Daughter of Mughal emperor Shah Jahaan.[54]

    Khurshid Jahan (P) خورشيد جهان: sun of the world.

    Nur Jahan (A+P) نور جهان: light of the world. Wife of Mughal emperor Jahangir.[55]

    Raunaq Jahan (A+P) رونق جهان: lustre of the world.

---

[53] "Jaanan Begum, that is, 'lives' in the plural. Names in the plural are not uncommon among the Arabs." See Colebrooke, T. E., 'On the Proper Names of the Mohammadans', *Journal of the Royal Asiatic Society of Great Britain and Ireland*, XIII, p. 278 (1881).

[54] See Majumdar, R. C., *An Advanced History of India*, p. 477.

[55] "In May 1611, Jahangir married Nur Jahan, originally known as Mihr-un-nisa." *Ibid.*, p. 458.

Female Names

Jala (A) جلاء (*jalaa'*): bringing to light, shining.

Jalila (A) جليلة (*jalilah*): great, exalted, magnificent; fem. of Jalil.

Jamia (A) جامعة (*jaami'ah*): gatherer, collector, author, writer; fem. of Jami'.

Jamila (A) جميلة (*jameelah*): beautiful, pretty; fem. of Jamil. Daughter of Khalifa Umar.

Janan (A) جنان (*janaan*) (جن): heart, soul. Comp. Jaanaan جانان (P), pretty.

Janna (A) جنة (*jannah*): garden, paradise.

Jannatul Firdaus (A) جنة الفردوس: Garden of Paradise. ان الذين آمنوا وعملوا الصالحات كانت لهم جنات الفردوس نزلا "Those who believe and do good works, the gardens of paradise are waiting for their welcome." (*surat al-Kahf* 18:107).

Jasmine (A). See Yasmine.

Jawda (A) جودة (*jawdah*): excellence, high quality, fineness.

Jawhara (A) جوهرة (*jawharah*) jewel, gem, essence.

Jazibiyya (A) جاذبية (*jaadhibiyyah*): attraction, charm, appeal.

Jibla (A) جبلة (*jiblah*): nature.

Jinan (A) جنان (*jinaan*): pl. of Jannat جنة, garden, paradise.

273

Female Names

Jumaina (A) جمينة (*jumainah*): diminutive of Jumana جمانة, small pearl.

Jumana (A) جمانة (*jumaanah*): pearl. See Luluah لؤلؤة. Jumana b. Abi Talib: a *sahaabia*.

Junna (A) جنة: shelter.

Juwayriyyah (A) جويريّة: diminutive of Juriyyah جوريّة, Damask rose.[56] Wife of Muhammad (s).[57]

---

[56] See *Al-Mawrid: A Modern Arabic-English Dictionary*, p. 439.

[57] See Haykal, M. H., *The Life of Muhammad*, p. 333.

Female Names

K

Kakuli[58] (P) كاكلي: curl or lock of hair.[59]

Kamila (A) كاملة (*kaamilah*): perfect, complete, genuine; fem. of Kamil.

Kaniz[60] (P) كنيز: female servant, virgin.

Karam[61] (A) كرم: generosity, bounty.

Karima (A) كريمة (*kareemah*): kind, generous, benevolent, open-handed, noble; fem. of Karim. See Karim (m.).

Karma (A) كرمة (*karmah*): vine, grapevine, kind, generous.

Kausar (A) كوثر (*kawthar*): abundance. See Kausar (m.).

Kawkab (A) كوكب: star. See Najm نجم, star.

---

[58] See Colebrooke, T. E., On the Proper Names of the Mohammadans, *Journal of the Royal Asiatic Society of Great Britain and Ireland*, XI, p. 237 (1879).

[59] *Ibid.*, p. 237; Steingass, F., *A Comprehensive Persian-English Dictionary*, p. 1007.

[60] *Ibid.*, p. 1057.

[61] See Abd-el-Jawad, 'A Linguistic and Socio-cultural Study of Personal Names in Jordan', *Anthropological Linguistics*, XXVIII, p. 83 (1986). It is also a well known Christian Lebanese family name. "Certain families, mainly Christian Lebanese, such as the Karam..." See Hitti, P, K., *History of the Arabs*, p. 670.

Female Names

Kazima (A) كاظمة (*kaazimah*): one who controls or suppresses her anger; fem. of Kazim. See Kazim (m.).

Khadija (A) خديجة (*khadeejah*): the first wife of Muhammad (s) who was the first to embrace Islam. She is known as *Khair al-Nisaa'*, 'the best of women'.

Khadra (A) خضراء (*khadraa'*): green, verdant.

Khair (A). See Khayr.

Khaleda (A). See Khalida.

Khalida (A) خالدة (*khaalidah*): immortal, eternal; fem. of Khalid. Khalida bint al-Aswad: a *sahaabia*. See Khalid (m.).

Khalisa (A) خالصة (*khaalisah*): pure, true, real; fem of Khalis.

Khanum (P) خانم (*khaanum*): princess, noble woman.

Khashia (A) خاشعة (*khaashi'ah*): pious, devout; fem. of Khashi'.

Khasiba (A) خصيبة (*khaseebah*): fruitful, fertile, prolific, prodigal, productive; fem. of Khasib.

Khatira (A) خاطرة (*khaatirah*): wish, desire, interest.

Khatun (P) خاتون (*khaatun*): noblewoman, lady. A courteous title used at the end of a woman's name.

Khayr (A) خير: good, blessing, boon, wealth, fortune. See Khayr (m.).

Female Names

Khayr-un-Nisa (A) خير النساء: best of women. Epithet of Khadija, the first wife of Muhammad (s).

Umm-ul-Khayr Salmaa (A) أم الخير سلمى: mother of Khalifa Abu Bakr.

Khayra (A) خيرة (*khayrah*): the best, prime, top, flower, cream; sing. of Khayrat خيرات. Khayra b. Abi Umayya: a *sahaabia*.

Khayrat (A) خيرات (*khayraat*) (خير): pl. of Khayra خيرة, blessing, good work. See Khayrat (m.).

Khayriya (A) خيريّة (*khayriyyah*): charity, benevolence, beneficence.

Khayriyya (A). See Khayriya.

Khudra (A) خضرة (*khudrah*): greenness, verdancy.

Khurshed (P) خورشيد: sun. See Aftaab افتاب (P); Mihr مهر (P); Shams شمس (A).

Khurshed Jahan (P) خورشيد جهان: sun of the world.

Khurshid (P). See Khurshed.

Khuzama (A). خزامى (*khuzaamaa*): lavender, tulip.

Khwurshed (P). See Khurshed.

Kishwar (P) كشور: country.

Kohinur (P+A) كوه نور (*kohinoor*): the mountain of light. A 109 carat

277

Female Names

diamond removed in 1849 from the Mughal jewels in India and added to the British crown jewels in London.

Kulsum (A) كلثوم (*kulthoom*): full of flesh about the face and cheeks.

Umm Kulsum (A) ام كلثوم (*umm kulthoom*): daughter of Muhammad (s), married to Khalifa Usman (*uthmaan*).[62]

Kulthum (A). See Kulsum كلثوم.

---

[62] See Haykal, M.H., *The Life of Muhammad*, p. 69.

L

Labiba (A) لبيبة (*labeebah*): intelligent, judicious, sagacious, wise, prudent, wise; fem. of Labib.

Laila (A). See Layla.

Lamia (A) لامعة (*laami'ah*) (لمع): brilliant, lustrous, shining, radiant.

Latifa (A) لطيفة (*lateefah*): pretty, charming, sweet, kind, friendly; fem. of Latif. See Latif (m.). Latifa al-Zayat: "a distinguished novelist." [63]

Layaan (A) ليان: gentleness, softness, tenderness.

Layla[64] (A) ليلى: (*laylaa*): night. A well-known character in Arabic literature. Layla bint Abu Hathma: a *sahaabia*.[65]

Leila (A). See Layla.

Leyli (A). See Layla.

---

[63] See Ahmed, Leila, *Women and Gender in Islam*, p. 196.

[64] It is a popular name for women throughout the ages all over the Muslim world. "A female proper name". See Steingass, F., *A Comprehensive Persian-English Dictionary*, p. 1135; "A woman's name"; see Cowan, J Milton (ed.) Hans Wehr, *A Dictionary of Modern Written Arabic*, p. 887; see Colebrooke, T. E., 'On the Proper Names of the Mohammadans', *Journal of the Royal Asiatic Society of Great Britain and Ireland*, XIII, p. 271 (1881).

[65] See Siddiqi, Muhammad Saeed, *The Blessed Women of Islam*, pp. 192-3.

Female Names

Lina (A) لينة (*leenah*) (لِين): gentle, soft, tender, 'a kind of palm'.[66]

Lubaba (A) لبابة (*lubaabah*) (لُب): innermost, essence, core. Wife of al-Abbas, uncle of Muhammad (s).[67]

Lubana (A) لبانة (*lubaanah*) (لبن): wish, desire.

Lubna (A) لبنى (*lubnaa*): a tree which yields an aromatic resin used in perfume and medicine (also called *lubnaa*). "[T]he girl who inspired the ancient Arab poet Qays."[68] Lubna b. Thabit: a *sahaabia*.

Lulu[69] (A) لؤلؤ (*lu'lu'*): pearls. وحور عين كامثال اللؤلؤ المكنون "And wide-eyed houris like hidden pearls." (*surat al-Waaqi'ah* 56:22-23). See Jumana جمانة, pearl. Badr al-Din Lu'lu': "Daughter of a king, the Atabeg of Mosul."[70]

Lulua[71] (A) لؤلؤة: (*lu'lu'ah*): pearl.

Lutf (A) لطف: kindness, friendliness, courtesy, delicate, grace, favour from Allah.

---

[66] See Steingass, F., *A Comprehensive Persian-English Dictionary*, p. 1135.

[67] See Al-Arnaut, Shafiq, *Qamus al-Asma' al-Arabiyya* [Dictionary of Arabic Names] (in Arabic), p. 136.

[68] See Schimmel, Annemarie, *Islamic Names*, p. 43.

[69] See Cowan, J Milton (ed.) Hans Wehr, *A Dictionary of Modern Written Arabic*, p. 852.

[70] See Mernissi, F. *The Forgotten Queens of Islam*, p. 98.

[71] See *Al- Mawrid: A Modern Arabic-English Dictionary*, p. 912. "Luulwa", see Yassin, M. Aziz F., 'Personal Names Address in Kuwaiti Arabic', *Anthropological Linguistics*, XX, p. 54.

Female Names

Lutf-un-Nisa (A) لطف النساء: grace of women. Wife of Siraj-ud-Dawlah, the last independent Nawab of Bengal (1757).[72]

---

[72] See Majumdar, R. C., *An Advanced History of India*, p. 656.

Female Names

M

Maaisa (A) مائسة (*maa'isah*): walking with a proud gait.

Maajida (A) ماجدة (*maajidah*): glorious, noble; fem. of Maajid.

Maaria (A). See Maria.

Maas (A) ماس for Almaas الماس: diamond. See Almas.

Maa' as-samaa' (A) ماء السماء: water from heaven.

Mabruka (A) مبروكة (*mabrookah*) (برك): blessed, prosperous, abundant; fem. of Mabruk.

Madiha (A) مديحة (*madeehah*) (مدح): praiseworthy.

Mah (P) ماه (*maah*): moon.

> **Mah Jabin** (P+A) ماه جبين (*maah jabeen*): (beautiful) brow like the moon.

> **Mah Liqa** (P) ماه لقا: moon-like (face).

> **Mah Naaz** (P) ماه ناز (*maah naaz*): beauty of the moon.

> **Mah Nur** (P+A) ماه نور (*maah noor*): moonlight.

> **Mah Rukh** (P) ماه رخ: cheeks as bright as the moon.

Female Names

Mahtab (P) ماهتاب (*maahtaab*): moonlight.

Maha (A) مهاة (*mahaah*): wild cow (representing beauty).

Mahabba (A) محبة (*mahabbah*): love, affection. Mahabba b. al-Rabi': a *sahaabia*.

Mahasin (A) محاسن (*mahaasin*): pl. of Mahsanah محسنة, beauty, charm, charming, attraction, virtue, merit.

Mahbuba (A) محبوبة (*mahboobah*): dear, beloved, sweetheart; fem. of Mahbub.

Mahdiya (A) مهديّة (*mahdiyyah*) (هدي): rightly guided; fem. of Mahdi. See Rashida رشيدة, rightly guided.

Mahdiyya (A). See Mahdiya.

Mahfuza (A) محفوظة (*mahfoozah*): safeguarded, well-protected; fem. of Mahfuz. See Mahfuz; Masun مصون (m.).

Mahiba (A) مهيبة (*maheebah*) (هيب): majestic, dignified, magnificent; fem. of Mahib.

Mahira (A) ماهرة (*maahirah*) (مهر): skilled, skilful, proficient; fem. of Mahir.

Mahjuba (A) محجوبة (*mahjoobah*): hidden, covered, screened; fem. of Mahjub.

Mahmuda (A) محمودة (*mahmoodah*): praised, praiseworthy, lauded,

283

laudable, commended, commendable; fem. of Mahmud. See Mahmud (m.).

Mahmudat-un-Nisa (A) محمودة النساء: praised (one) of the women.

Maimana (A) ميمنة (*maimanah*) (يمن): right, right-hand. اصحاب الميمنة "Companions of the right-hand." (*surat al-Waaqi'ah* 56:8).

Maimuna (A). See Maymuna.

Maisa (A). See Maaisa مائسة.

Maisara (A) ميسرة (يسر): prosperity, abundance, wealth, affluence, ease (*surat al-Baqarah* 2:280). See Yasaar يسار (m.).

Maisura (A) ميسورة (*maisoorah*) (يسر): easy, successful, fortunate, lucky, prosperous; fem. of Maisur.

Majd (A) مجد: glory, honour.

Majeeda (A) مجيدة (*majeedah*): glorious, noble; fem. of Majeed. See Majeed (m.).

Majida (A). See Maajida, Majeeda.

Makbula (A). See Maqbula.

Malaha (A) ملاحة (*malaahah*) (ملح): beauty, grace, elegance. See Husn حسن.

Malaika (A) ملائكة angels (*surat al-Ahzaab* 33:56).

Female Names

Malak (A) ملك: angel. فلما راينه اكبرنه وقطعن ايديهن وقلن حاش لله ما هذا بشرا ان هذا الا ملك كريم "When they saw him they exalted him and [in their amazement] cut their hands: they said, 'Allah preserve us! This is not a human being. This is no other than a noble angel." (*surat Yusuf* 12:31). See Jamal (m); Yusuf (m); Zulaykha (f.).
Malak Hifni Nasif (1886-1918): Egyptian writer who campaigned for women's rights.

Maliha (A) مليحة (*maleehah*) (ملح): beautiful, pretty, good-looking; fem. of Malih.

Malika (A) ملكة (*malikah*): queen; fem. of Malik. See Malik (m.)

> **Malika Jahaan** (A+P) ملكة جهان: wife of Delhi Sultan Jalal-ud-Din Firuz Shah.

Mamuna (A) مأمونة (*ma'moonah*): trustworthy, honest, faithful, reliable; fem. of Mamun. See Mamun (m.).

Manahil (A) مناهل (*manaahil*) (نهل): pl. of Manhal منهل, spring, pool, fountain.

Manal (A) منال (*manaal*) (نيل): attainment, acquisition.

Manar (A) منار (*manaar*) (نور): lighthouse.

Manara (A) منارة (*manaarah*): fem. of Manar. See Manar.

Manna (A) من (*mann*): gift, present, favour, benefit, boon. وانزلنا عليكم المن "We sent down the Manna upon you." (*surat al-Baqarah* 2:57).

285

Female Names

Mannana (A) مـنانة (*mannaanah*) (مـنّ): bountiful, generous; fem. of Mannan. See Mannan (m.).

Mansura (A) منصورة (*mansoorah*): assisted, victorious, triumphant; fem. of Mansur. See Mansur (m.).

Manzura (A) منظورة (*manzoorah*): approved of, chosen, promising; fem. of Manzur.

Maqbula (A) مقبولة (*maqboolah*): accepted, admitted, granted, approved; fem. of Maqbul.

Maqsuda (A) مقصودة (*maqsoodah*): intended, aimed at. See Murad مراد (m.).

Marab (A) مأرب (*ma'rab*) (أرب): wish, desire, purpose, use, aim; sing. of Marib مآرب. (see *surat Ta Ha* 20:18).

Maram (A) مرام (*maraam*) (روم): wish, desire, aspiration.

Mardiya (A). See Marzia.

Maria (A) مارِيَّة (*maariyyah*): kind of bird.[73] Wife of Muhammad (s) who gave birth to a son named Ibrahim.[74]

Mariam (A). See Maryam.

Marib (A) مآرب (*ma'aarib*) (أرب): pl. of Ma'rab مأرب, wish, use (see *surat Ta Ha* 20:18).

---

[73] See Steingass, F., *A Comprehensive Persian-English Dictionary*, p. 1140.

[74] See Haykal, M. H., *The Life of Muhammad*, p. 376.

Female Names

Marjaan (A) مرجان: small pearls, corals. كانهن الياقوت والمرجان
فباى آلاء ربكما تكذبان "[In beauty] like the rubies and the coral.
Then which of the favours of your Lord will you deny?" (*surat al-Rahman* 55:58).

Marufa (A) معروفة (*ma'roofah*) (عرف): famous, eminent, kindness, kind
act; fem. of Maruf. See Maruf (m.).

Marwa (A) مروة (*marwah*): flint-stone. See Marwa (m.).

Maryam (A) مريم: mother of Prophet 'Isa (Jesus), the Biblical Mary.
واذ قالت الملائكة يا مريم ان الله اصطفاك وطهرك واصطفاك على
نساء العالمين "And when the angels said: O Maryam! Behold, Allah
has chosen you and made you pure and raised you above all the women
of the world." (*surat Aal 'Imraan* 3:42).

Marziya (A) مرضيَّة (*mardiyyah*) (رضي): accepted, well-pleased, one
who is pleasing. يايتها النفس المطمئنة ارجعي الى ربك راضية
مرضية "O soul at peace! Return to your Lord well-pleasing,
well-pleased." (*surat al-Fajr* 89:27-28). An epithet of Fatima, daughter
of Muhammad (s). See Raazia راضية (*raadeeyah*).

Marzuqa (A) مرزوقة (*marzooqah*): blessed, fortunate, prosperous,
successful; fem. of Marzuq.

Masabih (A) مصابيح (*masaabeeh*): pl. of Misbah مصباح, lamp. See
Misbah (m.).

Masarrat (A) مسرة (*masarrah*) (سرّ): joy, delight, pleasure, gladness,
happiness.

Mashia (A) مشيئة (*mashee'ah*) (شيأ): wish, desire, will (of Allah).

287

Female Names

Masuda (A) مسعودة (*mas'oodah*): fortunate, happy, lucky; fem. of Masud. See Sa'eeda سعيدة.

Masuma (A) معصومة (*ma'soomah*): innocent, sinless, safe-guarded, protected; fem. of Masum. Daughter of Imam Musa al-Kazim. See Mahfuza محفوظة.

Masun (A) مصون (*masoon*): safeguarded, well-protected.

Mawadda (A) مودّة (*mawaddah*) (ودّ): friendship, intimacy, affection, love. ومن آياته ان خلق لكم من انفسكم ازواجا لتسكنوا اليها وجعل بينكم مودة ورحمة "And among His Signs is this: He created for you mates from yourselves that you may dwell in tranquillity with them, and He has put love and mercy between your [hearts]." (*surat al-Rum* 30:21).

Mawhiba (A) موهبة (*mawhibah*) (وهب): gift, talent; sing. of Mawaahib مواهب.

Mawhuba (A) موهوبة (*mawhoobah*) (وهب): gifted, talented, endowed, favoured; fem. of Mawhub.

Mawsufa (A) موصوفة (*mawsoofah*): worthy of description, portrayed, endowed with laudable qualities; fem. of Mawsuf.

Maymana (A). See Maimana.

Maymuna (A) ميمونة (*maymoonah*): auspicious, prosperous, lucky, fortunate, blessed; fem. of Maymun. Wife of Muhammad (s).[75]

---

[75] See Al-Tabari, *The Commentary on The Qur'an*, vol. 1, p. xv.; Haykal, M. H., *The Life of Muhammad*, p. 385; Colebrooke, T. E., 'On the Proper Names of the

288

Female Names

Maysara (A). See Maisara.

Mazida (A) مزيدة (*mazeedah*): increase, excess, high degree, maximum; fem. of Mazid.

Mehr (P). See Mihr.

Midha (A) مدحة: praise, eulogy.

Mihin (P) مهين (*miheen*): "[g]reater, greatest...fine, subtle, thin...name of a woman."[76]

Mihr (P) مهر: sun, affection. See Aftaab افتاب; Khurshid خورشد; Shams شمس.

Mihr-un-Nisaa (P+A) مهر النساء: sun of the women. Name of Nur Jahan, before her marriage to Mughal emperor Jahangir.[77]

Mihri[78] (P) مهري: sun. See Mihr.

Minnat (A) منّة (من): grace, kindness, favour, gift.

Mohammadans', *Journal of the Royal Asiatic Society of Great Britain and Ireland*, XIII, p. 271 (1881).

[76] See Steingass, F., *A Comprehensive Persian-English Dictionary*, p. 1357.

[77] "In May 1611, Jahangir married Nur Jahan, originally known as Mihr-un-nisa." See Majumdar, R. C., *An Advanced History of India*, p. 458.

[78] See Colebrooke, T. E., 'On the Proper Names of the Mohammadans', *Journal of the Royal Asiatic Society of Great Britain and Ireland*, XI, p. 237 (1879).

Female Names

Minu (P) مینو (meenoo): paradise, *behesht* بهشت.[79]

Misam (A) میسم (وسم): impression, mark, beauty, beautiful woman.

Mohsena (A). See Muhsina.

Mohsina (A). See Muhsina.

Momena (A). See Mumina.

Mona (A). See Muna.

Morsheda (A). See Murshida.

Mosammat (A). See Musammat.

Motia (A). See Mutia.

Muazzama (A) معظّمة (*mu'azzamah*): exalted, glorified; fem. of Muazzam.

Mubaraka (A) مبارکة (*mubaarakah*): blessed, fortunate, lucky, auspicious; fem. of Mubarak. Epithet of Fatima, daughter of Muhammad (s). See Mubarak (m.).

Mubina (A) مبینة (*mubeenah*) (بین): clear, plain, distinct; fem. of Mubin. See Mubin (m.).

Mufida (A) مفیدة (*mufeedah*) (فید): beneficial, advantageous, favourable, profitable.

---

[79] See Haim, S., *The Shorter Persian-English Dictionary*, p. 736.

Female Names

Muhayya (A) محيّا (حيو): countenance, face, look. Comp. Muhayya مهيّأ, prepared (m.). Muhayya bint Silkan: A *sahaabia*.

Muhja (A) مهجة (*muhjah*): heart, soul.

Muhra (A) مهرة (*muhrah*): filly, a female pony.

Muhsana (A) محصنة (*muhsanah*) (حصن): chaste, virtuous, pure, modest, married woman. والمحصنات من المؤمنات والمحصنات من الذين اوتوا الكتاب من قبلكم "[Lawful to you in marriage] the chaste women of the believers and the chaste women of the People of the Book." (*surat al-Maa'idah* 5:5).

Muhsina (A) محسنة (*muhsinah*): benevolent, beneficent, charitable, humanitarian; fem. of Muhsin. See Muhsin (m.).

Muida (A) معيدة (*mu'eedah*): teacher; fem. of Muid.

Mujahida (A) مجاهدة (*mujaahidah*) (جهد): one who struggles, strives, or fights for the cause of Islam; fem. of Mujahid. See Mujahid (m.)

Mukarrama (A) مكرّمة (*mukarramah*): honoured, revered, honourable; fem. of Mukarram. في صحف مكرمة "On honoured leaves." (*surat 'Abasa* 80:13).

Mulayka (A) مليكة: diminutive of Malak ملكة, angel. Mulayka b. Thabit: a *sahaabia*.

Muluk (A) ملوك (*mulook*): pl. of Malik ملك, king. See Shahan شاهان, (P) kings.

Mumina (A) مؤمنة (*mu'minah*): believer (in Islam), pious; fem. of

291

Female Names

Mumin مؤمن. ليدخل المؤمنين والمؤمنات جنات تجري من تحتها الانهار خالدين فيها ويكفر عنهم سيئاتهم "That He may bring the believing men and the believing women into Gardens underneath which rivers flow, wherein they will abide, and may remit from them their evil deeds." (*surat Fath* 48:5).

Mumtaz (A) ممتاز (*mumtaaz*) (ميز): distinguished, superior, outstanding.

Mumtaz Mahal (A) ممتاز محال: wife of Mughal emperor Shah Jahaan.[80]

Mumtaza (A) ممتازة (*mumtaazah*): fem. of Mumtaz. See Mumtaz.

Muna (A) منى (*munaa*): pl. of Munya منية, wish, desire.[81]

Muna as-Sabaah (A) منى الصباح wishes of the dawn.

Munawwara (A) منوّرة (*munawwarah*) illuminated, brilliant; fem. of Munawwar. The city of Medina is called *al-madina al-munawwara* المدينة المنورة.

Munia (A). See Munya.

Munifa (A) منيفة (*muneefah*): eminent, exalted, superior, high, lofty; fem. of Munif.

Munira (A) منيرة (*muneerah*): bright, brilliant, radiant, luminous; fem.

---

[80] "[T]o immortalise her name, Shah Jahan built on her grave the famous Taj Mahal." See Majumdar, R. C., *An Advanced History of India*, p. 481.

[81] See Steingass, F., *A Comprehensive Persian-English Dictionary*, p. 1336.

of Munir. See Munir (m.).

Munisa (A) مؤنسة (*mu'nisa*) (انس): sociable, friendly, kind, gentle; fem. of Munis. Daughter of Sultan Salah ud-Din Ayyubi. See Anisa أنيسة; Latifa لطيفة.

Munya[82] (A) منية (*munyah*): wish, desire, object of desire; sing. of Muna منى, wishes. See Arzu آرزو (P); Murad مراد (m.).

    Munyat al-Muna (A) منية المنى: wish of wishes.

Murshida (A) مرشدة (*murshidah*): leader, guide, adviser, counsellor; fem. of Murshid. See Murshid (m.).

Musammat (A) مسمات: "Names,...(in India) a title prefixed to the name of women; a lady",[83] no more in general use.

Musawat (A) مساواة (*musaawaah*): equality.

Mushira (A) مشيرة (*musheerah*): counsellor, adviser; fem. of Mushir. See Murshida مرشدة.

Mushtari (A) المشتري (*al-mushtarii*) (شرى): Jupiter.

Muslima (A) مسلمة (*muslimah*): (female) follower of the religion of Islam; fem. of Muslim. المسلمات "The Muslim women" (*surat al-Ahzaab* 33:35). See Muslim (m.).

Mutia (A) مطيعة (*mutee'ah*): obedient, pious, devoted, faithful; fem. of

---

[82] See Haykal, M. H., *The Life of Muhammad*, p. 62.

[83] See Steingass, F., *A Comprehensive Persian-English Dictionary*, p. 1239.

Female Names

Mutia (A) مطيعة (*mutee'ah*): obedient, pious, devoted, faithful; fem. of Muti'. Muti'a bint an-Nu'man: a *sahaabia*.

Muwaffaqa (A) موفّقة (*muwaffaqah*) (وفق): successful, prosperous, lucky, fortunate; fem. of Muwaffaq. See Naajiha ناجحة.

Muzaina (A) مزينة (*muzainah*): diminutive of Muzna مزنة, rain clouds. See Muzna.

Muyassar (A) ميسّر (يسر): successful, lucky, prosperous.

Muzna (A) مزنة (*muznah*): rain clouds. See Muzaina مزينة.

Female Names

N

Naabiha (A) نابهة (*naabihah*) (نبه): noble, famous, eminent, distinguished, brilliant; fem. of Naabih. See Nabiha نبيهة.

Naail (A). See Nail نائل.

Naaila (A). See Naila نائلة.

Naaima (A) ناعمة (*naa'imah*) (نعم): delicate, soft. See Ghaida غيداء. Comp. Naima نعيمة, happiness.

Naajia (A) ناجية (*naajiyah*) (نجو): saved, liberated; fem. of Naaji. Comp. Najia نجيَّة, intimate friend.

Naajiha (A) ناجحة (*naajihah*) (نجح): successful, prosperous; fem. of Naajih. See Muwaffaqa موفقة.

Naasia (A) ناصعة (*naasi'ah*): clear, pure; fem. of Naasi.

Naaz (P) ناز: glory, pride, elegance, gracefulness, fresh, tender, young.

Nabaha (A) نباهة (*nabaahah*): fame, nobility, intelligence, brightness, brilliance.

Nabawiyya[84] (A) نبوية: prophetic. Nabawiyya Musa (1886-1951):

---

[84] See Al-Arnaut, Shafiq, *Qamus al-Asma' al-Arabiyya* [Dictionary of Arabic Names], p. 144.

Female Names

Egyptian pioneer for women's education.[85]

Nabiha (A) نبيهة (*nabeehah*): noble, famous, eminent, distinguished, brilliant; fem. of Nabih. See Naabiha نابهة.

Nabila (A) نبيلة (*nabeelah*): noble, highborn, honourable; fem. of Nabil.

Nadaa (A) ندى: dew, generosity, liberality, magnanimity.[86]

Nadi (A) ندي (*nadiyy*): moist, damp, tender, delicate.[87]

Nadia (A) نديَّة (*nadiyyah*): fem. of Nadi. See Nadi (f.).

Nadida (A) نديدة (*nadeedah*): equal.

Nadima (A) نديمة (*nadeemah*): intimate friend, companion; fem. of Nadim. See Rafiqa رفيقة.

Nadira (A) نادرة (*naadirah*): rare, extraordinary; fem. of Nadir. Comp. Nadira ناضرة, radiant. See Nudra ندرة.

Nadira Begam (A+P) نادرة بگم: wife of Mughal prince Dara, son of Emperor Shah Jahan.

---

[85] See *The Oxford Encyclopaedia of the Modern Islamic World*, vol III, p. 179; Ahmed, Leila, *Women and Gender in Islam*, p. 171.

[86] See Madina, Maan Z., *Arabic-English Dictionary of the Modern Literary Language*, p. 658; Cowan, J Milton (ed.) Hans Wehr, *A Dictionary of Modern Written Arabic*, p. 952.

[87] See Cowan, J Milton (ed.) Hans Wehr, *A Dictionary of Modern Written Arabic*, p. 953.

Female Names

Nadira (A) ناضرة (*naadirah*): radiant, resplendent, bright, beaming (see *surat al-Qiyaamah* 75:22). Comp. Nadira نادرة, rare.

Nadiya (A). See Nadia.

Nadra (A) نضرة (*nadrah*): radiance, brightness, a light of beauty. تعرف في وجوههم نضرة النعيم "You will know in their faces the radiance of delight." (*surat al-Mutaffifin* 83:24).

Nadwa (A) ندوة (*nadwah*) council, club.

Nafia (A) نافعة (*naafi'ah*): beneficial, advantageous, profitable; fem. of Nafi.

Nafisa (A) نفيسة (*nafeesah*): precious, gem. A "great granddaughter of Ali."[88]

Nahar (A) نهار (*nahaar*): day. تولج الليل في النهار وتولج النهار في الليل "You (Allah) make the night to enter into the day and you make the day to enter into the night." (*surat Aal 'Imraan* 3:27).

    Shams-un-Nahaar (A) شمس النهار: sun of the day.

Nahid (P) ناهيد (*naaheed*): Venus.[89]

---

[88] See Hasan, Masudul, *History of Islam*, vol. I, p. 221. Also see Colebrooke, T. E., 'On the Proper Names of the Mohammadans', *Journal of the Royal Asiatic Society of Great Britain and Ireland*, XIII, p. 273 (1881); Schimmel, Annemarie, *Islamic Names*, p. 37.

[89] See Haim, S., *The Shorter Persian-English Dictionary*, p. 745.

Female Names

Nahida (P) ناهده (*naahida*), ناهيده (*naaheeda*): Venus.[90]

Nahla (A) نهلة (*nahlah*): a drink, a draught.

Nail (A) نائل (*naa'il*) (نيل): winner, achiever, gift. See Fazl فضل (*fadl*) (m.).

Naila[91] (A) نائلة (*naa'ilah*) fem. of Naail. See Naail (f.). See Atia عطية, gift. Naila bint Sa'id: a *sahaabia*.

Naima (A) نعيمة (*na'eemah*): happiness, peaceful, comfort, bliss; fem. of Na'im. See Naim (m.). Comp. Naa'ima ناعمة, delicate.

Najat (A) نجاة (*najaah*) (نجو): rescue, salvation, deliverance. See Najat (m.).

Najia (A). See Najiya.

Najiba (A) نجيبة (*najeebah*): noble, distinguished, aristocratic, of noble descent; fem.of Najib.

Najiya (A): نجيّة (*najiiyah*): intimate friend, bosom friend; fem. of Naji.

Najla (A) نجلاء (*najlaa'*): large-eyed, wide-eyed.

Najma (A) نجمة (*najmah*): star. See Kawkab كوكب; Najm نجم.

---

[90] See Steingass, F., *A Comprehensive Persian-English Dictionary*, p. 1382, 1383.

[91] See Haykal, M. H., *The Life of Muhammad*, p. 39. It is not a suitable name as it was the name of an idol in Makkah before Islam.

Female Names

Najwa (A) نجوى (*najwaa*) (نجو): confidential talk, secret conversation.

Najwan (A) نجوان (*najwaan*) (نجو): saved, liberated.

Na'ma (A) نعماء (*na'maa'*) (نعم): gift, present, grace, favour, kindness. See Atia عطية; Ihsan إحسان.

Naqiya (A) نقيّة (*naqiyyah*): pure, clean; fem. of Naqi.

Naqa (A) نقاء (*naqaa'*): purity, refinement, clarity.

Naqiba (A) نقيبة (*naqeebah*): mind, intellect.

Nargis (P) نرگس narcissus.[92] See Narjis نرجس.

Narjis[93] (A) نرجس: narcissus. See Nargis نرگس.

Nashat (A) نشاط (*nashaat*) (نشط): liveliness, vigour, energy, vivacity.

Nashita (A) نشيطة (*nasheetah*) (نشط): energetic, dynamic, lively, fresh, vigorous; fem. of Nashit.

Nashwa (A) نشوى (*nashwaa*) (نشو): elated, exalted, exuberant; fem. of Nashwan.[94]

---

[92] See Steingass, F., *A Comprehensive Persian-English Dictionary*, p. 1395.

[93] See Madina, Maan Z., *Arabic-English Dictionary of the Modern Literary Language*, p. 659; Cowan, J Milton (ed.) Hans Wehr, *A Dictionary of Modern Written Arabic*, p. 954; *Al-Mawrid: A Modern Arabic-English Dictionary*, p. 1175.

[94] See Cowan, J Milton (ed.) Hans Wehr, *A Dictionary of Modern Written Arabic*, p. 967; Madina, Maan Z., *Arabic-English Dictionary of the Modern Literary Language*, p. 668.

Female Names

Nasiba (A) نسيبة (*naseebah*): noble, highborn; fem. of Nasib.

Nasim (A) نسيم (*naseem*) (f.): breeze, gentle wind, fresh air, fragrant air.

Nasima (A). See Nasim.

Nasiman (P) نسيمن (*naseeman*): prayer, worship.

Nasira (A) نصيرة (*naseerah*): helper, protector, patron; fem. of Nasir. See Nasir (m.). See Naasira ناصرة.

Nasrin (P) نسرين (*nasreen*): wild rose.

Natiqa (A) ناطقة (*naatiqah*): one endowed with speech, eloquent, spokesperson; fem. of Natiq.

Naushin (P). See Noshin.

Nawal[95] (A) نوال (*nawaal*) (نول): gift, present, grant, favour, grace, kindness. See Atia عطية; Nawla نولة; Fazl فضل (*fadl*) (m.).

Nawfa (A) نوفة (*nawfah*): excess, surplus.

Nawla (A) نولة (*nawlah*): gift, present, grant, favour, grace. A *sahaabia*. See Nawal نوال, gift.

Nawra (A) نورة (*nawrah*): blossom, flower. See Zahrah زهرة;

---

[95] Abd-el-Jawad, Hassan, 'A Linguistic and Socio-cultural Study of Personal Names in Jordan', *Anthropological Linguistics*, XXVIII, p. 94 (1986). Name of a modern Egyptian writer.

Female Names

Nuwwaarah نوارة.

Naz (P). See Naaz.

Nazaha (A) نزاهة (*nazaahah*) (نزه): purity, chastity, virtue, honesty.

Nazanin (P) نازنين (*naazaneen*): elegant, delicate, beloved.

Nazara (A) نضارة (*nadaarah*): bloom, beauty.

Nazifa (A) نظيفة (*nazeefah*): pure, clean, innocent; fem. of Nazif.

Naziha (A) نزيهة (*nazihah*): pure, virtuous, honest; fem. of Nazih. See Afifa عفيفة; Adila عادلة; Sharifa شريفة.

Nazima (A) ناظمة (*naazimah*) (نظم): organiser; fem. of Nazim.

Nazira (A) نظيرة (*nazeerah*): equal, like, match, comparable; fem. of Nazir.

Nazli (A) نظلي (*nazlii*): delicate, feminine, beautiful.[96] Nazli Hanem: Egyptian princess.[97]

    Nazli Fadl (A) نظلي فضل: daughter of an Egyptian prince.[98]

Nesa (A). See Nisa نساء.

---

[96] See Cowan, J Milton (ed.) Hans Wehr, *A Dictionary of Modern Written Arabic*, p. 977.

[97] See Ahmed, Leila, *Women and Gender in Islam*, p. 142.

[98] *Ibid.*, p. 135.

Female Names

Nibras (A) نبراس (*nibraas*): lamp. See Misbah مصباح (m); Siraj سراج (m.).

Nida (A) نداء (*nidaa'*) (ندو): call. اذ نادى ربه نداء خفيا "When he [Zakariya] cried to his Lord in secret." (*surat Maryam* 19:3).

Nigar (P) نگار (*nigaar*): picture, portrait, beauty, sweetheart.

Nilufar (P) نيلوفر (*neeloofar*): water-lily.

Ni'ma (A) نعمة (*ni'mah*) (نعم): blessing, boon, favour, grace, bounty; sing of Ni'mat نعمات. See Ni'ma (m.).

Ni'mat (A) نعمات (*ni'maat*) (نعم): blessings, boons, favours, graces, bounties; pl. of Ni'ma نعمة, blessing. N'imat Fuad: well known Egyptian archaeologist.[99]

Nisa (A) نساء (*nisaa'*): women. *Al-Nisaa'* النساء 'The Women': title of the 4th *sura* of the Qur'an. نساؤكم حرث لكم "Your women (wives) are a tilth for you." (*surat al-Baqarah* 2:223).

    Qamar-un-Nisa (A) قمر النساء: moon of the women.

Nishat (P). See Nashat.

Noshin (P) نوشين (*nosheen*): sweet, pleasant.

Nubugh (A) نبوغ (*nuboogh*): distinction, eminence, excellence, superiority.

---

[99] *Ibid.*, p. 218.

Female Names

Nudar (A). See Nuzar نضار.

Nudra (A) ندرة (*nudrah*): rarity, rareness.　See Nadira نادرة;
Nudura ندورة.

Nudura (A) ندورة (*nudurah*): rarity, rareness.　See Nudra ندرة.

Nuha (A) نهى (*nuhaa*): intelligence, mind, intellect.

Nur (A) نور (*noor*): light, illumination.　See Nur (m.).

> **Nur Jahan** (A+P) نور جهان: light of the world.　Wife of
> Mughal emperor Jahangir.[100]

> **Nur-ud-Dunya**[101] (A) نور الدنيا: light of the world.

> **Nur-un-Nisa** (A) نور النساء: light of the women.

Nura (A) نورة (*noorah*): light; fem. of Nur.　See Nur.

Nuria (A). See Nuriya.

Nuriya (A): نوريّة (*nooriyyah*): light, luminous; fem. of Nuri.

Nuriyya (A). See Nuriya.

Nusayba (A) نسيبة (*nusaybah*): diminutive of Nasiba نسيبة, noble.

---

[100] "In May 1611, Jahangir married Nur Jahan, originally known as Mihr-un-nisa." See
Majumdar, R. C., *An Advanced History of India*, p. 458.

[101] See Colebrooke, T. E., 'On the Proper Names of the Mohammadans', *Journal of
the Royal Asiatic Society of Great Britain and Ireland*, XIII, p. 274 (1881).

Female Names

Nusayba bint Abi Talha: a *sahaabia*.

Nusrat (A) نصرة (*nusrah*) (نصر): help, aid, assistance, support.

Nuwwar[102] (A) نوّار (*nuwwaar*) (نور): pl. of Nuwwara نوّارة, blossom, flower. Nuwwar bint al-Harith: a *sahaabia*.

Nuwwara[103] (A) نوّارة (*nuwwaarah*): blossom, flower.   See Zahra زهرة.

Nuzar (A) نضار (*nudaar*): gold.

Nuzhat (A) نزهة (*nuzhah*): pleasure trip, promenade, recreation.

---

[102] See *Al-Mawrid: A Modern Arabic-English Dictionary*, p. 1194.

[103] *Ibid.*

O

Obaida (A). See Ubayda.

Ola (A). See Ula.

P

Pari (P) پری (*paree*): fairy, fairy-like beautiful.

> **Pari Bibi** (P) پری بیبی: daughter of Shaistah Khan (d.1688), viceroy of Bengal during Mughal period.[104] See Bibi.

Parsa (P) پارسا (*paarsaa*): chaste, devout, pious.

Parvin (P) پروین (*parween*) the Pleiades. See Surayya (A) ثریا.

---

[104] Her tomb and a mosque nearby of architectural importance are situated in Dhaka (Bangladesh).

Q

Qamar (A) قمر: moon. See Qamar (m.).

Qamar-un Nisa (A) قمر النساء: moon of the women.

Qamra (A) قمراء (*qamraa'*) (قمر): moonlight, moonlit, bright; fem. of Aqmar أقمر.

Qasima (A) قاسمة (*qaasimah*): distributor, divider; fem. of Qasim.

Qudsiya (A): قدسيّة (*qudsiyyah*): holiness, sacredness.

Qudsiyya (A). See Qudsiya.

Qurrat-ul-'Ayn (A) قرة العين: cooling, or, delight of the eye, joy, pleasure, darling, sweetheart. ربنا هب لنا من ازواجنا وذرياتنا قرة اعين "Our Lord! grant us wives and offspring who will be the comfort of our eyes." (*surat al-Furqaan* 25:74). Qurrat-ul-'Ayn bint 'Ubada: a *sahaabia*.

Female Names

R

Raabi'a (A) رابعة (*raabi'ah*): the fourth. Comp. Raabia رابية, hill; Rabi'a ربيعة, spring.

Raabia (of Basra) (713-801): famous saint.[105]

Raabia (A) رابية (*raabiyah*): hill, mound, knoll.   Comp. Raabi'a رابعة, the fourth; Rabi'a ربيعة. spring.

Raagiba (A). See Raghiba راغبة.

Raai (A) راعية (*raa'iyah*): guardian, custodian, patron, protector; fem. of Raai'.

Raaida (A) رائدة (*raai'dah*): explorer, guide, model, example; fem. of Raaid.

Raaiqa (A) رائقة (*raa'iqah*): pure, clear, tranquil, serene; fem. of Raaiq.

Raajia (A) راجية (*raajiyah*): hopeful, hoping, full of hope; fem. of Raaji. Comp. Raazia (*raadiyah*) راضية, satisfied.

Raazia (A) راضية (*raadiyah*): satisfied, contended, well-pleased; fem. of Raazi. يايتها النفس المطمئنة ارجعي الى ربك راضية مرضية "O soul at peace! Return to your Lord well-pleasing, well-pleased." (*surat al-Fajr* 89:27-28). An epithet of Fatima, daughter of Muhammad

---

[105] See Siddiqi, Muhammad Saeed, *The Blessed Women of Islam*, pp. 183-7.

(s).[106] See Raziya رضية (*radiyyah*).

Rabab[107] (A) رباب (*rabaab*): white cloud. Rabab bint Harith: a *sahaabia*.

Rababa (A) ربابة (*rabaabah*). See Rabaab.

Rabea (A). See Raabia.

Rabi'a (A) ربيعة (*rabee'ah*): spring, spring time; fem. of Rabi. Comp. Raabi'a رابعة, the fourth. A *sahaabia*.

Rabiha (A) رابحة (*raabiha*): winner, gainer; fem. of Rabih.

Rabita (A) رابطة (*raabita*): band, bond, link, nexus.

Radiya (A). See Raziya.

Rafat (A) رأفة (*ra'fat*) (رأف): mercy, compassion, pity.

Rafia (A) رفيعة (*rafee'ah*): high ranking, noble, eminent; fem. of Rafi. See Rafi (m.).

Rafida (A) رافدة (*raafidah*): support, prop.

Rafif (A) رفيف (*rafeef*): glittering, shining, gleaming.

Rafiqa (A) رفيقة (*rafeeqah*): intimate friend, companion; fem. of Rafiq.

---

[106] See Steingass, F., *A Comprehensive Persian-English Dictionary*, p. 36.

[107] *Ibid.*, p. 567; Al-Arnaut, Shafiq, *Qamus al-Asma' al-Arabiyya* [Dictionary of Arabic Names] (in Arabic), p. 115.

Female Names

Rafraf (A) رفرف: cushion. متكئين على رفرف خضر وعبقرى حسان "Reclining on green cushions and lovely carpets." (*surat al-Rahmaan* 55:76).

Raghada (A) رغادة (*raghaadah*): comfort, opulence, affluence.

Raghiba (A) راغبة (*raaghibah*): desirous, wishful, willing; fem. of Ragib.

Raghid (A) رغيد (*ragheed*): comfort, opulence, affluence.

Rahat (A) راحة (*raahah*) (روح): rest, comfort, ease, relief. See Sakina سكينة.

Rahifa (A) رهيفة (*raheefah*): sharp; fem. of Rahif.

Rahima (A) رحيمة (*raheemah*): kind, compassionate; fem. of Rahim. See Rahim (m.).

Rahil (A) راحيل (*raaheel*): wife of Prophet Yaqub (Jacob) and mother of Prophet Yusuf (Joseph). In the Bible she is mentioned as Rachel.[108]

Rahmat (A) رحمة (*rahmah*) (رحم): mercy, compassion, kindness. Wife of Prophet Ayyub and granddaughter of Prophet Yusuf.[109] See Rahmat (m.).

Raida (A). See Raaida.

---

[108] See Steingass, F., *A Comprehensive Persian-English Dictionary*, p. 561; Hanks, P. and Hodges, F., *A Dictionary of First Names*, p. 274.

[109] See Siddiq, Mohammad Sayed, *The Blessed women of Islam*, p. 4.

309

Female Names

Raihana (A). See Rayhana.

Raisa (A) رئيسة (*ra'eesah*): leader, superior; fem. of Ra'is.

Raja (A) رجاء (*rajaa'*) (رجو): hope, wish. See Amal أمل.

Rajab (A) رجب: the seventh month of the Muslim year. See Rajab (m.)

Rajia (A) رجية (*rajiyah*) (رجو): hope, expectation, wish. Comp. Raajia راجية, hopeful; Raziya (*radiyyah*) رضيّة, satisfied.

Rajiha (A) راجحة (*raajihah*): superior, predominant; fem. of Rajih.

Rajwa (A) رجوى: hope.

Rakhima (A) رخيمة (*rakheemah*): soft, pleasant, melodious (voice).

Rakina (A) ركينة (*rakeenah*): firm, steady; fem. of Rakin.

Ramadan (A) رمضان (*ramadaan*) (*ramazaan*): the ninth month of the Islamic calendar. See Ramadan (m.).

Ramazan (A). See Ramadan.

Ramla (A) رملة (*ramlah*): sand. Wife of Muhammad (s).[110] Her kunya is Umm Habibah.

Rana (A) رعناء (*ra'anaa'*): soft.

---

[110] See Haykal, M. H., *The Life of Muhammad*, p. 377.

310

Female Names

Randa (A) رندة (*randah*): scented, fragrant tree.[111]

Ranim (A) رنيم (*raneem*): singing, song, music.

Raqia (A) راقية (*raaqiah*): superior, high ranking, educated; fem. of Raqi.

Raqiqa (A) رقيقة (*raqeeqah*) (رق): delicate, fine, soft, slender, slim.

Rasha (A) رشاء (*rashaa'*): a fawn.[112]

Rashaqa (A) رشاقة (*rashaaqah*) (رشق): graceful stature, grace, elegance.

Rasheda (A) راشدة (*raashidah*): right minded, rightly guided; fem. of Rashed. See Rashed (m.).

Rashida (A) رشيدة (*rasheedah*): wise, prudent, judicious; fem. of Rashid. See Rashid (m.).

Rashiqa (A) رشيقة (*rasheeqah*): graceful, elegant; fem. of Rashiq.

Rasikha (A) راسخة (*raasikhah*): well-established, well-founded, stable, steady; fem. of Rasikh.

Rasima (A) راسمة (*raasimah*): planner, designer; fem. of Rasim.

Rasina (A) رصينة (*raseenah*): calm, composed.

---

[111] See Al-Arnaut, Shafiq, *Qamus al-Asma' al-Arabiyya* [Dictionary of Arabic Names] (in Arabic), p. 117.

[112] See Steingass, F., *A Comprehensive Persian-English Dictionary*, p. 577.

311

Female Names

Rasmiya (A) رسميّة (*rasmiyyah*): ceremonial, ceremonious, formal; fem. of Rasmi.

Ratiba (A) راتبة (*raatibah*): well-arranged, well-ordered, organised.

Raunaq (A) رونق: beauty, grace, glamour, splendour.

Raunaq Jahan (A+P) رونق جهان: lustre of the world.

Raushan[113] (P) روشن: light, luminous, bright, splendour

Raushan Ara Begum روشن آرا بگم: lady adorning light. Daughter of Mughal emperor Shah Jahan.

Raushan Jabin (P) روشن جبین: of radiant forehead.

Raushana (P) روشنا: light, splendour.

Rayhana (A) ريحانة (*rayhaanah*): a handful of sweet basil. Wife of Muhammad (s).[114] See Rayhan ريحان (m.).

Razan[115] (A) رزان (*razaan*): calm, composed, self-possessed; fem. of Razin.

Razia (A). See Raziya.

---

[113] See Colebrooke, T. E., 'On the Proper Names of the Mohammadans', *Journal of the Royal Asiatic Society of Great Britain and Ireland*, XIII, p. 275 (1881).

[114] See Haykal, M. H., *The Life of Muhammad*, p. 634.

[115] *Al-Mawrid: A Modern Arabic-English Dictionary*, p. 583.

Female Names

Razina (A) رزينة (*razeenah*): calm, composed, self-possessed; fem. of Razin. A *sahaabia*.

Raziya (A) رضيَّة (*radiyyah*): satisfied, contended, pleased; fem. of Razi. See Raazia (*raadiyah*) راضية, satisfied. Delhi Sultana (1236-40).[116]

Rehab (A). See Rihab.

Rehana (A). See Rayhana.

Rezwan (A). See Rizwaan (*ridwaan*).

Ridwan (A). See Rizwaan (*ridwaan*).

Ridwaana (A). See Rizwaana (*ridwaana*).

Rif'at (A) رفعة (*rif'a*) (رفع): high rank, high standing. See Rif'at (m.).

Rifqa (A) رفقة (*rifqah*): kindness, gentleness, company, companionship. Wife of Prophet Ishaaq.

Rihab (A) رحاب (*rihaab*): pl. of Rahbah رحبة, vastness, expanse.

Rihana (A). See Rayhana.

Rim (A) ريم (*reem*): white gazelle, antelope.

---

[116] She was the first woman to rule over India. "She read the Koran with correct pronunciation" (Ferishta). She "was endowed with all the admirable attributes and qualifications necessary for kings." (Minhaj-us-Siraj). See Majumdar, R. C., *An Advanced History of India*, pp. 277-9. Also see Mernissi, Fatima, *The Forgotten Queens of Islam*, p. 13.

Female Names

Rima (A) ريمة (*reemah*): white gazelle, antelope.

Riyaz (A) رياض (*riyaad*): pl. of Rawza (*rawdah*) روضة, garden.

Rizwaan (A) رضوان (*ridwaan*) (رضي): satisfaction, contentment. See Rizwaan (*ridwaan*) (m.).

Rizwaana (A) رضوانة (*ridwaanah*): fem. of Rizwaan (*ridwaan*). See Rizwaan (*ridwaan*) (m.).

Rokea (A). See Ruqayya.

Rokhsha (P). See Rukhsha.

Roya (A). See Ruya

Ruba (A) ربى (*rubaa*): pl. of Rubwa, Rabwa ربوة, hill[117] (*surat al-Baqarah* 2:265). See Rubiy ربي.

Rubaba (P) ربابه (*rubaaba*): a stringed musical instrument.[118]

Rubiy (A) ربي (*rubiyy*): pl. of Rubwa ربوة,[119] hill. See Ruba ربى.

Rubwa (A) ربوة (*rubwah*): hill.

---

[117] See Cowan, J Milton (ed.) Hans Wehr, *A Dictionary of Modern Written Arabic*, p. 324; Steingass, F., *A Comprehensive Persian-English Dictionary*, p. 568; Madina, Maan Z., *Arabic-English Dictionary of the Modern Literary Language*, p. 247.

[118] See Steingass, F., *A Comprehensive Persian-English Dictionary*, p. 567.

[119] See Madina, Maan Z., *Arabic-English Dictionary of the Modern Literary Language*, p. 247.

Female Names

Rukhshana[120] (P) رخشان (*rukhshaan*):[121] bright, brilliant, shining.

Rumana (A). See Rummana.

Rumman (A) رمان (*rummaan*): pl. of Rummana رمانة, pomegranate. فيهما فاكهة ونخل ورمان "Wherein [paradise] will be fruits and dates and pomegranates." (*surat al-Rahmaan* 55:68).

> **Umm Rumman** (A) ام رمان: mother of Aisha (wife of Muhammad (s)).[122]

Rummana (A) رمانة (*rummanah*): pomegranate. See Rumman.

Ruqa (A) روقة (*rooqah*): pretty, beautiful.

Ruqayya (A) رقيَّة (*ruqayyah*): charming, attractive, captivating. Daughter of Muhammad (s), married to Khalifa Usman (*uthmaan*). See Ruqya رقية.

Ruqya (A) رقية (*ruqyah*): charm.[123] See Ruqayya رقيَّة.

Rushdiya (A) رشديَّة (*rushdiyyah*): rightly guided, on the right way, following the right path; fem. of Rushdi. See Rushd (m.).

Ru'a (A) رؤى: pl. of Ru'yaa رؤيا, dream.

---

[120] See Schimmel, Annemarie, *Islamic Names*, p. 70.

[121] See Steingass, F., *A Comprehensive Persian-English Dictionary*, p. 572.

[122] See Ahmed, Leila, *Women and Gender in Islam*, p. 49.

[123] See Madina, Maan Z., *Arabic-English Dictionary of the Modern Literary Language*, p. 272; Cowan, J Milton (ed.) Hans Wehr, *A Dictionary of Modern Written Arabic*, p. 355.

Female Names

Ruwaa' (A) رواء (روى): beauty, grace, prettiness, comeliness.

Ruya (A) رؤية (ru'yah) (رأي): vision, sight.　Com. Ru'yaa رؤيا, dream.

Ru'yaa (A) رؤيا (رأي): dream.　Comp. Ruya رؤية, vision.

Female Names

S

Saabiha (A) صابحة (*saabihah*): coming or arriving in the morning; fem. of Saabih. Comp. Sabiha صبيحة, morning.

Saabira (A) صابرة (*saabirah*): patient, tolerant; fem. of Saabir. والصابرين والصابرات "Men and women who are patient." (*surat al-Ahzaab* 33:35). See Saabir (m.).

Saadat (A) سعادة (*sa'aadah*) (سعد): happiness, bliss, felicity, success, luck.

Saadiqa (A) صادقة (*saadiqah*): true, truthful, honest, sincere, devoted; fem. of Saadiq. الصادقات "Women who speak the truth." (*surat al-Ahzaab* 33:35). See Saadiq (m.).

Saafia (A) صافية (*saafiyah*): pure, clear, crystal; fem. of Saafi. See Safia صفيّة.

Saaida (A) صاعدة (*saa'idah*): rising, ascending; fem. of Saaid. Comp. Saaida ساعدة, branch.

Saaida (A) ساعدة: branch, tributary, affluent. Comp. Saaida صاعدة, rising.

Saaima (A) صائمة (*saa'imah*) (صوم): fasting; fem. of Saaim. والصائمين والصائمات "Men who fast and women who fast." (*surat al-Ahzaab* 33:35).

Saalima (A) سالمة (*saalimah*): safe, secure, perfect, complete; fem. of

317

Saalim.

Saamia (A) سامية (*saamiyah*): eminent, exalted, high minded, sublime; fem. of Saami.

Saamira (A) ثامرة (*thaamirah*): fruit-bearing, fruitful, productive; fem. of Saamir.

Saba (A) صبا (*sabaa*): east wind.

Sabah (A) صباح (*sabaah*): morning.

Sabaha (A) صباحة (*sabaahah*) (صبح): beauty, gracefulness, handsomeness.

Sabat (A) ثبات (*thabaat*): firmness, stability, certainty, endurance, boldness, truth.

Sabeera (A) صبيرة (*sabeerah*): patient, tolerant; fem. of Sabeer.

Sabera (A). See Saabira صابرة.

Sabha (A) صبحى (صبح): pretty, beautiful, graceful, radiant; fem. of Subah صباح.

Sabia (A) سابية (*saabiyah*): captivating, enchanting, charming.

Sabih (A) صبيح (*sabeeh*) (صبح): pretty, beautiful, graceful. Comp. Saabih صابح, coming or arriving in the morning. See Saabih (m.).

Sabiha (A) صبيحة (*sabeehah*) (صبح): morning. Comp. Saabiha صابحة, coming or arriving in the morning. Sabiha Malika Qurtaba: wife of the

318

Female Names

Umayyad Khalifa al-Hakim al-Mustansir.[124]

Sabiqa (A) سابقة (*saabiqah*): first, winner; fem. of Sabiq.

Sabira (A). See Saabira, Sabeera.

Sabita (A) ثابتة (*thaabitah*): well established, certain, sure; fem. of Sabit (*thaabit*).

Sabriya (A) صبريـة (*sabriyyah*): patient; fem. of Sabri.

Sabuh (A) صبوح: shining, brilliant.

Sadeka (A). See Saadiqa.

Sadia (A). See Sadiya.

Sadida (A) سـديدة (*sadeedah*): correct, right, sound, appropriate; fem. of Sadid. See Sadid (m.).

Sadiqa (A) صديقة (*sadeeqah*): friend, companion; fem. of Sadiq. See Sadiq (m.).

Sadiya (A) سعدية (*sa'diyah*): happy, lucky, blissful fortunate; fem. of Sadi.

Sadiyat (P) سعديت (*sa'diiyat*): auspiciousness, felicity, bliss.[125]

---

[124] She was known as "queen of Cordova". See Mernissi, Fatima, *The Forgotten Queens of Islam*, p. 44.

[125] See Steingass, F., *A Comprehensive Persian-English Dictionary*, p. 682.

Female Names

Saduh (A) صدوح: singer, singing.

Saduq (A) صدوق: honest, truthful, sincere, trustworthy.

Saeeda (A) سعيدة (*sa'eedah*): happy, lucky; fem. of Sa'eed. A *sahaabia*. See Saeed (m.).

Safa (A) صفا (*safaa*): a hill near the sacred Kaaba. See Marwa (m.). Comp. Safaa صفاء.

Safaa (A) صفاء (*safaa'*) (صفو): purity, clarity, serenity. Comp. Safa صفا.

Safiya (A) صفيّة (*safiyyah*): pure, sincere and honest friend; fem. of Safi صفي. Wife of Muhammad (s).[126] See Saafia صافية, pure.

Safiyya (A). See Safiya.

Safura (A) صافورا (*saafuraa*): wife of Prophet Musa.

Safwa[127] (A) صفوة (*safwah*): the best part, elite, top, prime, flower.

Sahab (A) سحاب (*sahaab*): clouds.

Sahar (A) سحر: early dawn, early morning.

Sahla (A) سهلة (*sahlah*): smooth, simple, fluent, facile, easy, even; fem. of Sahl. Sahla bint Suhayl: a *sahaabia*.

---

[126] See Haykal, M. H., *The Life of Muhammad*, p. 373.

[127] "Padishah Khatun took the title of *Safwat al-dunya wa al-Din* (purity of the earthly world and of the faith)." See Mernissi, Fatima, *The Forgotten Queens of Islam*, p. 101.

Female Names

Saima (A). See Saaima.

Sajeda (A). See Sajida.

Sajida (A) ساجدة (*saajidah*): prostrate in worship, bowing in adoration; fem. of Sajid. See Sajid (m.).

Sakhaa (A) سخاء (*sakhaa'*) (سخو): generosity, liberality.

Sakhiya (A) سخيَّة (*sakhiyyah*) (سخو): generous, liberal, open handed.

Sakiba (A). See Saqiba ثاقبة.

Sakina (A) سكينة (*sakeenah*) (سكن): calmness, tranquillity, repose, serenity, "In Islam the word designates a special peace, the 'Peace of God' which settles upon the heart."[128] هو الذي انزل السكينة في قلوب المؤمنين ليزدادوا ايمانا مع ايمانهم "It is He who sent down peace of mind into the hearts of the believers, that they may add faith to their faith." (*surat al-Fath* 48:4).

Salam (A) سلام (*salaam*) (سلم): peace, safety, security. See Salam (m.)

Salama (A) سلامة (*salaamah*) (سلم): peace, safety, security; fem.of Salam سلام. Salama b. Mas'ud: a *sahaabia*.

Salama (A) سلمة (*salamah*): peace; fem. of Salam سلم. Umm Salama: See Umm.

Saleha (A). See Saliha.

---

128 See Glasse, Cyril, *The Concise Encyclopaedia of Islam*, p. 343.

Female Names

Salema (A). See Saalima.

Saliha (A) صالحة (*sáalihah*): pious, righteous, upright, just, virtuous, devoted; fem. of Salih. فالصالحات قانتات حافظات للغيب بما حفظ الله "So the righteous women are obedient, guarding in secret that which Allah has guarded." (*surat al-Nisaa'* 4:34).

Salima[129] (A) سليمة (*saleemah*): sound, perfect, complete, safe, secure; fem. of Salim. See Salim (m.); Saalima سالمة (f).

Salima Sultana (A) سليمة سلطانة: niece of Mughal emperor Humaayun.[130]

Salma[131] (A) سلمى (*salmaa*): beloved, sweetheart. Wife of Hamzah, uncle of Muhammad (s);[132] wife of Khalifa Abu Bakr.[133] Comp. Salama سلمة, peace.

Salsabil (A) سلسبيل (*salsabeel*): a spring in Paradise. تسمى عينا فيها سلسبيلا "The water of a spring therein, named Salsabil." (*surat al-Dahr* 76:18)

---

[129] See Abd-el-Jawad, Hassan, 'A Linguistic and Socio-cultural Study of Personal Names in Jordan', *Anthropological Linguistics*, XXVIII, p. 84 (1986).

[130] She was "authoress of several Persian poems."See Majumdar, R. C., *An Advanced History of India*, p. 572.

[131] See Abd-el-Jawad, Hassan, 'A Linguistic and Socio-cultural Study of Personal Names in Jordan', *Anthropological Linguistics*, XXVIII, p. 84 (1986); Steingass, F., *A Comprehensive Persian-English Dictionary*, p. 694. Salmaa (A)سلمى: Umm al-Khair Salmaa سلمى أم العبير: mother of Khalifa Abu Bakr.

[132] See Haykal, M. H., *The Life of Muhammad*, p. 385.

[133] *Ibid.*, p. 433.

Female Names

Salwa (A) سلوى (*salwaa*): quail.[134] (see *surat al-Baqarah* 2:57). Comp. Salwah سلوة, comfort.

Salwah (A) سلوة: comfort, ease, amusement.[135] Comp. Salwa سلوى, quail.

Sama (A) سماء (*samaa'*): heaven, sky (see *surat al-Tariq* 86:1).

Samah (A) سماح (*samaah*) (سمح): generosity, bounty, good-heartedness, large-heartedness.

Saman (A) ثمن (*thaman*): price, value. فلا تخشوا الناس واخشون ولا تشتروا بآياتي ثمنا قليلا "Therefore fear not men, but fear Me, and sell not My Signs for a small price." (*surat al-Maa'idah* 5:44).

Samar (A) سمر: pleasant conversation, evening or nightly conversation.

Samia (A). See Saamia سامية.

Samiha (A) سميحة (*sameehah*): generous, kind, good-hearted, large-hearted, open-handed; fem of Samih.

Samim (A) صميم (*sameem*) (صم): sincere, genuine, pure, true. essence, heart.

Samina (A) ثمينة (*thameenah*): valuable, precious, priceless; fem. of Sameen.

---

[134] See Madina, Maan Z., *Arabic-English Dictionary of the Modern Literary Language*, p. 324.

[135] *Ibid.*

Female Names

Samira (A) سميرة (*sameerah*): companion (in nightly conversation), entertainer (with stories, music etc.); fem. of Samir.

Samiqa (A) سامقة (*saamiqah*): lofty, towering.

Sanaa (A) سناء (*sanaa'*) (سنو): brilliance, radiance, splendour, majestic. A *sahaabia*. Comp. ثناء, praise.

Sanaa (A) ثناء (*thanaa'*) (ثنو): praise, commendation, eulogy. Comp. سمله, brilliance.

Sanad (A) سند: support, prop.

Sania (A). See Saniya سنيّة.

Saniya (A): سنيّة (*saniyyah*): brilliant, majestic, exalted, eminent, splendid; fem. of Sani.

Sanjida (P) سنجيدة: weighty, proved.

Saqiba (A) ثاقبة (*thaaqiba*): penetrating, piercing, sharp-witted, sagacious, acute; fem. of Saqib. See Saqib (m.).

Sara[136] (A) سارة (*sarah*): wife of Prophet Ibrahim.

Sarab (A) سراب (*saraab*): mirage.

---

[136] See Al-Arnaut, Shafiq, *Qamus al-Asma' al-Arabiyya* [Dictionary of Arabic Names] (in Arabic), p. 120; Haykal, M. H., *The Life of Muhammad*, p. 24. In Steingass, F., *A Comprehensive Persian-English Dictionary*, p. 640, the word is classified as Persian: "سارا, Pure, excellent."

Female Names

Sarah[137] (A). See Sara.

Sarwa (A) ثروة (*tharwah*): fortune, wealth, riches.

Sauda (A). See Sawda.

Sausan (A) سوسن: lily of the valley, iris. In Persian, Susan.

Sawda (A) سودة (*sawdah*): date-palm garden. Wife of Muhammad (s).[138]

Sayeda (A). See Sayyida.

Sayyeda (A). See Sayyida.

Sayyida (A) سيِّدة (*sayyidah*): lady, Mrs; fem. of Sayyid.

> **Sayyidat-un-Nisa** (A) سيِّدة النساء: chief of women. Honorific title of Fatima, daughter of Muhammad (s).

Selima (A). See Salima.

Setara (P). See Sitara.

Shaad (P). See Shad.

Shaahida (A) شاهدة (*shaahidah*): witness; fem. of Shaahid. See Shaahid (m.).

---

[137] "...Abraham's aged and barren wife, Sarah..." See Armstrong, Karen, *Jerusalem: One City Three faiths*, p. 26.

[138] See Haykal, M. H., *The Life of Muhammad*, p. 183.

Female Names

Shaahin (P). See Shahin.

Shaban (A) شعبان (*sha'baan*): the eighth month of the Muslim year. See Shaban (m.).

Shabnam (P) شبنم: dew, a pendant of pearls.

Shad (A) شاد (*shaad*): happy.

Dilshad (P) دلشاد (*dilshaad*): of happy heart, happy, glad. See Dilshad.

Shadman (P) شادمان (*shaadmaan*): glad, cheerful, joyful.

Shadia (A) شادية (*shaadiyah*): singer.[139]

Shadin (A) شادن (*shaadin*): fawn, young deer.

Shafaqat (A) شفقة (*shafaqah*) (شفق): compassion, pity, kindness, tenderness.

Shafia (A) شفيعة (*shafee'ah*) (شفع): mediatress; fem. of Shafi. See Shafi (m.).

Shafiqa (A) شفيقة (*shafeeqah*): compassionate, kind-hearted, affectionate, warm-hearted; fem. of Shafiq.

---

[139] See Cowan, J Milton (ed.) Hans Wehr, *A Dictionary of Modern Written Arabic*, p. 461; Madina, Maan Z., *Arabic-English Dictionary of the Modern Literary Language*, p. 344.

Female Names

Shahana[140] (P) شاهانه (*shaahaanah*), شهانه (*shahaanah*): royal, kingly, splendid, magnificent.

Shaheda (A). See Shaahida.

Shahida (A) شهيدة (*shaheedah*): martyr in the cause of Islam and as such held in very high esteem and honour; fem. of Shahid. See Shahid (m.).

Shahin (P) شاهين (*shaaheen*): a royal white falcon, the beam of scales. See Shahin (m.).

Shahiqa (A) شاهقة (*shaahiqah*): high, towering, lofty, tall; fem. of Shahiq.

Shahira (A) شهيرة (*shaheerah*): famous, eminent, renowned; fem. of Shahir.

Shahnaaz (P) شهناز: a musical note.[141]

Shahrazad (P). See Shahrzad.

Shahrbanu (P) شهر بانو: lady of the city. Mother of the fourth Shi'ite Imam Zaynul Abidin.

---

[140] See Steingass, F., *A Comprehensive Persian-English Dictionary*, pp. 726, 768; Haim, S., *The Shorter Persian-English Dictionary*, p. 426.

[141] See Steingass, F., *A Comprehensive Persian-English Dictionary*, p. 770. "The name denotes a woman so beautiful that she would be the pride and glory even of a king." See Baker, M., 'Common Names in the Arab World', in Hanks, P. and Hodges, F., *A Dictionary of First Names*, Supplement I, p. 432.

Female Names

Shahrin (A) شهر (*shahr*): month. *Shahrin*, the fully inflected form of *shahr* appears in verse 3 of *surat al-Qadr* (no. 97) . The Qur'an was revealed on *Lailat al-Qadr* (the Night of Power). The importance of this night is described in this verse. ليلة القدر خير من الف شهر (*Laylatul-Qadri khayrum-min alfi shahrin*) "The Night of Power is better than a thousand months."

Shahrzad (P) شهرزاده (*shahrzaad*): offspring of the city. The vizier's daughter married to King Shahryar in the tales of *The Thousand and One Nights*.

Shahzadi[142] (P) شاه زادي: princess.

Shaila (A) شعيلة (*sha'eelah*) (شعل): burning candle.

Shaima (A) شيماء (*shaimaa'*): daughter of Halima, the wet nurse of Muhammad (s).[143]

Shaira (A) شاعرة (*shaa'irah*) (شعر): poetess, endowed with deep insight or intuition; fem. of Sha'ir شاعر. وما هو بقول شاعر "It is not the word of a poet." (*surat al-Haaqqah* 69:41)

---

[142] In Persian, a princess is Shahzada Khanum شاهزاده خانم. (see Haim, S., *The Shorter Persian-English Dictionary*, p. 427). "[O]ne finds a tendency in [the subcontinent of] India to invent feminine forms by adding the Hindi suffix -i to any name:...and the Persian -zad 'born' is changed into zadi, like Shahzadi, 'princess'". See Schimmel, Annemarie, *Islamic Names*, p. 48.

[143] See Haykal, M. H., *The Life of Muhammad*, p. 49; Lings, Martin, *Muhammad*, p. 307; Siddiqi, Muhammad Saeed, *The Blessed Women of Islam*, p. 187-8.

Female Names

Shajarat al-Durr[144] (A) شجرة الدر: the tree of pearls. Mamluk Sultana (1250).[145]

Shajia (A) شجيعة (*shajee'ah*): courageous, bold, brave; fem. of Shaji.

Shakila (A) شكيلة (*shakeelah*): well formed, beautiful; fem. of Shakil.

Shakera (A). See Shakira.

Shakira (A) شاكرة (*shaakirah*): thankful, grateful; fem. of Shakir. See Shakir (m.).

Shakufa (P) شكوفه (*shakoofa*): blossom, opening bud.

Shakura (A) شكورة (*shakoorah*): thankful, grateful; fem. of Shakur. See Shakur (m.).

Sham'a (A) شمعة (*sham'ah*): candle.

Shamikh (A) شامخ (*shaamikh*): high, lofty, towering.

Shamim (A) شميم (*shameem*): perfume, scent.[146]

---

[144] See Colebrooke, T. E., 'On the Proper Names of the Mohammadans', *Journal of the Royal Asiatic Society of Great Britain and Ireland*, XIII, p. 274 (1881).

[145] "The foundation of Mamluk power was laid by Shajar al-Durr, widow of the Ayyubid al-Salih...For eighty days the sultanah, the only Moslem woman to rule a country in North Africa and Western Asia...She struck coins in her own name and had herself mentioned in the Friday prayer." See Hitti, Philip K., *History of the Arabs*, pp. 671-2. "She brought the Muslims a victory ...routed [the French] army during the Crusades and captured their king, Louis IX." See Mernissi, Fatima, *The Forgotten Queens of Islam*, p. 14.

[146] See Steingass, F., *A Comprehensive Persian-English Dictionary*, p. 761.

Female Names

Shamima (P) شمیمه (*shameema*): sweet smell.[147]

Shamma (P) شمه: perfume, fragrant.

Shams (A) شمس: sun. See Shams (m.).

Shams-un-Nahaar (A) شمس النهار: sun of the day.

Shamshad (P) شمشاد (*shamshaad*): tall and upright tree, graceful figure.

Shaqraa (A) شقراء (*shaqraa'*): blond, fair-haired, fair-complexioned; fem. of Ashqar اشقر.

Sharaf (A) شرف: nobility, high rank, eminence, distinction, honour. Sharaf bint Khalifa: a *sahaabia*.

Sharifa (A) شریفة (*shareefah*): noble, honourable, highborn; fem. of Sharif. See Sharif (m.).

Shazi (A) شذي (*shadhiyy*) (شذو): fragrant, aromatic.

Sharmin[148] (P) شرمن: shy, bashful, modest, coy.

Sherifa (A). Sharifa.

Shifa (A) شفاء (*shifaa'*) (شفی): cure, healing, satisfaction, gratification. Shifa bint 'Awf: a *sahaabia*.

---

[147] See Haim, S., *The Shorter Persian-English Dictionary*, p. 444.

[148] See Al-Arnaut, Shafiq, *Qamus al-Asma' al-Arabiyya* [Dictionary of Arabic Names] (in Arabic), p. 184. Sharmanda شرمنده: covered with shame. See Steingass, F., *A Comprehensive Persian-English Dictionary*, p. 742.

Female Names

Shikufa (P) شكوفه: blossom.

Shirin[149] (P) شيرين (*shireen*): sweet, pleasant, gracious, delicate. A character in Persian literature. See Farhad (m.).

Shuhrah (A) شهرة: fame, renown.

Shukr (A) شكر (*shukr*): thanks, gratitude, gratefulness.

Shukriya (A) شكرية (*shukriyyah*): thanking and acknowledging gratefulness to Allah; fem. of Shukri.

Shuqra[150] (A) شقراى (*shuqraa*): fair-complexioned, blonde.

Shula (A) شعلة (*shu'lah*) (شعل): flame, blaze.

Siddiqa (A) صديقة (*siddeeqah*): righteous, very truthful, honest; fem. of Siddiq. وامه صديقة "His ('Isa) mother was a righteous woman." (*surat al-Maa'idah* 5:75). See Siddiq (m.).

Sidra (A) سدرة (*sidrah*): the "Lote-tree at the farthest boundary" in paradise (*surat al-Najm* 53:14).

Silma (A) سلمة (*silmah*): peace; fem. of Silm سلم (see *surat al-Baqarah* 2:208)

Silmi (A) سلمى (*silmii*): peaceful.

---

[149] See Steingass, F., *A Comprehensive Persian-English Dictionary*, p. 774.

[150] Al-Arnaut, Shafiq, *Qamus al-Asma' al-Arabiyya* [Dictionary of Arabic Names] (in Arabic), p. 124.

Female Names

Simin (P) سیمین (*seemeen*): silvery, made of silver.

Sitara[151] (A) ستارة (*sitaarah*): veil, screen, curtain, drape.

Sofia (A). See Sufiya.

Suad[152] (A) سعاد (*su'aad*): happiness. Su'ad bint Rafi': a *sahaabia*.

Subaha (A) صباحة (*subaahah*): beautiful, graceful.

Subh (A) صبح: dawn, aurora, morning. والصبح اذا اسفر "And by the dawn when it shines forth." (*surat al-Muddaththir* 74:34). Mother of Spanish Umayyad Khalifa Hisham II (976-1009).

Sufia (A). See Sufiya.

Sufiya (A) صوفیّة (*soofiyyah*): a mystic, someone believing in Sufi mysticism; fem. of Sufi.

Sufiyya (A). See Sufiya.

Suha (A)سها (*suhaa*): "dim star in Ursa Minor".[153]

---

[151] In Persian, ستاره (*sitaara*): star, morning star, Venus. See Steingass, F., *A Comprehensive Persian-English Dictionary*, p. 654.

[152] "[T]he women mentioned in classical Arabic love poetry are still favourites; thus Salmaa,... Su'aad (for whom Ka'b ibn Zuhayr wrote his famous ode *Baanat Su'aad...*" See Schimmel, Annemarie, *Islamic Names*, p. 43.

[153] See Steingass, F., *A Comprehensive Persian-English Dictionary*, p. 648.

Female Names

Suhir (A) سهير (*suheer*) name of a star.[154]

Sukayna (A) سكينة (*sukaynah*): diminutive of Sakina سكينة, calmness. See Sakina.

Sulayma (A) سليمى (*sulaymaa*): diminutive of Salma سلمى, beloved. See Salma.

Sultana (A) سلطانة (*sultaanah*): queen, wife of a Sultan; fem. of Sultan. See Sultan (m.).

Sulwa (A) سلوة (*sulwah*): comfort, ease, amusement. See Salwa سلوة, comfort.

Sumaya (A) سمية (*sumayyah*) (سمو): diminutive of Saamia سامية, high. Sumayya bint Khubbat: a *sahaabia* who "was the first to be martyred in Islam."[155] See Saamia.

Sunbula (A) سنبلة: ear of corn. في كل سنبلة مائة حبة "In every year a hundred grains." (*surat al-Baqarah* 2: 261). Umm Sunbula: a *sahaabia*.

Sundus (A) سندس: silk brocade. ويلبسون ثيابا خضرا من سندس "[The inhabitants of paradise] will wear green robes of finest silk." (*surat al-Kahf* 18:31).

Suraya (A). See Surayya.

---

[154] See Al-Arnaut, Shafiq, *Qamus al-Asma' al-Arabiyya* [Dictionary of Arabic Names] (in Arabic), p. 123.

[155] See Sa'd, Muhammad Ibn, *The Women of Madina*, p. 186.

Female Names

Surayya (A) ثريًا , ثريَّة (*thurayyaa*): the Pleiades.   See Parvin (P) پروين.

Susan (P) سوسن: lily of the valley, iris.[156] In Arabic, Sausan.   See Sausan.

---

[156] See Steingass, F., *A Comprehensive Persian-English Dictionary*, p. 708.

Female Names

T

Tabassum (A) تبسّم (بسم): smile. *Tabassama* فتبسم "[Sulayman] smiled" (*surat al-Naml* 27:19).

Taghrid (A) تغريد (*taghreed*): singing, song.

Tahani (A) تهانئ (*tahaani'*) (هنء): pl. of Tahniat تهنئة, congratulation, felicitation, well-wishing.

Tahira (A) طاهرة (*taahirah*): chaste, pure; fem. of Tahir. Name of Khadija, the first wife of Muhammad (s).[157] Epithet of Fatima, daughter of Muhammad (s).

Tahiya (A) تحية (*tahiyyah*) (حي): greeting, salutation, cheer, welcome. وإذا حييتم بتحية فحيوا بأحسن منها أو ردوها "When you are greeted with a greeting, greet with one better or [at least] return it equally." (*surat al-Nisaa'* 4:86).

Tahmina (P) تهمينه: wife of the famous Persian hero Rustam and mother of Sohrab.

Tahseen (A) تحسين (حسن): adornment, ornament, decoration, embellishment, betterment.

Taiba (A) تائبة (*taa'ibah*): repentant, penitent; fem. of Ta'ib, تائبات "Who turn to Allah in repentance..." (*surat al-Tahreem* 66:5).

---

[157] See Siddiq, Muhammad Sayed, *The Blessed Women of Islam*, p. 9.

335

Female Names

Taif (A) طيف: vision, spectre.

Taj (A) تاج (*taaj*): crown.

Taliba (A) طالبة (*taalibah*): student, seeker, pursuer; fem. of Talib.

Tamanna[158] (A) تمنى (*tamannaa*) (مني): to wish, to desire, to hope. See Tamanni تمنّي, wish.

Tamanni (A) تمنّي (*tamanniy*) (مني): wish, wishing (for), desire.[159] See Tamanna تمنى, to wish.

Tanjia (A) تنجية (*tanjiyah*) (نجو): rescue, salvation, deliverance.[160]

Tanzila (A) تنزيلة (*tanzeelah*) (نزل): revelation, sending down; fem. of Tanzil. See Tanzil (m.).

Taqiya (A) تقيّة (*taqiyyah*) (وقي): Godfearing, devout, pious; fem. of Taqi. See Taqi (m.).

Taqiyya (A). See Taqiya.

Tarana (P) ترانه (*taraana*): melody, song.

Tarib (A) طرب: lively, gleeful, merry.

---

[158] It should be noted that 'Tamanna' is a verb while 'Tamanni' is a noun.

[159] See *Al-Mawrid: A Modern Arabic-English Dictionary*, p. 372; Madina, Maan Z., *Arabic-English Dictionary of the Modern Literary Language*, p. 641.

[160] See Madina, Maan Z., *Arabic-English Dictionary of the Modern Literary Language*, p. 654.

Tarifa (A) طريفة (*tareefah*): rare, exquisite thing or object.

Tarub (A) طروب (طرب): lively, gleeful, merry.

Taslima (A) تسليمة (*tasleemah*): greeting, salutation; fem. of Taslim. See Taslim (m.).

Tasnim (A) تسنيم (*tasneem*): a spring in paradise (*surat al-Mutaffifin* 83:27).

Tasniya (A) تثنية (*tathniyah*) (ثني): praise, commendation.

Taufiqa (A). See Tawfiqa.

Tawfiqa (A) توفيقة (*tawfeeqah*): prosperity, good luck, good-fortune, success (granted by Allah); fem. of Tawfiq. See Tawfiq (m.).

Tawaddud (A) تودّد (ودّ): endearment, showing love or affection to, gaining the love of another.

Tayyiba (A) طيّبة (*tayyibah*): good, good-natured, generous, good-tempered; fem. of Tayyib. والطيبات للطيبين والطيبون للطيبات "Good women are for good men and good men are for good women." (*surat al-Nur* 24:26). See Tayyib (m.).

Tayyibat-un-Nisa (A) طيّبة النسا: good-natured (one) of the women.

Tazima (A) تعظيمة (*ta'zeemah*): glorification, exaltation, honour; fem. of Tazim.

Tuhfa (A) تحفة (*tuhfah*): gift, present.

Turfa (A) طرفة (*turfah*): rarity, rare object, novelty.

Female Names

U

Ubayda (A) عبيدة (*ubaydah*): female servant of lower rank; fem. of Ubayd. See Ubayd (m.).

Ula (A) على (*'ulaa*): high rank, prestige, glory. See Rifat رفعة.

Ulya[161] (A) عليا (*'ulyaa*): higher, highest; fem. of A'laa أعلى. See Asma أسمى.

Umayma (A) أميمة: diminutive of mother Umm أمّ, mother. Umayma bint Ruqayqa: a *sahaabia*.

Umm (A) أمّ: mother. Used as a *Kunya*, to make a compound of which the first part is Umm.

> **Umm Ayman** (A) أم أيمن: mother of the blessed. Nurse of Muhammad (s).[162] See Ayman.

> **Umm Fazl** (A) أم فضل (*umm fadl*): mother of favour, bounty. Nickname of the wife of Abbas, uncle of Muhammad (s).[163]

> **Umm Habiba** (A) أم حبيبة: Wife of Muhammad (s). Her name is Ramla; Umm Habiba is her *kunya* (nickname) after the name of her daughter Habiba.

---

[161] See *Al-Mawrid: A Modern Arabic-English Dictionary*, p. 778.

[162] See Haykal, M. H., *The Life of Muhammad*, p. 47.

[163] *Ibid.*, p. 384.

Female Names

Umm Kulsum[164] (A) أم كلثوم (*umm kulthoom*): daughter of Muhammad (s), married to Khalifa Usman (*uthmaan*) after the death of her sister Ruqayya. See Ruqayya.

Umm Salama (A) أم سلمة: wife of Muhammad (s).[165] Her name was Hind. Umm Salama is her *kunya* (nickname) derived from her child Salama.

Ummid (P) أميد, hope.

Umniya (A) أمنية (*umniyah*): wish, desire, hope. See Amani.

Unquda (A) عنقودة (*'unqoodah*): bunch of grapes.[166]

Uzma (A) عظمى (*'uzmaa*) (عظم): more magnificent, more glorious; fem. of Azam أعظم. See Azam (m.).

---

[164] *Ibid.*, p. 251.

[165] *Ibid.*, p. 291.

[166] See Steingass, F., *A Comprehensive Persian-English Dictionary*, p. 871.

Female Names

W

Waasiqa (A) واثقة (*waathiqah*): confident, sure, certain; fem. of Waasiq (*waathiq*).

Wadad (A) وداد (*wadaad*): love. See Widad وداد.

Wadi (A) وديع (*wadee'*) (ودع): gentle, calm.

Wafa (A) وفاء (*wafaa'*) (وفى): faithfulness, fidelity, loyalty, faith. See Amanat أمانة; Ikhlas إخلاص.

Wafiqa (A) وفيقة (*wafeeqah*): companion, friend; fem. of Wafiq. See Rafiqa رفيقة.

Wafiya (A): وفيّة (*wafiyyah*): true, trustworthy, reliable, perfect, complete; fem. of Wafi. See Saliha صالحة (f.); Wafi (m.).

Wafiyya (A). See Wafiya.

Wahida (A) وحيدة (*waheedah*): unique, matchless, singular; fem. of Wahid. See Farida فريدة.

Wajida (A) واجدة (*waajidah*): finder, lover; fem. of Wajid.

Wajiha (A) وجيهة (*wajeehah*): high, honoured, well-esteemed, illustrious; fem. of Wajih. See Wajih (m.).

Wallada (A) ولاّدة (*wallaadah*): prolific, fertile, fruitful. A renowned poetess (1087).[167]

---

[167] "This beautiful and talented Walladah, renowned alike for personal charm and liberty, was the Sappho of Spain." See Hitti, Philip K., *History of the Arabs*, p. 560.

Female Names

Wardah (A) وردة: rose. Wardatan وردة "rosy" (see *surat al-Rahmaan* 55:37).

Wasama (A) وسامة (*wasaamah*): beauty, gracefulness, prettiness.

Wasima[168] (A) وسيمة (*waseemah*): beautiful, pretty, graceful; fem. of Wasim.

Wasiqa (A). See Waasiqa.

Wasma (A) وسماء (*wasmaa'*): a pretty face, beautiful, graceful.

Widad (A) وداد (*widaad*) (ودّ): love, friendship.

Wisam (A) وسام (*wisaam*): decoration, medal, badge of honour.

---

[168] See Steingass, F., *A Comprehensive Persian-English Dictionary*, p. 1468.

Female Names

Y

Yakta (P) يكتا: unique, incomparable.

Yaqut (A) ياقوت (*yaaqoot*): ruby, sapphire, topaz (*surat al-Rahmaan* 55:58). Eminent thirteenth-century historian who "wrote *Mujam ul Adaba*, a literary history."[169]

Yasim (P) ياسم (*yaasim*): jasmine.

Yasmin[170] (A) يسمين (*yasmeen*), ياسمين (*yaasameen*): jasmine.

Yumna (A) يمنة (*yumnah*): happiness; fem. of Yumn يمن.

Yusra (A) يسرى (*yusraa*): easy, state of ease. ونيسرك لليسرى "And We shall ease your way to the state of ease." (*surat al-A'ala* 87:8).

Yumnaa (A) يمنى (يمن): right-hand, right, lucky, blessed; fem. of Ayman أيمن. See Ayman.

---

[169] See Hasan, Masudul, *History of Islam*, vol. I, p. 646.

[170] See Madina, Maan Z., *Arabic-English Dictionary of the Modern Literary Language*, p. 787.

Female Names

Z

Zaahira (A) زاهرة (*zaahirah*) (زهر): bright, brilliant, shining, luminous.

Zaaida (A) زائدة (*zaa'idah*): increasing, exceeding, excessive, growing, surplus; fem of Zaaid.

Zaakia (A) زاكية (*zaakiyah*). See Zakia زكيّة.

Zabya (A) ظبية (*zabyah*): female gazelle.

Zafira (A) ظافرة (*zaafirah*): victorious, triumphant, winner, conqueror; fem. of Zafir.

Zaghlula (A) زغلولة (*zagloolah*): young pigeon; fem. of Zaghlul.

Zaheda (A). See Zahida.

Zahia (A) زاهية (*zaahiyah*) (زهو): beautiful, brilliant, glowing; fem of Zahi.

Zahida (A) زاهدة (*zaahidah*): devout, ascetic.

Zahira (A) ظهيرة (*zaheerah*): helper, supporter, protector, patron; fem. of Zahir. See Zahir (m.).

Zahra (A) زهراء (*zahraa'*) (زهر): bright, brilliant, radiant, shining, luminous; fem. of Azhar أزهر. Al-Zahra: an epithet of Fatima, daughter of Muhammad (s). See Azhar (m.). Comp. Zahrah زهرة.

Zahrah (A) زهرة (زهر): flower, blossom, beauty. See Nuwwara نوارة. Comp. Zahraa' زهراء, bright.

343

Female Names

Zahrat-un-Nisa (A) زهرة النساء: flower of women.

Zahrat (A). See Zahrah.

Zaina (A). See Zayna.

Zainab (A). See Zaynab.

Zakia (A). See Zakiya.

Zakira (A) ذاكرة (*dhaakirah*): one who glorifies or eulogises Allah; fem. of Zakir (see *surat al-Ahzaab* 33:35). See Zakir (m.).

Zakiya (A): زكيّة (*zakiyyah*): pure, chaste, sinless, fem. of Zakiy زكي (see *surat al-Kahf* 18:74). Epithet of Fatima, daughter of Muhammad (s). Comp. ذكيّة (*dhakiyyah*), intelligent, brilliant, sharp-witted. See Zaki (m.).

Zakiyya (A). See Zakiya.

Zarifa (A) ظريفة (*zareefah*): elegant, witty, graceful; fem. of Zarif.

Zarin (P) زرين (*zareen*): golden.

Zarina (P) زرينه (*zareena*): golden.

Zayan (A) زيان (*zayaan*) (زين): beautiful, graceful, pretty.

Zayna (A) زينة (*zaynah*): fem. of Zayn. See Zayn (m.).

Zaynab (A) زينب: scented flower. Names of two wives and one daughter of Muhammad (s) and one daughter of Khalifa Ali.

Zeb (P) زيب: ornament, beauty.

Female Names

Zeb Ara (P) زیب آرا: adorning ornament.

Zeb-un-Nisa (P+A) زیب النساء: adornment of women. Daughter of Mughal emperor Aurangzeb.[171]

Zeba (P) زیبا (*zeebaa*): beautiful, pretty. Comp. Ziba (A) ظباء, gazelles.

· **Ziba** (A) ظباء (*zibaa'*): pl. of Zaby ظبی, gazelle.

Zinat (A) زینة (*zeenah*) (زین): adornment, ornament, decoration. ولا يبدين زينتهن الا ما ظهر منها "[And tell the believing women *mu'minaat*] not to display their beauty and ornaments except that which is apparent." (*surat al-Nur* 24:31).

Zinat-un-Nisa (A) زینة النساء: ornament of women. Daughter (d.1721) of Mughal emperor Aurangzeb.[172]

Zinaat (A) زینات (*zeenaaat*): pl. of Zinat زینة, ornament. See Zinat.

Ziyadat (A) زیادة (*ziyaadah*) (زید): increase, addition, surplus, superabundance.

Ziyan (A) زیان (*ziyaan*) (زین): ornament, decoration. See Zinat زینة.

Zohra (A). See Zuhra.

Zubaida (A) زبیدة (*zubaydah*): diminutive of Zubda زبدة, butter, cream. Elite, choicest part, quintessence, essence, prime, flower. Wife

---

[171] "Besides being a fine Arabic and Persian scholar, Zeb un-Nisa was an expert in calligraphy and had a rich library." See Majumdar, R. C., *An Advanced History of India*, p. 573.

[172] "Zeb un-nisa and Zinat un-nisa 'ornament of the women' were two of the Mughal emperor Aurangzeb's daughters." See Schimmel, Annemarie, *Islamic Names*, p. 48.

Female Names

of Abbasid Khalifa Harun al-Rashid.

Zuhaira[173] (A) زهيرة (*zuhayrah*): floret, small flower.

Zuhra[174] (A) زهرة (الزهرة): Venus. See Nahid, Nahida (P).

Zuhur (A) زهور (زهر): pl. of Zahrah زهرة, flower.   Comp. Zuhur ظهور, fame (m.).

Zulaikha (A). See Zulaykha.

Zulaykha (A) زليخا (*zulaykhaa*): wife of Aziz who was attracted by the beauty of Prophet Yusuf (see *surat Yusuf* 12:51).   The Qur'an however does not mention her by name . See Jamal (m); Malak (f.); Yusuf (m.).

Zulekha (A). See Zulaykha.

Zulfa (A) ذلفاء (*dhulfaa'*): having a small and finely chiselled nose.

Zurafa (A) ظرفاء (*zurafaa'*) (ظرف): elegant, witty, graceful; fem.of Zarif ظريف.

---

[173] See *Al-Mawrid: A Modern Arabic-English Dictionary*, p. 611.

[174] *Ibid.*

BIBLIOGRAPHY

Books on Names

Ahmed, Salahuddin, *Muslim Names* (in Bengali), with quotations from the Qur'an (Dhaka, Bangladesh: 1992).

Al-Arnaut, Shafiq, *Qamus al-Asma' al-Arabiyya* [Dictionary of Arabic Names] (in Arabic) (Beirut: Dar El-Ilm Lilmalayin, 1988).

Hanks, P. and Hodges, F., *A Dictionary of First Names* (Supplement I: Baker, M., 'Common Names in the Arab World' (Oxford University Press, 1990).

Haroon, Mohammed, *Cataloguing of Indian Muslim Names* (Delhi: Indian Bibliographies Bureau, 1984).

Huq, A. M. Abdul, 'A Study of Bengali Muslim Personal Names to Ascertain the Feasibility of Application of a Mechanistic Rule for their Arrangement' (Ph.D. dissertation, University of Pittsburgh, 1970).

Khurshid, Anis, *Cataloguing of Pakistani Names* (University of Karachi, 1964).

Schimmel, Annemarie, *Islamic Names* (Edinburgh University Press, 1989).

Articles on Names

Abd-el-Jawad, Hassan, 'A Linguistic and Socio-cultural Study of Personal Names in Jordan', *Anthropological Linguistics*, XXVIII, pp. 81-94 (1986).

Anglo American Cataloguing Rules, 2nd edn, revised (1988).

Ashoor, M. S., 'The Formation of Muslim Names' in *Int. Libr. Rev.*, IX, pp. 491-500 (1977).

Chaplin, A.H., 'Names of Persons: Arabic Names', *National Usages for Entry in Catalogues* (IFLA/FIBA, 1967).

Colebrooke, T. E., 'On the Proper Names of the Mohammadans', *Journal of the Royal Asiatic Society of Great Britain and Ireland*, XI,

347

Bibliography

pp. 171-237 (1879); XIII, pp. 237-80 (1881).

Dil, Afia, 'A Comparative Study of the Personal Names and Nicknames of the Bengali-Speaking Hindus and Muslims' in Gunderson, W. M., *Studies on Bengal* (Michigan State University, 1976).

Dogra, R C., 'Cataloguing Urdu Names', *Int. Libr. Rev.* V, pp. 351-77 (1973).

Elahi, Fazl; Khurshid, Anis; Kaisar, S Ibne Hasan, 'Cataloguing of Oriental Names', *Quart. J. Pak. Lib. Asso.*, II, pp. 5-16 (1961).

Habibi, Nader, 'Popularity of Islamic and Persian names in Iran before and after the Islamic Revolution', *Int. J. Middle East Stud.*, XXIV, pp. 253-60 (1992)

Huq, A M Abdul, 'Problems and Prospects in the organisation of Bengali Materials', *Libri: International Library Review*, XXIX, pp. 51-65 (1979).

Khurshid, Anis, 'Is Uniformity in Cataloguing Muslim Names Feasible or Possible?', *Libri: International Library Review*, XXVII, pp. 282-95 (1977).

Majid, Abul Fazal Fazlul, 'Cataloguing of Bengali Muslim Names', *Eastern Library*, I, pp. 15-19 (1966-7).

Paxton, Evelyn, 'Arabic Names', *Asian Affairs*, LIX, pp. 198-200 (1972).

Saif-ul-Islam, 'Cataloguing Bengali Muslim Names: problems and possible solutions', Librarianship & Archives Administration, *UNESCO J. of Information Science*, II, pp. 35-41 (1980).

Sheniti, Mahmud, 'Treatment of Arabic names', *International Conference on Cataloguing Principles Report*, 1961, pp. 267-76 (London: 1963).

Yassin, M. Aziz F., 'Personal Names Address in Kuwaiti Arabic', *Anthropological Linguistics*, XX, pp. 53-63.

Bibliography

General Books

Ahmad, Aziz, *An Intellectual History of Islam in India* (Edinburgh University Press, 1969).

Ahmed, Leila, *Women and Gender in Islam* (New Haven: Yale University Press, 1992).

Ali, Ameer, *A Short History of the Saracens* (London: Macmillan, 1955).

Armstrong, Karen, *Jerusalem: One City Three faiths.* (London: HarperCollins, 1996).

Bosworth, C. E., *The Islamic Dynasties*, Islamic Surveys 5 (Edinburgh University Press, 1967).

Choueiri, Youssef, *Islamic Fundamentalism* (London: Pinter, 1990).

Coulson, N. J., *Conflicts and Tensions in Islamic Jurisprudence* (University of Chicago Press, 1969).

Denffer, Ahmad Von, *'Ulum Al-Qur'an* (Kuala Lumpur: A. S. Noordeen, 1991).

Doi, Abdur Rahman, *Shariah: The Islamic Law* (Kuala Lumpur: A. S. Noordeen, 1984).

Donohue, John J., and Esposito, John L., *Islam in Transition* (Oxford University Press, 1982).

Esposito, John L., *The Islamic Threat* (Oxford University Press, 1992).

Fyzee, Asaf A. A., *Outlines of Muhammadan Law*, 4th edn (Delhi: Oxford University Press, 1977).

Fernandez-Armesto, Felipe, *Millennium* (Black Swan, 1996).

Hardy, P., *The Muslims of British India* (Cambridge University Press, 1972).

Hasan, Masudul, *History of Islam*, vols I & II, 2nd edn (Lahore: Islamic Publications Ltd., 1992).

Haykal, Muhammad Husayn, *The Life of Muhammad* (North American Trust Publications, 1976).

Hitti, Philip K., *History of the Arabs*, 7th edn (London: Macmillan, 1960).

Bibliography

Ikram, S. M., *History of Muslim Civilization in India and Pakistan*, 5th edn (Lahore: Institute of Islamic Culture, 1993).

Kepel, Gilles, *Allah in the West*, translated from the French (Cambridge: Polity Press, 1997).

Keller, *Reliance of the Traveller* (translation of *'Umdat al-Salik* in Arabic by Ahmad ibn Naqib al-Misri) (Evanston, IL: Sunna Books).

Lewis, Bernard, *Islam in History* (Chicago: Open Court, 1993).

--, *The Middle East* (London: Weidenfeld & Nicolson, 1995).

Lings, Martin, *Muhammad* (London: George Allen & Unwin, 1983).

Majumdar, R. C., Raychaudhury, H.C., Datta, Kalikinkar, *An Advanced History of India*, 3rd edn (New York: St Martin's Press, 1967).

Mernissi, Fatima, *The Forgotten Queens of Islam*, translated by Mary Jo Lakeland (Cambridge: Polity Press, 1993).

Martin, Gilbert, *A History of the Twentieth Century*, vol. I (London: HarperCollins, 1997).

Mujahid, Sharif Al-, *Quaid-i- Azam Jinnah* (Karachi: Quaid-i-Azam Academy, 1981).

Munson, Henry, *Islam and Revolution in the Middle East* (New Haven: Yale University Press, 1988).

Pipes, Daniel, *In the Path of God: Islam and Political Power* (New York: Basic Books, 1983).

Sa'd, Muhammad Ibn, *The Women of Madina* (London: Ta Ha Publishers, 1995).

Sabiq, Sayyid, *Fiqh us-Sunnah*, vols I-IV translated from the Arabic (Beirut: Dar El Fikr, 1996).

Siddiq, Muhammad Sayed, *The Blessed Women of Islam* (Delhi: Taj Company, 1990).

Shourie, Arun, *The World of Fatwas* (New Delhi: ASA Publications, 1995).

Tabatabai, Allamah Sayyid Muhammad Husayn al-, *Shi'ite Islam*, translated and edited by Nasr, Seyyed Hossein (London: George Allen & Unwin, 1975).